Expelling Hope

SUNY Series, INTERRUPTIONS:
Border Testimony(ies) and Critical Discourse/s
Henry A. Giroux, Editor

Expelling Hope

The Assault on Youth
and the Militarization of Schooling

CHRISTOPHER G. ROBBINS

Cover image: "Snagged," by Natasha Mayers (digital image). Courtesy of the artist.

Published by
State University of New York Press, Albany

© 2008 State University of New York

For information, contact State University of New York Press, Albany, NY
www.sunypress.edu

Production by Eileen Meehan
Marketing by Michael Campochiaro

Library of Congress Cataloging-in-Publication Data

Robbins, Christopher G.
  Expelling hope : the assault on youth and the militarization of schooling / Christopher G. Robbins.
       p. cm. — (Suny series, interruptions—border testimony(ies) and critical discourse/s)
  Includes bibliographical references and index.
  ISBN 978-0-7914-7505-8 (hardcover : alk. paper)
  1. Education—Political aspects—United States.   2. Critical pedagogy—United States.   3. Democracy—United States.   I. Title.

LC89.R63 2008
371.5'430973—dc22   2007035103

10 9 8 7 6 5 4 3 2 1

This book is dedicated to my late mom, Linda Robbins,
whose patience, support, and deep understanding were instrumental
in developing my outlook and life in myriad ways.

Contents

Acknowledgments

Books are difficult to write and are never the creation of a sole author. They require the direct and indirect support of very many colleagues, friends, and family. This book is no exception, especially considering the disturbing and complex character of the subject matter. It is also the result of innumerable conversations that I had with incredibly insightful scholars by way of the important works they had the civic courage to make public. These courageous scholars, I assume and hope, will recognize the respect I have for their work and the intellectual debt I owe them.

I am grateful to Henry A. Giroux, the impacts of whose mentorship and friendship are probably clearly etched throughout the project, and whose ongoing guidance, intellectual acuity and generosity of thought will be appreciated long after the ink dries on this project. I thank him for perceiving something in me years ago and having confidence in that something eventually emerging as a result of the patient and critical tutelage he graciously provided me as his research assistant. During the early stages of this project, Jacqueline Edmondson, Patrick Shannon, and Chongdae Park were incredibly helpful and supportive. Without Kevin Tavin's instruction and friendship, the project might not have been possible. Doug Morris has been a great friend, whose civic courage is a model to follow. Valerie Polakow has been a tremendous source of insight, solidarity, and friendship. I would like to also thank my colleagues Joe Bishop, Jeanne Pietig, Rebecca Martusewicz, Rob Carpenter, PK Smith, and Stephanie Daza for their collegiality and friendship. Vernon Polite, Michael Bretting, and Donald Bennion (my deans and department head) have been supportive of me in various endeavors. For this, I am grateful. My extended family, the Farvar's, have provided much-needed assistance during this stage of my career and beyond; I

am thankful in ways far exceeding my facility with language for everything they have done and continue to do. I also thank my "brothers,"
Scott, George, Ed, and Dennis, for their patience with me (and my indignation), especially in the early stages of this work. Many thanks go to Eileen
Meehan and Michael Campochiaro at SUNY Press for their patience and
assistance. Of course, my students provide me with much needed engagement, intellectual stimulation, and hope. I thank my dad, Gary Robbins, for
his support and encouragement. My younger sister, Liz, deserves much
praise for the many lessons she has taught me about tolerance and respect.
Thanks go to Natasha Mayers (mayersnatasha@gmail.com) for gener-
ously granting permission to use "Snagged," one of her many insightful
pieces of art, on the cover.

Lastly and most importantly, I extend my deepest appreciation and
love to my wife and partner, Aryana, for her wide-ranging support,
commitment, patience, generosity, and love. She deserves partial credit
for this project, as she not only listened to every argument from its
inception to its provisional completion and read (and reread) the whole
book, but also shored up financial deficits, performed unpaid shifts at
home, and endlessly devoted her time and love to our wonderful daughter,
Mandana, as various periods in the development of this project placed
additional demands on my time. I thank Aryana for everything she is
and does. With her caring and gentle spirit, curiosity, sense of humor,
and playfulness, Mandana is a true inspiration for me.

It is my wish that this book critically contributes to a much
needed public conversation about and movement against the social
injustices wreaked on youth today, so that Mandana and other children
in her generation can create, participate in, and share a world that
develops and relishes—instead of stigmatizes and expels—the hope for
and commitment to a just and humane society and future.

Expelling Hope

Zero Tolerance and the Attack on Youth, Public Schooling, and Democracy

A culture of fear plays a primary role in provoking private anxieties and redefining public issues in contemporary American society. This is another way of saying that a disparate set of free floating and seemingly self-perpetuating fears, rather than a coordinated set of shared social responsibilities, currently mobilizes and organizes dominant social relationships in the U.S. Fear guides a War of Terror that, as such, is not only presented as perpetual and unending, but is also, in actuality, enacted pervasively. Its reach extends sweepingly—to definable and redefinable geo-political targets and foreign nationals of Middle Eastern descent to university professors and the U.S. Constitution and civil liberties with the passing of the USA PATRIOT Act and other covert operations like the National Security Agency's wiretapping scheme enacted by the federal government under the administration of President Bush. The mainstream media has exacerbated the culture of fear by silencing groups and discourses that question the commonsense ideology of fear. Instead of portraying and including diverse voices and perspectives as being central to democratic public life, the media portrays dissent as unacceptable, dangerous, and treasonous. The wide-ranging fear associated with the current War of Terror resonates with nightly newscasts that focus on anything from "outbreaks" of West Nile virus to new dangers lurking in public spaces and to upgraded, downgraded, and false terror alerts. Fear also is the framing device for the plots of innumerable crime shows that advertise the high-tech surveillance devices being tested and deployed daily in public and private settings—all under the guise of assuaging societal fears and moral panics about dangerous others, whoever or whatever they might be at any point in time. Prior to the tragedies of September 11, 2001, (White) suburban fears of young African American males, coded as superpredators, purportedly spreading violence and drugs, were (and continue to be) motivating factors in the formulation of official social policies such as random searches and seizures, zero tolerance, three-strikes and mandatory minimum sentencing, and informal variants, such as police harassment and brutality, that implicitly profile and disproportionately punish urban, poor, citizens of color.

The mobilization of this repressive fear, what Corey Robin (2004) calls political fear, is not new. As Robin documents, fear is not only a preoccupation of prominent philosophers meditating on the shifts from feudal society to modern, state-based regimes but also and, more recently, can be seen to have played a crucial role at various points across the 20th century in the United States. Think of the Red Scare, the Palmer Raids of 1919–1920, the McCarthy witch hunts of the early 1950s that sought to smoke out the perpetrators of the Red Menace, and the COINTEL program of the 1960s (Cole, 2003), and, now recall the revelations, in December 2005, of President Bush's secret National Security Agency (NSA) spying program that has targeted a range of individuals and groups under the guise of national security and the Orwellian protection of civil liberties. In all cases, various levels of government and multiple actors in civil society—such as churches, employers, the media, and schools—were instrumental in reproducing fear through silencing and punishing individuals in the name of protecting and maintaining national security. Thus, a culture of fear benefits those with power, because it allows powerful social actors and institutions to squelch opposition to their interests by referring to a broader set of domestic and/or foreign threats (e.g., communists, Black radicals, terrorists), while diverting attention from and reinforcing the asymmetrical conditions of power that underpin and provoke social tensions.

In this way, a culture of fear promotes a low intensity warfare of sorts not only on the principles of democracy and democratization but also on individuals and groups who bear the brunt of stigmatization, punishment, social exclusion, and the related limitations of civil rights, liberties, and life chances. If democracy is understood to be an inclusive political form concerned with protecting and expanding the rights and life chances of all citizens and democratization can be understood as a social agenda and set of processes and relationships that enable citizens to participate in the redistribution of resources so as to encourage more representative forms of being governed and inclusive forms of governing, then political fear and the supporting modes of culture through which it is mobilized are antithetical to democracy.

Unfortunately, two dominant—sometimes overlapping and occasionally contradictory—groups in the United States reproduce and manage the conditions for defining democracy and democratization at this point in history. The neoliberal faction sees democracy as merely an economic form of social organization, in which democracy is understood to be increased and unfettered corporate control of both material, immaterial, public and private resources, and an expanding horizon of consumer choice. The neoliberal faction has had devastating impacts on the *form* and *function* of a range of public goods ranging from healthcare and social welfare to social security, the environment and public schools, subjecting public services to privatization, commercialization, and strict cost-benefit analyses that reduce the complexity of human existence to the barebones ethic of the bottom line. The other faction, the neoconservatives, understands democracy more as a cultural form that serves the interests of religious fundamentalism, jingoistic patriotism, macho paternalism, homogeneity, and rugged individualism. The neoconservative faction has produced troubling changes in the content of public institutions and services, sometimes in coordination with neoliberal efforts, other times simply overlaying neoliberal interests. The neoconservative regime justifies the erosion of public goods and civil liberties through promoting the notion that only individuals are responsible for their fates, individuals need to take initiative, and the standard of the White middle-class, heterosexual family is the one to which citizens are suppose to aspire. Clearly, the intersecting battle lines of the market revolution and conservative restoration circumscribe and exclude scores of individuals such as the poor, the sick, the elderly, people of color, single women (with children or pregnant), gays, lesbians and any individual or group unwilling to toe the mutually constitutive lines of militarism, commercialism, and religious and political conformism. This, in short, can be seen as the conditions of possibility for zero tolerance: a Manichean praxis of absolutes—U.S. versus them, good versus evil, patriotic versus unpatriotic, appropriate versus inappropriate, inside versus outside, and so forth.

However, one profound and often overlooked expression of the culture of fear is the persistent, retrograde war that is being waged against youth, and poor students of color. While public schools have historically failed in providing this population appropriate, equitable, and meaningful learning/social opportunities, the current attack on youth mediated by public schools is fundamentally different and more intense than previous battles. This attack on both youth and public schools is different and more intense because zero tolerance, as legislated by the Gun-Free Schools Act of 1994 (Public Law 103-227, 1994), has legalized the exclusion of primarily poor youth of color from schools. This attack on youth is also being waged at a time when the purpose and viability of public schools are put under sustained public scrutiny, fiscal disciplining and redefinition as a result of largely neoliberal cultural-economic initiatives of school choice, privatization, and accountability. Exclusion is no longer the excess of a stable but hierarchical system linked to the division of labor. Exclusion is a functional component of a system that has eroded the conditions that made it possible for citizens to reflect on and occasionally contest its excesses. Further, with the extreme restructuring of the division of labor that is attendant to the neoliberal economic and social policies associated with negative globalization, it is unclear if, how, and in what ways public schools, especially urban ones, are linked to the division of labor. But the incursion of zero tolerance policies on public schools is not simply a mechanism to enforce the narrow winner-take-all philosophy of the new world order that pervades education policy, school organization and administration, and classroom practice under the new testing-punishment regime; within the culture of fear, *zero tolerance marks the routinization of a growing "war" mentality that is central to a militarizing social order in which brute force, fear, and exclusion prevail over dialogue and critical debate, democratic engagements with difference and inclusion, and mutual responsibility for a shared social fate.* In this way, zero tolerance also chimes well with neoconservative interests in promoting patriotic education, where the purpose of schooling invariably is to cultivate in students the values and propensities to support a revolutionary neoconservative and militarizing social order (Gingrich, 2005). Thus, zero tolerance must be explored because it is crucial to not only understanding the ongoing militarization of schools but also the larger assault being waged on democracy vis-à-vis its attack on youth, particularly youth of color.

What is Zero Tolerance?

Zero tolerance is a general school discipline policy that responds with similar punishments to both nonviolent behaviors that are perceived to be disruptive and weapons and drug related infractions of school discipline codes. Russell Skiba and Reese Peterson (1999) note that zero tolerance was first documented in 1983 as a Navy response to substance use by service members. Zero tolerance was expanded in 1986 by the U.S. Attorney in San Diego "to impound seacraft carrying any amount of drugs" and in 1988, by the Federal government as a customs policy to curtail drug traffic. As these uses of zero tolerance became more widely noted, other social policies became infused and defined by the tactic. Under the rubric of quality of life policing, criminal justice policies were defined by zero tolerance, mandatory minimum sentencing, and other get-tough initiatives in cities like New York, Los Angeles, and Philadelphia. Social problems such as homelessness and nonviolent previously noncriminal issues like youth curfews, skateboarding and loitering also became susceptible to zero tolerance. Many urban public school systems embraced zero tolerance by the late 1980s.

In response to an apparent increase in youth violence, particularly in public schools, congress passed the Gun-Free School Zones Act of 1990, which banned guns within a distance of one thousand feet of schools and municipal playgrounds, in the hope of ridding public schools of violence. As the media continued to focus on both real and exaggerated or disparate incidents of school violence, public concern with school safety reached the point at which the legitimacy and future of public education was at stake (Noguera, 1995). Senators Diane Feinstein (CA) and Byron Dorgan (ND) coauthored the Gun-Free Schools Act of 1994, which Dorgan tellingly tagged "the law of the land" in a senate floor speech (see also Feinstein, 1994). As Title VIII in the renewal of the Elementary and Secondary Education Act of 1965, the Gun-Free Schools Act of 1994 mandated the following:

> No assistance may be provided to any local educational agency
> under this Act unless such agency has in effect a policy requiring
> the expulsion from school for a period of not less than one year
> of any student who is determined to have brought a weapon to a
> school under the jurisdiction of the agency. (Public Law 103–
> 227, 1994)

Within the first year after GFSA 1994 was mandated, all states except
Vermont instituted a state-level zero tolerance policy, 94% of public
schools had drafted zero tolerance policies for firearms, 91% of public
schools drafted policies for weapons other than firearms, 87% of schools
implemented zero tolerance policies for alcohol-related incidents, while
79% of schools rewrote or drafted zero tolerance policies for tobacco-
related crimes and violent behavior (U.S. Department of Education,
1999). However, like the sweeping use of zero tolerance that took hold
of other social policies, zero tolerance in schools grew into a far-
reaching practice from which children have had criminal charges brought
against them for behaviors as trivial as tossing peanuts on a bus, eight-
year-old suspended for pointing a chicken finger at a teacher and saying
"pow-pow," and any other range of behaviors that teachers and administrators have deemed disruptive to the classroom environment or threatening to school officials. These are common practices of zero tolerance
at the local level, not statistical aberrations. The overwhelming majority
of documented exclusions due to zero tolerance are for disruptive
behaviors or behaviors defined as disorderly conduct alone (Browne,
2003, 2005; Fuentes, 2003). What's more, students of color are subjected
disproportionately to school exclusion as a result of zero tolerance. As
I discuss in chapter 1, many of these zero tolerance practices are consequences not only of the particular policy process through which zero
tolerance was passed, where the policy went through various levels of
definition and distortion between the Federal mandate to state law and
then to local policy formulation (Sughrue, 2003), but also because of
the inconsistent comprehension, interpretation and practice of the law
by local administrators and teachers (Dunbar & Villarruel, 2002).

   Much has been written about and, unsurprisingly, against the
policy and practice of zero tolerance in schools. The broad questions
guiding the various studies on zero tolerance can be broken down into
three rough interest areas and sets of assumptions: the social and cultural

context in and of public schools; the legal aspects of zero tolerance; and, the implications of zero tolerance on educational opportunity and life chances. Questions that resonate throughout studies of zero tolerance are: How does zero tolerance change teacher-student relationships? How does zero tolerance alter both the structural relationships and material conditions of schools? In what ways and how does zero tolerance deny due process and civil rights? How does zero tolerance support broader dominating and derogatory conceptions and receptions of youth? What does zero tolerance do to students' educational opportunity and future civic and economic viability?

Critiques of zero tolerance have appeared commonly in venues ranging from alternative rags like *LA Weekly* (Kuipers, 2001) to esteemed legal journals such as *The Michigan Journal of Race and Law* (Zweifler & DeBeers, 2002). At least six book-length studies of zero tolerance have been published by teachers, social science and education scholars, lawyers and legal advocates (Advancement Project/Harvard Civil Rights Project, 2000; Ayers, Dohrn, & Ayers, 2001; Browne, 2003; Casella, 2001; Johnson, Boyden, & Pittz, 2001; Skiba and Noam, 2002). In addition to legal and child advocacy groups like the Student Advocacy Center, the Harvard Civil Rights Project, the Advancement Project, End Zero Tolerance, and Building Blocks for Youth, the American Bar Association (2001), American Academy of Pediatrics (2003), and the National Mental Health Association (2003) have issued unequivocal condemnations of the practice of zero tolerance for reasons varying from the abridgment of "anti-discrimination policies" (ABA, 2001) to "potential physical health, mental health, and safety concerns that arise from suspension from school" (AAP, 2003) and the failure to meet "mental health or educational needs" of students (NHMA, 2003). Nonetheless, federal law still supports and encourages the practice of zero tolerance in public schools. The most general themes that have emerged from the policy and practice of zero tolerance should thus be introduced.

The punitive rationale for zero tolerance, coupled with a non-reflective/-thinking method of application, has undermined the social relations in and everyday practices of (public) schools (Dohrn, 2001; Giroux, 2001; Noguera, 1995; Robbins, 2005). As the sociologist A. Troy Adams (2000) states, zero tolerance is clearly "a get-tough approach reminiscent of sixteenth-century draconian practices." In using zero tolerance in public schools, teachers, administrators, and security personnel deploy two primary tactics: the weeding out of troublemakers; and the public punishment of students, a tactic that has been variably defined as weed and seed, search and destroy, detect and punish. These are, as the respected sociologist Emile Durkheim pointed out in the early 1900s, techniques used by authority figures to create the image that an individual is entirely culpable for a particular behavior and thus accountable to some form of punishment. The objective is to instill fear in the rest of the group while maintaining a fragile institutional consensus by hiding the social and structural conditions of the behavior.

The search element of zero tolerance is demonstrated by numerous examples: the installation of cameras and closed circuit television systems that monitor nearly every aspect of the students' days; metal detectors and biometric scanners that detect the possession of weapons, drugs, and drug paraphernalia; random police sweeps replete with search-and-sniff dogs; emergency lockdowns of students and most faculty to expedite search procedures; and undercover agents posing as students to search out juicy leads on possible fights, weapons, or drug possession, even verbal threats made in reference to school personnel.

Punishment eagerly waits on the other side of these practices and devices. For example, it was reported that a student was suspended for five days for having two Tylenol found in her backpack during a drug sweep while she attended gym class and her bag was left unattended (Scaife, 2004). Whether the girl needed the Tylenol for a recent illness, just had them in the event she would need them or, more centrally, if this action violated her fourth amendment rights under the search and seizure clause were all beside the point. In New York City public schools, school security officers—members of a force that exceeded 4600 as of March 2007—regularly arrest students for disorderly conduct when they contest apparent violations of their fourth amendment rights during the police force's daily metal detector searches of upwards of 93,000 students (Muhkarjee & Karpatkin, 2007). The patent objective here is not simply to scare or teach a group through spectacle (e.g., the frightening image of uniformed police officers and dogs storming through schools) that anyone of them could experience the same punishment and exclusion from school life, if they, too, choose to transgress a school's well-fortified boundaries of zero tolerance. More precisely, zero tolerance more powerfully links fear and authority through spectacle. Again, as a blanket approach, zero tolerance practices operate regardless of students' rationales and the conditions of possibility for their actions, however nonviolent or violent.

The search and destroy logic and symbolic function of zero tolerance undermine school social relations and practices in a more general and perhaps more fundamental way. The idea and the practice of zero tolerance impose a climate of fear, mistrust, and alienation instead of fostering a school-community culture built on practices of respect, trust, and belonging. As the various contributors to *Zero Tolerance: Resisting the Drive for Punishment in Our Schools* explicitly state or tacitly suggest, the traditional responsibilities of the teacher, such as providing guidance and support, are traded for the "policing of schools" where "[l]aw enforcement rather than education becomes a prime vehicle of socialization for students" (Dohrn, 2001, p. 98). Through sting operations and the example set by undercover agents, students have learned quickly that both their teachers and the police (and sometimes individuals who look like other students) are not primarily involved in school life to guide and protect them, but to set up conditions that make it easier for professionals and other authority figures to find, frame, and forbid certain students from school life. Fear becomes one of the primary elements in student-teacher relationships, and it promotes a perpetual cycle of *mistrust* (Dohrn, 2001; Giroux, 2004a), student *misbehavior* (as certain students receive different sets of expectations than other students in the school) (Casella, 2001), professional *misfeasence* as teachers abdicate responsibility for their classrooms and schools (Beger, 2002), and *alienation* as students are divided against themselves and professionals, making it possible for individuals to become the sole sites onto which responsibility for the social relations and material conditions of schools are projected (Noguera, 1995, 2003; Robbins, 2005). These and other issues concerning the social and cultural contexts of schools under the guiding metaphor of zero tolerance will be addressed throughout the project. There are, nonetheless, two other major themes that animate studies of zero tolerance.

Zero tolerance disinvests in (the idea of) youth. Despite, or perhaps masking, the steady decrease in youth violence in schools over the last thirteen years (Brooks, Schiraldi, & Ziedenberg, 2000; Gagnon & Leone, 2002; Office of Juvenile Justice and Delinquency Prevention, 2003), the practice of zero tolerance reinforces, taps, and exacerbates disproportionate media representation of the alleged criminal state of youth affairs (Males, 1996; Schiraldi & Ziedenberg, 2001). Zero tolerance participates in this social-political trend by ultimately defining nonviolent, noncriminal and violent criminal behavior the same through providing the same punishment—exclusion—for incongruent behaviors that occur under equally disparate circumstances. For example, a fifteen-year-old girl in Louisiana was recently expelled for a year, after a teacher found Advil in her purse during a search for cigarettes (Brumble, 2003). An honors student in Wisconsin was also suspended with an expulsion pending for supposedly committing a crime the equivalent of "making a bomb threat" by "threatening" the school's principal in a lyric on a homemade rap CD (Epstein, R. J., 2003). Additionally, Christopher Dunbar and Francisco Villarruel (2002) have found that some rural school districts in Michigan allow students to possess firearms in their cars during hunting season, while urban schools in Michigan have been found to exclude students for merely being disruptive. Regardless of the fact that the first two examples referred to above fall outside of the purview of the federal zero tolerance mandate, these responses are currently legal according to their respective local zero tolerance policies. In a media environment and political climate that is predisposed to representing youth as a menace to society, these instances of zero tolerance all too easily reinforce the predominant framing of youth as being more of a problem than promise.

What's more, the public disinvests in youth through zero tolerance by using the law to frame and punish youth behaviors in devastating ways. The practice of zero tolerance has been found in some instances to violate students' and families' rights to due process (Rubin, 2004; Zweifler & DeBeers, 2002) and civil rights (Harvard Civil Rights Project, 2000; Eskenazi, Eddins, & Beam, 2003). Administrators and some school resource officers are not required to issue Miranda rights, but they can still use evidence they gather from students to press criminal charges. In other instances, special education laws codified in the Education for All Handicapped Children Act (1975) (renamed the Individuals with Disabilities Education Act [1990]) can be/are also abridged and circumvented by school zero tolerance policies. But, further and possibly more telling, zero tolerance can start an entire criminal process for students based on behaviors for which adults are spared punishment of any kind. For example, zero tolerance infractions can result in a student's placement in a detention center. As I will discuss further in chapter 1, this student is subjected to potentially overcrowded and violent conditions without educational provisions. Unsurprisingly, students subjected to this process often find it difficult to return to school, at which point they are sent back to the criminal justice system or turned out to the streets in which they are susceptible to punitive policing tactics and an increased likelihood of being arrested and charged for criminal violations. Thus, a law such as zero tolerance that was purportedly designed as a tool to protect students becomes a weapon to batter much of their life chances by way of the structural enmeshing of "nurturing institutions" such as public schools with the punishment system in the era of mass incarceration (Rios, 2006).

Hence, *zero tolerance also threatens educational opportunity and the life chances of most youth, and particularly poor youth of color.* Judith A. Browne (2003) notes how zero tolerance shifts former, de facto tracking mechanisms to a criminal, juvenile justice track—what she names the "schoolhouse to jailhouse track." In the past, students were partitioned in academic, business, and vocational tracks in schools in ways that were largely reflective of race and class hierarchies in the division of labor, and this still occurs—the division of labor in a post-industrial, globalized market has simply been reordered, thus altering the functionality and viability of the less valued schoolhouse tracks. As public funds for public schools are transferred to other areas (e.g., the military, policing and mass incarceration, tax cuts for the wealthy, etc.), many public schools are forced to eliminate vocational programs and extracurricular activities. As a consequence, youth who were previously directed (for better or worse) into these school-related areas are increasingly channeled into systems of punishment, as schools use zero tolerance as a safety valve to dispose students for whom they do not have the structural or personnel resources or for students who require more intense academic resources (e.g., additional staff or staff with specialized certifications, curricular materials or, simply, extra time) to perform adequately on standardized tests (Noguera, 2003; Zweifler & DeBeers, 2002). Accordingly, zero tolerance undermines already-tested educational opportunities. Further, increased suspensions and expulsions due to zero tolerance extend a previously established link between school exclusion and later school dropout (Skiba, 2000). Moreover, common to most studies of zero tolerance is an emphasis on the highly unequal impact on the life chances for youth of color. While the rates cannot be explained by differences in or degrees of severity of behaviors under like circumstances, African American youth are suspended and expelled from schools at a rate of 1.5 to 2.5 times their representation in school populations,[1] whereas white students of all classes experience school suspension and expulsion rates far below or equal to their representative school populations. Consequently, increased suspension and expulsion as a result of zero tolerance, whether leading to school pushout or insertion into the criminal justice system, limit the future social, political, and economic viability of youth, especially youth of color.

Zero tolerance inflicts academic and social damages on all youth, even if in different ways for those who remain in or are excluded from school. Those who elude the wrath of zero tolerance are left to perceive their educational opportunity as tentative and others must accommodate the social fact that their educational opportunity comes as a result of the denial of the same opportunity to other students (regardless, as Dewey would have put it, of how this social fact is rationalized), while excluded students pay the ultimate social, political, and economic price for a society that appears to have zero tolerance for the idea of youth. The sheer severity of zero tolerance creates or justifies a system of school relations and practices that make it difficult to have zero tolerance for legitimately dangerous behaviors and tolerance for students who are simply unwanted in certain school environments. All students, albeit in different ways, must navigate this Scylla and Charybdis of punishment and alienation in schools. All youth are thus denied the fullest and most meaningful, supportive and trusting democratic public education possible.

A Clarification of Values and Overview

These primary points of criticism—devastating impacts on school contexts and individual development, the abrogation of civil rights and the denial of educational opportunity, and disinvestment in (the idea of) youth—might be considered the observed and well-documented consequences of zero tolerance, and I will address them in significant detail in chapter 1. However, zero tolerance acts in a wider social context as a condensation point—or catchword—for sometimes divergent, otherwise caustically convergent discourses and processes associated with the ascendance and restoration of the dominating social formations of neoliberalism and social conservatism.[2] The discourses and processes that involve these social formations fragment social relationships; atomize issues of social risk; stigmatize personal troubles; celebrate the new and more rugged individual; valorize the market and military as the penultimate models of social organization and control; codify public issues of race and racism in color-blind terms of "crime," "cultural deficit," or private pathology instead of social justice and structural inequality; and expel educated hope from the social field of struggle and possibility—the ultimate effect of which is the undermining of the conditions of democracy and the relationships crucial for democratization.

I will address these social, political, cultural, and economic moorings and consequences of zero tolerance in different ways and at different times in the critical study that follows, and I will be concerned with how the articulation of zero tolerance with cultural practices and material relationships particularly impacts the social realm, youth, race, and racial justice. These are three specific categories of interest, among others, that are crucial to democracy and democratization and which are particularly threatened in the current political climate, especially by zero tolerance and its relationships to the processes of criminalization and militarization.

The vitality of the social realm has been long held as a crucial facet of democracy. Historically, the social has been defined as the political space that stands between private people in their roles as citizens in public life (Arendt, 1958). As Hannah Arendt (1958) describes it, the social realm is comparable to a table around which individuals are seated; it "relates and separates [people] at the same time" (p. 52). As the social relates separate(d) citizens through a space shared in common, it increases the likelihood that individualized interests can be held in common or made common. The social, in other words, provides a space in which citizens can translate private sufferings into ones publicly intelligible and of common importance (Bauman, 1999). Consequently, the social performs another vital function to democratic public life. By orienting individual people around common or contested interests, the social leaves open the possibility for the past to be a guiding authority of public decision-making, and for discipline (that is, self-governance and social governance) to become a public and democratized—that is, inclusive, positive, and shared—feature of a common public life. Without the social in real or imaginary terms, separate individuals remain separate and unrelated by increasingly separated life projects and worldviews and the extremely polarized bifurcation of life chances. But, obviously, the social is contingent upon material spaces, time, and vocabularies in which the private-public translation can become operative. Space-time defined by, and a lexicon replete with, equality (of being) and justice can only become operative if "everyone [is] included in power sharing and decision making, from the rich to the poor" (Difazio, 2003, p. 160). This means that the social is limited if political or economic inequalities structurally exclude citizens from the social as a space held in common. The social is a product of unequal human relations and is thus contingent upon the reproductive capacities of future generations to whom it is articulated.

It is a given that if youth are denied the skills of democratic public life and deprived of the opportunities, spaces, and vocabularies to internalize and practice them, the possibility for reproducing—let alone extending—future democratizing impulses is dramatically diminished. Hence the centrality of (the idea of) youth to democratic public life. While the category of youth has been defined differently across historical contexts and troubled by contradictory systems of support and abuse across time and place in the United States (Finkelstein, 2000; Giroux, 1999; Giroux & Giroux, 2004), youth were conceived and received across the twentieth century as a political promise and a social responsibility. The drafting of compulsory education laws, the prohibition on child labor, social support for families victimized by economic downturns, the definition of "child abuse as a legally punishable social offense" (Finkelstein, 2000, p. 22), and the decision to ban segregated and unequal schools as unconstitutional through *Brown v. Board of Education* (1954) were manifestations of social struggles that demonstrated a commitment to the promise of youth. As Lawrence Grossberg (2001) notes, "Youth became" during much of the twentieth century, "the trope of the universal faith in futurity . . . [a] symbolic guarantee that America still had a future, that it still believed in a future, and that it was crucial to America to invest its faith in that future" (p. 133. See also Grossberg, 2005). Clearly, the symbolic and the material are interlaced in the category of youth: to invest materially in youth presupposes immaterial—symbolic—investment in youth as a promise for future society and the future of democracy. However, the troubled history of social investments in youth is related to the history of, and contemporary practices that revolve around, issues of racial justice.

Racialized practices in society, politics, culture, and the economy impeded democracy in the United States and abroad from the time of the state's formation. Under slavery and later Jim Crow, African Americans were completely disenfranchised and systematically excluded from social, cultural, and economic life. Racialized power was simply but devastatingly explicit and explicitly accepted even when it wasn't legalized. U.S. democracy is still deterred and deferred by racial injustice. This racial condition that undermines democratization in the United States and abroad is suspended from public understanding and judgment by the contemporary hegemony of the discourse of colorblindness, which ignores racial hierarchies in both society and the economy. This discourse hides the social fact that inequalities are built into the system of governance (e.g., rigging voting districts, the criminalization of social problems that exist in areas of high poverty, and racial segregation); into segregated residential housing and thus re-segregated public schools; and into structurally exclusive employment practices. Those economic opportunities that are still viable glom onto suburban, exurban, and largely white labor bases, creating cumulative patterns of investment and disinvestment. The discourse of color blindness then latches onto the myth of individual responsibility and merit, and casts individuals marginalized by economic and political structures of opportunity as completely culpable for their lot—as participants in allegedly pathological subcultures, not victims of a sick social order. Consequently, the contemporary dis-engagement with the abuses of racial profiling and retreats from racial justice actively masks the dis-accumulation of power and privileges over time for racialized groups (Brown, Carnoy, Currie, Duster, Oppenheimer, Shultz, et al., 2003). Therefore, any effort at democratization must recognize and democratically address how the racial hierarchy persists, if only under a different name (e.g., multiculturalism, color blindness, post-multiracial society), and how "its ubiquity, its presence [is demonstrated] in both the 'smallest' and the 'largest' features of social relationships, institutions, and identities" (Winant, 2001, p. 313).

In chapter 2, I address the realm of the social, youth, race, and racial justice, with a specific and sustained focus on the relationships between the hidden curriculum of schooling and the liberal democratic social contract. In particular, I focus on how zero tolerance, in coordination with the ascendant neoliberal market order, contravenes the modern, democratic social contract's obligations to youth by redefining them as social threats or disposable, and alters the function of public schools by subjecting the provision of education to scarcity through privatization and commercialization, the broad processes in which the testing, funding, punishment regime operates and gains meaning. Zero tolerance institutionalizes, illuminates, and normalizes the most egregious tendencies of the hidden curriculum. Marginalization, stigmatization, sorting, and exclusion, in the light of market pressures and other perversions of the democratic social contract undermine the life chances of youth. These subversions of the democratic purposes of public schools and deformations of the social contract are racially and class structured, disproportionately producing severe social injuries for both poor students and students of color.

The reconfiguring of school space and time under the process of militarization and in relation to zero tolerance is discussed in chapter 3. Following Doreen Massey (1994), I explore the categories of space and time as space-time, in which space and time are interdependent and interconstitutive. That is, they are dialectically related categories of social interaction that gain meaning and power through the social relationships that produce space-time—and are produced by it. Certain definitions of time and configurations of space are crucial to processes of democratization. This is because the ordering of space and the objects and bodies in it is a pedagogical practice. Space teaches participants the values, knowledges, and range of behaviors appropriate to it. Space, and the values it promotes, are conditioned by, as well as condition, the definition of time applied to it. This is important for understanding both the blatant and latent consequences of zero tolerance, as the social in schools is rewired in soft and hard terms, teachers and students are provided with and enter into different systems of signification or meaning-making, and zero tolerance's rewiring of space and altered definition of time operate in relation to predominant racial politics. Chapter 3 also allows for an investigation of how the processes of criminalization and militarization have penetrated public schools through the security industry and programs such as Junior Reserve Officers' Training Corps. It will be seen that zero tolerance reinforces and is reinforced by the school relationships promoted by criminalization and militarization, and, when their combined effects on school social relationships are considered, the space-time of urban public schools appears antithetical to the space-time social relationships of democracy and processes of democratization that make it operative.

By this point, the implications of zero tolerance should be clear—and harrowing. In chapter 4 I am concerned with exploring two related questions. One, what role does color-blindness perform as the ideology of the new racial politics, and in what ways does it share common ground with zero tolerance? Two, what type of society and state make sense of the different types of social exclusion that color blindness and zero tolerance perform?

I provide a tentative conclusion in chapter 5. The total picture sketched throughout chapters 1 through 4 will be necessarily bleak. The picture is dismal because the following analyses demonstrate that zero tolerance underscores a lack of social vision regarding the democratic legacy and promise of schooling. This produces dangerous impacts not only on youth but also on the fabric of democratic public life. In chapter 5, I work through the rough outlines of an oppositional vision to zero tolerance that take seriously the utmost urgency of engaging a struggle over both schooling and democratic public life as well as basing that struggle in the promise and *hope* of a democratic future.

A Final Introductory Statement

Intolerance, alienation, exclusion, and the denial of educational opportunity are the documented consequences of zero tolerance in public schools—or at least the informal tendencies of public schools that zero tolerance institutionalizes. Tolerance, proximity, inclusion, and the production of the capacities and propensities to participate in the world of work and the work of citizenship are, however, preconditions for democratic public life and the democratization of social relations and cultural practices. Rights should also be included in this list, as the *right* to equal educational opportunity was a moderate triumph in social thought and governance and as its support given by the decision in *Brown v. the Board of Education* (1954), signaled the centrality of public school life to the reproduction and extension of a democratic polity. A crucial caveat must be entered here. Public schools never operated in an ideal state that served the interests of an inclusive democracy. Rather, public schools represented more prominently in previous eras a *contested terrain* over which various groups struggled publicly to define their form, content, and purpose. In other words, public schools were always, and still are, sites of social reproduction *and* production. However, as demonstrated by the efficacy of zero tolerance, the type of reproduction has changed, and the dominant public debates concerning public schools largely exclude the role of public schools as democratic public spheres, opting instead to cast them as spheres of achievement, accountability, and private advance.[3] Thus, considering the long-documented primacy of public education to the reproduction and promotion of democratic public life through developing and augmenting the skills and knowledges youth need to be productive citizens—a legacy extending from Horace Mann, John Dewey, W. E. B. Dubois, and George Counts to educational philosophers and social critics like Paulo Freire, Henry A. Giroux, Donaldo Macedo, Pedro Noguera, and Jonathan Kozol—the following questions should be held open throughout the book. If public schools can be used to deny basic rights of citizenship and create new modes of racial exclusion, what other institutions or social forms can protect the preconditions for and expand the conditions of democratic public life? If public schools are used to reinforce a corporate and militaristic order, what other institutions will be able to, as Horace Mann (1848) notes, guard against the "fatal extremes of overgrown wealth and desperate poverty" that set the conditions for sweeping structural, symbolic, and physical violence used by overgrown wealth to protect its interests and, less frequently, by those in desperate poverty to oppose those interests? If public schools are no longer the sites through which society, in part, defines and makes its commitment to youth as a symbolic guarantee of a democratic future, what other sites can define and assume these responsibilities to youth and the future? Unless these questions frame or guide analyses and interpretations of the consequences of zero tolerance, the meaning of zero tolerance for democratic public life will remain elusive. Is the promise and hope of a democratic future something for which we, as a society, will have zero tolerance and are also willing to expel?

CHAPTER 1

The Problems of Zero Tolerance and the Problem for Democracy

A Critical Analysis

Introduction

*Z*ero tolerance is a complex and dangerous phenomenon eating away at the democratic possibilities of public schools, the rights of students, and the autonomy of teachers. This is more than a political charge. It is a theoretical position that has been intensively researched by a number of authors concerned with zero tolerance policies. Various studies demonstrate how zero tolerance, as both an ideology and policy, reinforces the culture of fear in schools, uses schools to criminalize youth, creates antidemocratic forms of authority and atomizes discipline. Many studies have shown how zero tolerance permits schools to circumvent students' Fourth and Fourteenth Amendment rights, in addition to propelling primarily students of color into a despairing process that removes them from public purview by bouncing them between dangerous social situations in their communities and institutions of the criminal justice system. Yet, other studies have documented the many ways zero tolerance undermines teacher autonomy by providing an easy, quick, and irresponsible mechanism to deal with the disruptions embedded in unequal social and educational conditions. Thus, it is important to explain how zero tolerance works and to review the research that substantiates how counterproductive the policy is for public education.

In this chapter, I review key studies of zero tolerance. I do so by considering the themes that emerge from these analyses and are pertinent to understanding its legal aspects, its impacts on educational opportunity, and its function in the changing social-cultural contexts of public schools. In part 2 of the chapter, I review a representative critical analysis of zero tolerance (Giroux, 2001a). Giroux's study considers the elements missing in other literature on zero tolerance (e.g., the political and economic), but his analysis omits the centrality of the perceived threat of violence in public schools as the motivating element in mobilizing support for zero tolerance, something that is addressed by other studies of zero tolerance. By interpreting the combined observations of all the studies reviewed here, the following approach to zero tolerance will help construct a more comprehensive picture of the phenomenon. From this more complete picture, politicized definitions of zero tolerance and violence can be devised and show the underlying tendencies of zero tolerance and violence, its foundational threat to youth, and the threat to democratic public life.[1]

I also introduce an important background consideration that should be factored into responses to zero tolerance, namely the role schools must play in structuring and maintaining democratic social spheres capable of curtailing both school violence and the inordinate exclusion of students for behaviors that are primarily disruptive or might be the symptoms of antidemocratic social relationships and unequal material conditions in schools and their wider communities.

Zero Tolerance and the Law

Much can be learned about zero tolerance by looking at its direct and indirect legal implications: (a) Zero tolerance has been found to abridge certain student rights. Zero tolerance encourages other practices such as random searches that also threaten the integrity of constitutional rights. (b) The law, policy and practice of zero tolerance achieve greater power in relation to other policies (e.g., funding schemes; accountability). (c) Studies that demonstrate the legal aspects and implications of zero tolerance also point to diminished educational opportunity in general.[2] Before turning toward the key themes of zero tolerance and law, it is necessary to understand the policy formation process of zero tolerance.

Policy Formulation

In part, the legislative process through which zero tolerance passed explains why zero tolerance continues to be practiced inconsistently, if not punitively. Zero tolerance, as explained in the introduction, was legislated under the Gun-Free Schools Act 1994. The federal law explicitly codified the stipulations that states (and local education agencies) had to follow in drafting their policies.[3] While the federal government respects states' rights in allowing them to draft zero tolerance policies according to their perceived needs, states roundly expanded, if not disrespected, the letter of the federal law. This is what Jennifer Sughrue (2003) calls the first deviation (pp. 241–42) of GFSA 1994 from law to practice. Some states tailor their definitions in ways that merely replicate the federal law, whereas others extend the state law to include drugs, harassment, or in some cases, even forms of speech they deem threatening or disruptive. The first deviation can be seen in the juxtaposition of Pennsylvania's and Michigan's zero tolerance policies. In Pennsylvania, the zero tolerance policy states:

> A school district . . . shall expel, for a period of not less than one year, a student who brought onto or is in possession of any weapon on any school property, at a school or a school-sponsored activity or onto any public conveyance providing transportation to a school or school-sponsored activity. (Safe Schools and Possession of Weapons, BEC 24 P.S.§13–1317.2, 2002)

While Pennsylvania's zero tolerance policy adheres closely to GFSA 1994, Michigan takes greater liberty with its definition. Michigan legislates zero tolerance for "assaults committed against other students at school (even if no weapon was involved) [and] verbal assaults committed against school employees or volunteers" (Institute for Public Policy and Social Research, 2002, p. 2). But it also implements zero tolerance policies in instances when:

> A teacher in a public school has good reason to believe that a pupil's conduct in a class, subject, or activity constitutes conduct

for which the pupil may be suspended from a class, subject, or
activity according to the local policy . . . [T]he teacher may [then]
cause the pupil to be suspended from the class, subject, or
activity for up to 1 full school day. (Michigan Compiled Laws
380.1309 2006)[4]

Sughrue's extensive research of school district and local school zero
tolerance policies found that local education agencies repeatedly drafted
distorted versions of GFSA 1994, resulting in the continued expansion
and confusion over the intent and practice of the law at the classroom
level. Christopher Dunbar and Francisco Villarruel (2002) demonstrate
the ways by which school administrators and teachers further distort
the law, which is not entirely their fault or an unpredictable outcome
of the law, as it reached local school systems in versions quite different
from the federal formulation of it.

After studying administrator and teacher responses to zero tolerance in urban schools in Michigan, Dunbar and Villarruel (2002) found
gaps and distortions in the comprehension and interpretation of the law.
In this study, the authors found large gaps in administrator comprehension, that is, what they remembered of the law, its intent, and conditions
for its application. Furthermore, Dunbar and Villarruel agree that not
only is Michigan's law on zero tolerance far reaching, but also that
teachers and administrators broadly interpret the policy, and practice it
inconsistently. Teachers have indiscriminately applied the law, such as in
cases where "teachers made snap suspensions even if students [only]
'rolled their eyes' allegedly at [them]" (p. 96) and in situations where
administrators overrode the teacher's decision either because the teacher's
choice was rash or because out of school suspension wouldn't provide
appropriate punishment to the student (p. 99).

Nonuniformity, however, should not be confused with the notion
that GFSA 1994 is exercised in specific and deliberate ways that are
mindful of both the policy and democratic sensibilities. But administrators and teachers generally hold differing views on what the original
law states and how to interpret and practice GFSA 1994 according to
their schools' policies. That teachers and administrators misinterpret the
law itself might be a function of the degree to which they distort the
perceived need for it, particularly around issues of weapons and drugs.
In other words, teachers and administrators approach school relationships as a result of local community pressures attendant to changing

demographics. This latent feature of the law and the practice of zero tolerance comes with potentially dangerous consequences for students' constitutional rights.

Abridging Student Rights

While many urban public schools employed police officers before the legislation of zero tolerance, suburban schools have gradually employed police, school resource officers, and plainclothed agents since zero tolerance policies were implemented, especially in light of the Columbine tragedy. In recent years, both suburban and urban public schools have introduced security technologies such as cameras and closed-circuit television systems, free standing and hand held metal detectors and, in some instances, biometric scanning devices. Much of this enters schools relatively uncontested—uncontested because their intended purpose is to promote safety (Goldberg, 2003; Kennedy, 2004; Sansbury, 2003).[5] But, as demonstrated by zero tolerance, the wider policy that frames the support for these incursions on public school environments, intended purpose and use are not the same as actual use and its actual consequences. Randall Beger (2002) provides three related caveats about the rise of security technologies in schools in the punishing climate of zero tolerance. On the one hand, security corporations provide special packages for schools to do trial runs of new devices. This has the effect of making students into "guinea pigs" in "learning prisons," (p. 120). On the other hand, it comes as no small surprise that when these technologies are coupled with school resource officers, undercover cops and the framing of zero tolerance, students' Fourth amendment rights—to privacy and protection against unreasonable search and seizure—are reduced markedly, if not completely obliterated, for some students. Further, public schools have support for these "hidden" consequences of zero tolerance as state and federal courts define "police search conduct [in schools] as 'minor' or 'incidental' to justify application of the reasonable suspicion standard" (p. 126). Probable cause is a remote consideration, and the burden of proving the unreasonableness of the suspicion falls entirely upon the student. As another scholar notes, the success of students and families in proving the unreasonableness of a search is next to nil because state and federal courts defer to a public school's choice of actions to maintain safety and limit disruptions in the school environment. However, the abridgment of Fourth Amendment rights teaches a more sweeping lesson, possibly showing that the abridging of certain student rights is based on the distortion of school needs for frequent searches and zero tolerance.

Joe Blankenau and Mark Leeper (2003) studied administrators' rationales for school searches in terms of what they call "morality policy." Morality policies such as zero tolerance and its related random school searches are simply used to "teach a lesson," regardless of the stated intent, the perceived need for them, and the policy's efficacy in reducing school violence. Their study found that administrators use searches not because they have been successful or they perceive a high degree of drug or weapon prevalence in their schools. On the contrary, administrators were found to employ random searches and sweeps because of pressure from local interest groups such as school boards and influential parents (p. 580. See also Bartlett, Frederick, Gulbrandsen, & Murillo, 2002). This tendency is problematic in other ways. One way random searches and threats to students' Fourth Amendment rights is questionable is that they are performed without a concern for efficacy; this lack of interest in whether or not a particular policy's practices and consequences match its intent is a primary feature of morality policies (p. 567). As Blankenau and Leeper suggest, another primary, possibly more powerful way this encroachment on Fourth Amendment rights is damaging, is that students have little autonomy to resist and question these searches due to their age and relatively low position in a school's hierarchy. This has the implicit effect of teaching students that not only are their rights tenuous and limited at best, but also that a purportedly democratic government and its institutions can "search without cause, individualized suspicion, or apparent purpose" and "waive privacy protections for many purposes (e.g., a war on drugs or a war on terror)" (p. 582) as well as, potentially, a war on youth since they are ultimately the targets and victims of school exclusions that result from the altercations these intrusive practices sometimes provoke.[6]

Threatening Students' Rights

Other constitutional rights of students have been threatened by zero tolerance and related school (discipline) practices.[7] Another student right abbreviated by zero tolerance is due process as codified in the Fourteenth Amendment.[8] The abbreviation of due process for students occurs on two primary levels. As David Rubin (2004) effectively demonstrates in his exhaustive case study review, due process for students is rendered procedural at the level of the law itself. *Goss v. Lopez* (1975), the case from which education was deemed a property right and thus subject to due process, suggests how due process might be provided but it did not devise or implement a mechanism to guarantee that the right was operative in any substantive capacity. *Goss* only suggested that local schools provide a more formal hearing process for exclusions greater than ten days. For lesser exclusions, schools are only culpable for providing minimal due process.

Because due process is given only a procedural valence, the use of cross-interrogation and the viability of appeals are limited. For example, Rubin, in affiliation with the Student Advocacy Center in Ann Arbor, Michigan, represented a case in which a student was permanently expelled for an after-school altercation in which s/he allegedly threatened a bystander. When student witnesses were later questioned, it was found that the particular threat for which he was expelled was convoluted in hearsay. If the school allowed for cross-interrogation, the student could have been given a much lesser punishment. In another situation, a parent found out one year after a child's expulsion that it could have been appealed. The only problem in this instance was that the local statute on appeals was only operative for five days, something the district neglected to tell the parent. Consequently, as Rubin brilliantly notes

> Due to the imbalance of knowledge between parents and school districts, failing to inform a parent of their right to appeal at the time of expulsion . . . often has the same practical effect as denying the parent that right altogether." (p. 10)

What's more, Rubin finds, similar to Beger (2002), that state and Federal courts consistently side with the school's decision, whether or not they agree with the severity of the punishment because, as they argue, " 'public confidence in the disciplinary authority of schools is bolstered when schools carefully adhere to their own written disciplinary policies if suspending students' " (Rubin, p. 23). Further, while all states must respect due process in protecting educational opportunity, some states (e.g., Michigan) fail to require local schools to find alternative placements for excluded students (Rubin, 2004; Zweifler & DeBeers, 2002).

But, in the case of zero tolerance exclusions, due process can be and is circumvented in other ways. This occurs through the increasing practice of *school-based arrest* (Browne, 2005; Mukharjee & Karpatkin, 2007), something not entirely unrelated to the increased presence of police in schools and the threats they pose to students' Fourth Amendment rights. If a student can be charged criminally for a perceived zero tolerance infraction such as resisting a search, due process is rendered beside the point. Judith Browne (2003, 2005) found that punishments such as *school-based arrest* are given regularly for behaviors that are not patently violent or criminal, and which were formerly handled within schools or between schools and parents. Additionally, Browne found that students with special needs are subjected to criminal charges for behaviors that are accommodated in their education plans or should be understood in terms of their specific disabilities (an infringement of educational rights legislated by Individuals with Disabilities Education Improvement Act 1990), because criminal charges allow schools to circumvent the right to the least restrictive environment for students with disabilities.[9]

Zero Tolerance, Other Laws and Policies, and Contexts

Like any other law and policy, zero tolerance cannot be understood outside of the variables of the contexts in which it is practiced. These include, but are not necessarily limited to: the demographics of a community; the resources allocated to a particular community; and the wide-ranging public and educational policies that structure and legitimate the relationships between demographics and resources. In this way, central questions must be asked not only of the perceived need for zero tolerance as a law, but also what factors contribute to the perceived need for zero tolerance as a practice. What are the most frequent behaviors punished by exclusion through zero tolerance? What students manifest these behaviors? Are the students who are most frequently subjected to zero tolerance exclusions already marginalized by class inequality, racial injustices, or both? Is this an intraschool or interschool (district) dynamic? If it's the former, what school structures influence certain student behaviors more so than others? If it's the latter, what interschool and community factors promote certain behaviors of students in one community, as opposed to another?

Michael Eskenazi, Gillian Eddins, and John M. Beam (2003) studied the relationships between demographics, resource allocation, and exclusion in New York City public schools. They found that mainly poor African American and Latino students are subjected to exclusion in New York State. This is partly the consequence of their high concentration in New York City public schools, as opposed to suburban districts. Their exclusions, however, are not only due to their concentrated populations in urban schools. African American and Latino concentration in urban schools is also propounded by unequal resource allocation between suburban and urban schools in New York. Suburban districts have lower student-competent teacher ratios, while urban schools have a dearth of competent teachers and indisputably larger student populations and class sizes. What's more, sound infrastructure and softer variables like quality libraries, functioning computer systems, and current and adequate curricular materials are wanting in New York City public schools and near givens in suburban districts, due to New York's school funding formula. These factors (e.g., the lack of engaging educational contexts) produce conditions in which disruptive behaviors not only occur more frequently, but also in which under-qualified school professionals have more difficulty in resolving the behaviors.[10] For New York City students, the paucity of resources, both in terms of competent professionals and learning materials, is compounded by a school security force of over 4600 agents and a city-wide policy (Safe Schools Against Violence in Education Act 2000) that permits teachers and school officers to exclude students for up to four days without administrative oversight (Eskenazi, Eddins & Beam, p. 8)—which eliminates the prospects for due process—and it does nothing to resolve the conditions that are promoting disruptive student behaviors in the first place, if they are, in fact, even disruptive.

This is a legal concern, however broad it may be, if not for any other reason, than because the law of zero tolerance is made more sensible and logical by other laws, policies, the relationship between resource allocation and demographics, and the combined consequences of these factors that are manifested in the systemic denial of educational opportunity. Zero tolerance helps rationalize unequal school funding and its conditions of possibility—it not only reduces educational opportunity through promoting more exclusions; zero tolerance shifts the concerns from structural issues to those of behaviors allegedly endemic to poor, urban African American and Latino youth, legitimating the general loss of educational opportunity that results from iniquitous funding schemes. Thus, zero tolerance remains federal law and local practice because it exists amidst a complex of social, political, and economic forces, and it helps justify the social and economic structure of those forces as schools and communities vie for resources.

Zero Tolerance and Educational Opportunity

Zero tolerance's impacts on educational opportunity can be approached in various ways. An insightful way of understanding the loss of educational opportunity through zero tolerance is to define both the behavior and the expulsion as moments in a process, rather than isolated events (Morrison, Anthony, Storino, Cheng, Furlong, & Morrison, 2002). The idea of expulsion-as-process clarifies the consistently disproportionate patterns of exclusion experienced by students with disabilities and students of color. As zero tolerance creates an objective link between schools and the juvenile and criminal justice system, the idea of expulsion as process also underscores the ways in which educational opportunity is further jeopardized and diminished long after the exclusion itself.

Loss of Educational Opportunity Does not Begin or End with Zero Tolerance

Rarely are mishaps in other areas of society perceived merely as accidents; extensive efforts are made to identify the conditions of the accident, the factors that might have contributed to it, and what could be done to ensure that those factors and precipitating conditions are mitigated to prevent future accidents.[11] When it comes to schools, however, a different approach is generally used (see Henry, 2000). Disruptive behaviors and the rare incidents of violence in schools are often considered discrete, aberrant events. This is not only an inadequate way of understanding school disruptions, but it is also a counterproductive method that professionals use as a basis for correcting inappropriate behavior while providing and protecting educational opportunity.

Morrison, Anthony, Storino, Cheng, Furlong, & Morrison (2002) suggest that educators and policy makers think of disruptive behavior and subsequent exclusion as a process. This comes with at least two important consequences for understanding the relationship between loss of educational opportunity and zero tolerance. The first is disruptive behaviors generally follow an identifiable pattern, or trajectory (p. 53). This is especially true for students with disabilities, diagnosed or undetected, or with other identifiable risk factors such as poverty, family upheaval, or other community strains to which particular students are subjected. A particular learning disability, if not accommodated environmentally, pedagogically, or with curricular modifications, might provoke student frustration and thus disruptive behavior. Or, for students of color and class minorities, White, middle-class teachers have been found to perceive—and punish—their communication styles as disruptive or threatening (Akom, 2001; Noguera, 2001; Skiba, 2000). In both instances, educational opportunity is diminished by teacher failures to accommodate a student's learning need or cultural capital; frustration and alienation are sound bases for disruptive behaviors.[12] Simply, *disruptive behaviors in many instances are the symptoms of a process of denial of educational opportunity.*

The second insight of seeing behavior-exclusion as a process is that exclusion—temporary or permanent—continues the process of denial of educational opportunity. While some states do not require schools to find alternative placements for excluded students other states require the provision of alternative education settings but don't enforce it (Rubin, 2004; Zweifler & DeBeers, 2002), or alternative education settings are unsupervised or undersupervised, of poor quality, or simply nonexistent, depending on the type of institution in which the student is placed (Bell, 2001; Eskenazi, Eddins, & Beam, 2003; Blumenson & Nilson, 2002). Thus, *the loss of educational opportunity for some students continues long after the exclusion "event" ends.*[16]

Who Loses Educational Opportunity through Zero Tolerance?

Generally, all students lose educational opportunity through zero tolerance. This is because the absence of tolerance frames both purportedly disruptive behavior and resulting exclusion as isolated events. Zero tolerance explicitly conveys that there is no other way of understanding and addressing the contingencies of classroom and school life. This is another way of saying that zero tolerance limits or eliminates school capacities to become more human(e) by sharing in learning processes that could resolve at least some of the conditions and relations that provoke inappropriate behaviors. But, of course, this general observation ignores who suffers most from zero tolerance.

Since zero tolerance was legislated, students with disabilities and students with identifiable risk factors have been consistently and disproportionately excluded from educational opportunity, and primarily for nonviolent and previously noncriminal(ized) behaviors. These exclusions also follow age and race lines, and they are correlated with later school dropout rates. For example, during the school year 1999–2000, 71% of students in a study on expulsion in Michigan had either identified special needs or identifiable risk factors (Zweifler & DeBeers, 2002, p. 206). At the same time in Michigan, 83% of an estimated 3600 expulsions were for zero tolerance infractions unspecified in GFSA 1994, that is, these infractions involved no firearms or dangerous weapons. African American students were 66% of these expulsions (2.4 times their representative population), while White students were 28.5% of expulsions (a rate less than their representative population) (Michigan Public Policy Initiative, 2003, pp. 6, 7–8).[14]

Since GFSA 1994 was legislated, the general increases in suspension/expulsion are telling. The data are suggestive on both city and state levels. Chicago public schools had ten expulsions during the 1993–1994 school year, but 571 during the 1997–1998 school year (Gordon, Della Piana, & Keleher, 2000, p. 12). In Wisconsin, four hundred students were expelled statewide in the 1991–1992 school year, but 1299 were expelled during 1997–1998 (Zweifler & DeBeers, p. 203). Nationally, upwards of 3 million students have been suspended annually in recent years (Fuentes, 2003), and nearly another 1 million expelled. These numbers are purposefully scattershot, to demonstrate that zero tolerance has devastating consequences wherever it is used.

One major consequence of denying educational opportunity is the relationship between school exclusion and later school dropout rates. Most exclusions occur between the sixth and ninth grades and, again, predominantly for students of color (Skiba, 2000; Zweilfer & DeBeers, 2002). African American and Latino youth drop out of school at a rate of two to three times that of Whites (Cross, 2001, pp. 6–7). Dropout and push-outs occur most often in tenth grade, following the most prevalent years (sixth to ninth grades) of school exclusion. While other factors such as high-stakes testing and overall climate of the school and community contribute to this trend (Madaus and Clarke, 2001), increased suspension and expulsion as a result of zero tolerance are also central factors. However, zero tolerance bears another consequence, not entirely unrelated to school dropout, creating another process in the denial of educational opportunity.

Detaining Educational Opportunity

Zero tolerance created a direct link between public schools and the juvenile and criminal justice system. In fact, according to the Harvard Civil Rights Project (HCRP), "41 states require schools to report students to law enforcement agencies for various conduct committed in school" (2000, p. 13). Arguably, in some instances, such as knowingly possessing a firearm or large knife and intending to use it, police involvement might be an appropriate measure to take. Regardless, this school juvenile and criminal justice system link comes with consequences for educational opportunity. For example, as of 2000, Maryland state zero tolerance policy allowed for districts to "refer students to law enforcement agencies for the first incident of possession of a paging device; the second offense requires referral to law enforcement" (HCRP p. 13).[15] Students have been taken into custody for wearing "inappropriate" clothes (see Rimer, 2004). Skiba and Knesting (2002) present the case where two second graders were charged criminally with making "terroristic threats" because they pointed paper folded like a gun at students and said, "I am going to kill you all" (p. 22). HCRP (2000) provides the incident where an African American male seventh grader won a bet, and his classmate accused the boy of "threatening him for payment." The school skipped due process altogether, and the local law enforcement charged the boy with "felony extortion and [he was] expelled" (p. 4).[16] This list could be continued ad infinitum.

The general point here is that public schools can and do subject students of all races and classes to these bizarre and devastating punishments. The specific point, however, is that students of color are subjected far more frequently than White students to these "unintended consequences" of GFSA 1994. Importantly, if students of color and White students were all provided these heinous punishments, their consequences are not nearly the same. Brown et al. (2003) found in their study of the intersection of race and crime that youth of color (despite class location or family stability) are more than twice as likely than White youth to be referred to a juvenile (or, in some cases, adult) detention center, whereas White youth are returned to parental custody—

and this is for similar "crimes." Further, this trend also has racial and gender dynamics, where girls of color are directed to crowded public facilities with older detainees and White girls generally receive placements in private institutions (Dohrn, 2001, pp. 104–105). In both instances, youth of color are propelled into crowded systems with older detainees and presented with despairing safety threats (e.g., isolation, harassment, physical abuse, and even rape) (Abramsky, 2001; see also Olson, 2003). If students are directed to a juvenile facility, their education is not closely monitored (Bell, 2001). When students are directed to an adult facility as a result of a zero tolerance infraction, they don't receive any education, as the facility is not equipped for their needs, if it has any educational services at all (Blumenson & Nilsen, 2002). What's more, placement in detention centers for noncriminal offenses generally positions youth with individuals who have committed more serious and sometimes violent crimes and, as noted above, subjects them to a potential wrath of psychological and physical trauma. Educational opportunity is truly suspended in these ways, as rates of recidivism increase with each stint in a facility (See Olson, 2003), and as youth have increasing difficulty in readjusting to school and community demands after these experiences in juvenile and adult detention centers. Most of this educational opportunity is suspended as a result of proverbial youth behaviors that were formerly handled by school staff and parents.

The loss of educational opportunity through the increased suspensions/expulsions that have occurred since GFSA 1994 does not stop at the time of exclusion. It is a cumulative process that obviously impacts the students directly subjected to it. Less obviously, schools and society in general lose out, if they are not fundamentally changed, as public schoolings' central objective of providing at least minimal academic or vocational and civic competencies is transformed into an explicit partnership with the criminal justice system.

Zero Tolerance and the Social and Cultural Contexts of and in Public Schools

Zero tolerance operates inside and outside of public schools. This means that zero tolerance plays a role not only in the social relations and cultural practices *in* schools but also in the social relations and cultural practices of the larger society in which schools exist—the contexts *of* schools. A number of studies have addressed this aspect of zero tolerance. The questions they ask about zero tolerance can be posed roughly as follows: How do the images and discourses constructed about youth and schools in the broader society inform punitive policies like zero tolerance, and how does this impact schools and ultimately youth? What is the relationship between zero tolerance in schools and wider social relations and cultural practices concerning youth? The studies argue that a relationship exists between media representations of youth and violence and their concomitant political discourses. This relationship is one of the primary factors involved in the production of draconian policies that criminalize youth, zero tolerance being just one of them. These studies also demonstrate clearly that zero tolerance is imposed on preexisting modes of school organization that already impede constructive teacher-student relationships. Importantly, these studies also consider the potential reality of violence in schools.

Criminal Images of Youth Help Create Policies that Criminalize Youth

In 1997, former Princeton political scientist John DiIulio announced again the formerly unspeakable but, evidently, not unthinkable. He stated in the *Wall Street Journal* that urban youth were "super-predators" who were "more savage than salvageable young criminals" (DiIulio, 1997, A.23; see also DiIulio, 1995). Of course, savage pronouncements like this carried and still carry a large cache for mostly suburbanized whites of all classes, especially after seeing nearly a decade of gangsta videos, *Cops,* and nightly news reports on the war on drugs, all of which portrayed urban African Americans as the primary perpetrators of violence and the drug trade. Shortly after DiIulio's offensive and misleading pronouncement, Senator McCollum (R–FL) proposed the Super-predator Incapacitation Act of 1997 that was renamed the Juvenile Crime Control Act of 1997, calling for the automatic transfer of youth to adult courts for certain crimes (see Ayers, 1997/1998). This position became routinized in developing policy to respond to youth and crime. In fact, by 2001, 48 states had drafted social policies that allow youth—sometimes as young as 12—to be tried as adults in adult courts of law. While these policies came after GFSA 1994, they certainly reinforced in the public mind the popularity of zero tolerance in schools.

This example is demonstrative of a theme prevalent in the work of Dohrn (2001), Ladson-Billings (2001), and Schiraldi & Ziedenberg (2001): the relationship between the media, beliefs about youth, and social policy.[17]

The media has been instrumental in changing the discourse on youth, as Dohrn (2001) notes, from "innocence to guilt, from possibility to punishment, from protection to fear" (p. 92). Central to this transformation of the definition of youth is the repeated warnings presented in the news media and popular culture about the threats that youth pose to society. These threats are seen in the mass reporting on the extremely rare "hyperviolent" acts "presented out of context" such as the Columbine and West Paduchah tragedies (Schiraldi & Ziedenberg, 2001, p. 114) and in popular movies like *187* and television dramas such as *Boston High*. In these reports and representations, it is innocent and impotent but well-intentioned adults in "inefficient" public bureaucracies that are held under a persistent state of siege by rudderless "thugs."

Two interrelated features underpin this construction of youth as a threat over the last fifteen years. One, the threat itself is racially coded. The crimes allegedly committed by Black youth are presented as the consequences of biological pathologies or cultural deficits, whereas those allegedly perpetrated by White youth are typically framed as responses to middle-class alienation or the consequences of proverbial teen angst gone mad. For example, the reports on Kliebold and Harris, the Columbine shooters, framed them as a good kids and students who were subjected to bullying and harassment, whose frustrations resulted in a horrific tragedy. Meanwhile, urban and generally Black and Latino youth have been described repeatedly as super-predators and other animal-like beings (Dohrn, 2001, p. 91). Ladson-Billings argues that this dual conception of youth allows zero tolerance to be used irrespective of the broader social and economic conditions of most Black and White youth (p. 82). A subtle racialized definition of youth is operative, in which African American youth are perceived to be inured, hardened to their life situations, and thus supposedly grow up more quickly and should be held completely responsible for their actions, while White youth are constructed as innocent, in need of protection from the dangers that lurk out there.

Two, racialized representation of youth violence is made all the more powerful by a widening gap between data on the actuality of violence and the social policies devised to counter it (Schiraldi & Ziedenberg, 2001, p. 115). As Dohrn (2001) notes, the criminalization of youth "makes full use of racial, ethnic, and gender stereotyping" (p. 90), the result being the creation of conditions in which fear instead of facts guides social policy. For example, 66% "of Americans think juvenile crime is on the increase, while there has been a 68% decline in violent juvenile crime since 1993" (Schiraldi & Ziedenberg, 2001, p. 118). Schiraldi and Ziedenberg also note that while students had a "one in three million chance of being killed in school" during the 1997–1998 school year, "71 percent of respondents to a *Wall Street Journal* poll believed that such a killing was likely in their school" (p. 118). Of course, with the media repeatedly framing African-American youth as criminal and violent, most people believe that Black youth are the perpetrators of violent school crime, when under like circumstances rates of reported violence for Black youth are not significantly higher than those of White youth (Eitle & Eitle, 2003). Thus, morality policies such as zero tolerance are devised a priori more on suspicion than substance, more on racist beliefs than racial realities.

What happens when these social constructions of youth and ill-conceived policy responses to violence meet the traditional grammar of public schooling and the changing youth cultures that participate in schools? In other words, what can be learned about the efficacy of zero tolerance when the social and cultural context *in* schools is considered?

Zero Tolerance and School Contexts

Pedro Noguera (1995) and Ronnie Casella (2001) provide similar analyses of the long-embedded modes and codes of public school organization.[18] Both authors claim that zero tolerance must be seen in relation to the trajectory or inertia of public school administration, the role of teachers, and the cultures that youth now produce and inhabit.[19] Analyzing zero tolerance from this perspective provides insights as to why zero tolerance has been so readily embraced by school professionals, and how zero tolerance allays adults' fears about school violence, while reproducing the very school relations that influence or promote school violence when it does occur.

Noguera (1995) and Casella (2001) turn to the rise of public schooling in the late 1800s, in order to demonstrate the guiding rationale for public schools, its concomitant organizational vision, and the remnants of that vision that still persist today in schools. While public schools were always believed to provide at least a modicum of the skills central to citizenship, public schools rose to prominence in the late 1800s as a way to reduce tensions between rivaling ethnic groups and to fill a suspected void left by poverty and the fragments of their home cultures. Casella positions this objective within the child-saving missions of the nascent helping professions (pp. 45–48), while Noguera suggests explicitly that child-saving in the late 1800s and early 1900s was about social control, the need to baptize immigrants in American values, and to produce future workers (p. 194). Consequently, both authors are correct in noting that school organization and administrative and teacher duties were concerned with efficiency and routinization of the school day. Efficiency and routinization can be produced and enforced best by fragmenting school time, space, and labor for both students and school personnel. Work periods were split into distinct units, a process over which neither teachers nor students had or have control, and school space was divided in a cellular fashion—separate offices for executive and vice principals, separate lounges for faculty and custodial staff, separate classrooms for groups of students, and separate work areas for students. Obviously, these were models lifted directly from industrial organizational forms, and they were to serve the same purpose in schools: to reinforce a hierarchy of governance, so that the power to and over discipline would be as far removed from those who were to benefit from it—students and future workers. It goes without saying: This organizational form still predominates in public schools.

Though Noguera (1995) and Casella (2001) give different names to an immediate consequence of this form of governance, the conclusions are relatively similar. Noguera is concerned with how students are *alienated* from processes of learning and governance in schools, especially in light of the traditional organization of schools. For Noguera, this alienation is produced on two levels: (1) the cellular organization of schools, as it splits professionals from professionals, students from students, and professionals from students; and (2) the traditional role of teachers, coupled with class and racial backgrounds that differ from students, as these factors create desolate stretches of social distance between teachers and their students. These two primary levels of alienation leave students feeling (sometimes correctly enough) that they are misunderstood, disrespected and often feared and unwanted in all of their cultural and racial complexity (pp. 203–204). For Casella (2001), the alienation produced by traditional school organization as it butts up against changing youth cultures and social demands can be renamed as "emotional distance." As teachers are "pull[ed] away from the emotional life of students," emotional and behavioral problems are directed to "guards, police, and the courts" (p. 121). Despite the different names these authors give to the fragmentation of school life, the consequences are the same: Teachers are removed further from the most pressing and meaningful aspects of students' lives, laying the grounds for the cycle of fear, mistrust, and alienation. Of great importance, both authors justly note that zero tolerance rationalizes this destructive cycle by leaving fear untouched as both the structure and substance of student–teacher relationships, not to mention by also ignoring the material conditions such as poverty that magnify teacher–student and student–student tensions (Casella, pp. 72–73). Only intensified by zero tolerance practices, this condition is totally counterproductive to both safety and educational goals, as Noguera (1995) notes: "[W]hen fear is at the center of student–teacher interactions, teaching becomes almost impossible, and concerns about safety and control take precedence over concerns about teaching" (p. 204).[20]

When zero tolerance is observed in the trajectory or inertia of traditional public school organization and disciplinary objectives, it is a quite rational, though obviously not necessarily effective, approach to school violence. Beyond providing a quick and fragile solution to school disruptions, whether violent or nonviolent, zero tolerance reinforces the hierarchy of power endemic to the predominant model of school governance. And it does so by disregarding the varied racial and ethnic cultures that students bring to schools and by dealing with school violence as if it were a problem unrelated to the violence that pervades the rest of society (Casella, 2001, p. 2; Noguera, 1995, p. 189).

Violence in Society

Casella (2001) calls attention to the following features of American history and culture, which are important for understanding how school violence is only one point on a continuum of social violence. U.S. culture is steeped in the alleged glories of military might, and citizens learn repeatedly how the United States has become great due to the violent interventions of the U.S. military in founding the country, in creating its wealth by using paramilitary groups to protect the slave system, in expanding the nation's boundaries through the mass removal and killing of Native Americans, and in using its military prowess around the world throughout the twentieth century and into the 21st century. This long history of violence, Casella suggestively notes, also includes the incursion of JROTC programs in middle schools and high schools during the 1990s, where students were trained in the virtues of military culture while also learning a certain form of discipline, and the power of a sizable gun culture, where influential gun lobbies headed by the National Rifle Association saturate the media and policy initiatives with the belief that individuals, not guns or their manufacturers, are the root of violence (pp. 2–3, 141–168). School violence can and should be approached in its specificity, but it certainly cannot be bracketed entirely from these albeit contradictory celebrations of violence in the broader society. This is potentially one reason why zero tolerance was so readily embraced by politicians, school administrators, teachers, and parents who had not yet dealt with its implications vis-à-vis their children's experience with it: Zero tolerance is an easy response to what Dohrn (2001) calls the "hackneyed mantra to 'do something' " (p. 94), since it subjects a relatively powerless group to punishment, while carefully avoiding the difficult challenge of questioning and transforming U.S. cultural priorities that support violence in many facets of society outside of schools.

Clearly, the authors of studies on media representation of youth and crime, public discourse, and policy, and the authors of representative studies of zero tolerance and the social context in and of schools, provide momentous insights on the social mooring and consequences of zero tolerance. But most of the studies of zero tolerance are beset by the failure to address the underlying causes of how and why the United States came to a point where having zero tolerance for youth was even thinkable. Nor do they provide a critical analysis of the conditions in the broader society that make violence so prevalent in the United States at this point in time. In part, this is due to the lack of a discourse on inclusive democracy and a programmatic concern with how the cultural politics of our contemporary economy, neoliberal global capitalism, provides the frames through which zero tolerance is

perceived as a favorable method for dealing with youth and the consequences of our shared social conditions.

A Critical Approach to Zero Tolerance

In what follows, my critical analysis of zero tolerance recognizes and
respects the insights provided by the studies concerning its legal aspects,
its impacts on educational opportunity, and what it means in terms of
the social-cultural contexts in and of schools. However, critical ap-
proaches to zero tolerance not only bring these broad findings together,
attempt to understand how zero tolerance fits into neoliberal economic
practices and cultural politics, and further theorize what zero tolerance
coupled with neoliberalism portends for youth and public schools. They
also examine the impacts of zero tolerance and neoliberalism on democratic public life in general. Nonetheless, the goal of *this* critical approach is not to suggest that one study is necessarily better than another.
On the contrary, my objective in this final section is to provide a clearer
picture of the threats that zero tolerance and violence poses to the
social-cultural contexts of schools and youth of color and thus processes
crucial to democracy and democratization.[21]

Neoliberalism, Criminalization, Militarization

Henry A. Giroux (2001a) argues that democracy is threatened by
neoliberal economic policy and cultural politics in two closely related
ways: (1) Public life is eviscerated persistently by the privatization of
public space and the commodification of vocabularies once central to
the realm of the social; (2) citizenship is being emptied of its "critical
social and political content" (p. 29).[22] Over the last 30 years but more
intensively over the last 20 years, a common sense ideology has been
produced in the United States that claims free markets promote democracy and an allegedly burdensome government impedes it. Central
to this process was the selling off of public spaces, land, and institutions
to private corporations that could manage them more effectively and
efficiently than their previous public entities. Giroux suggests that by
having allowed corporate interests to inject their "discourses, identities,
and practices" into formerly public venues, the government helped

create conditions in which "[d]emocracy [could be] reduced to a metaphor for the alleged 'free' market" (p. 30). A foundational consequence of this transformation in government and society—the rapidly shrinking public life under neoliberalism—is that citizens are systemically denied the "connection with each other that transcends the selfishness, competitiveness, and brutal self-interests unleashed by an ever-expanding market economy" (p. 29). Citizens are denied, in other words, the conditions and the terms by which they can engage each other as *citizens* instead of as merely consumers and competitors.

With these changes in how citizens view government and public institutions have come new ways of explaining and responding to what were previously recognized as *social* problems, and of explaining and responding to the problems these changes create or exacerbate. In terms of society, socially created problems such as poverty are no longer ameliorated through social welfare but punished through so-called welfare reform.[23] Problems related to the social forces of poverty, such as homelessness, substance abuse, or participation in alternative economies are now treated not primarily with jobs, social support, or therapy, but with zero tolerance, three strikes, and mandatory minimum policies.

Schools are not free from these processes that Giroux elaborates as rampant privatization, the "criminalization" of social policy, and domestic militarization. As public funding for public schools erodes and schools are subsequently commercialized and thrown into choice and testing schemes, educational practices become even more intensively driven by "individualism, self-interest, and brutal competitiveness" (p. 46). This is, in other words, how public schools become central sites through which neoliberalism's hyper-individualism and ruthless "social Darwinism" are reproduced (p. 31). As is the case with social problems in the broader society, problems previously understood as school/educational concerns (e.g., discipline, and what is now called "low performance") receive less support and more punishment, if not criminalization. Zero tolerance officializes these exclusionary educational practices under neoliberalism, and it does more. Zero tolerance, enforced by teachers, administrators, and police officers—in other words, the hyper-criminalization and "militarization of public schools" (p. 51)—makes it easier for administrators to promote the codes of individualism and competition and sever the school-community link (pp. 48–49) than to promote "the conditions necessary within schools and other public spheres to produce the symbolic and material resources . . . to engage in the struggle for critical citizenship, freedom, democracy, and justice" (p. 51).

Clearly, the space of the social, and neoliberalism's assault on it, figure prominently into this analysis of zero tolerance. Giroux's critical approach to zero tolerance consequently adds a crucial variable to the social-cultural analyses reviewed earlier. Zero tolerance is not simply the effect of possibly ignorant adults who misunderstand data on youth violence; it is not simply the resulting social policy of ill-spirited adults who carelessly toe the line of pejorative media representations of youth; it is not simply another devastating practice of traditional top-down, corporate models of school governance. When democracy and the threat of neoliberalism—the authority of the economic and its cultural politics—are used in analyzing zero tolerance, the policy is seen as all of these things, together, as a symptom of the whole way of life in the United States at this point in history. Since neoliberal economic policies and cultural politics so efficiently eliminate public space and demean "substantive citizenship," zero tolerance is a response chosen by adults in a society that has permitted its public venues and desires for learning about and debating data on youth violence to be effectively downsized; it is the consequence of pejorative media representations of youth, not just because of the representations, but because a densely corporatized media environment has no interest in presenting youth as needy, well-intentioned, curious, meaning-seeking beings—such representations evoke responsible social identities for adults not individualistic, privatized, or competitive ones. Zero tolerance is another powerful form of top-down corporate authority in public schools, not simply because it mimics that model of organization, but because public school organization and objectives are no longer systemically checked by democratic ideals, discourses, or practices.

What does this mean? The processes of meaning-making, of creating common long-term objectives and visions, and of democratizing social, political, and economic life have been fundamentally short-circuited by neoliberalism, its evisceration of the social, and its selling off of vocabularies fundamental to democratic public life. From Giroux's critical approach, an important conclusion can be drawn: Zero tolerance naturalizes an entire way of life in which a certain largely corporate faction benefits from the denial of one of the preconditions to social existence—

the shared, cooperative search for and production of meaning and significance. This is the basic condition of violence preexisting to school
violence, media violence, the militarization of society, the criminalization
of youth and social issues, and this is where one can incorporate the
idea of violence into Giroux's observations and close by presenting a
critical definition of zero tolerance that integrates the central concerns
of all the studies presented here.

Meaning, Zero Tolerance, and Violence

Giroux's critical approach to zero tolerance underplays the idea of
violence while clearly enumerating the total social condition under
neoliberalism that makes certain forms of violence possible. The social-
cultural analyses of zero tolerance omit the role of the economic, while
presenting violence as a central feature to the popularity of zero tolerance. Taken together, the basic violence of the neoliberal cultural-
economic order can be understood as the founding element of zero
tolerance and the underlying threat to democratization justified by zero
tolerance. This requires that violence be reformulated, both in terms of
how it is addressed in studies of zero tolerance and how it is related to
two of the perceived primary roles of public schools and public life in
general—learning and the search for meaning.

Casella (2001) outlines various forms of violence in his study of
zero tolerance. As I stated earlier, he sees individual acts of violence in
schools as points on a broader continuum of violence that pervades
society. Casella also notes how violence is produced on an institutional
level by promoting exclusionary practices, such as tracking and the
profiling of students by race and class. He understands violence as
bullying and sexual harassment that repeatedly go unchecked by school
professionals who are uncomfortable in addressing those problems.
Noguera (1995) explains violence as the consequence to dominating
forms of school administration and teaching and their related processes
of alienation. These conceptions of violence are allegedly and fairly
credibly the acts to which zero tolerance responds. But all of these
conceptions of violence and their relationship to zero tolerance can be
better understood and extended by considering Giroux's conclusions
about the disappearing social under neoliberalism.

Violence in its most basic, and potentially most pervasive, form
was described by Paulo Freire (1970) as any condition or act that

prevents a person or group from learning or stifles any person's or group's ability to participate as fully as possible in a shared social existence—that is, any act that prevents an other or another group from becoming more human and achieving human dignity (see also, Freire 1997, 2004). This definition has two important implications: the person or people preventing others from learning are themselves stunted in their desire for a full social existence, as the diversity, richness, and complexity of a shared world are reduced by prohibiting others from having equal access to it; a democratic social life is, by consequence, impeded if any of its members are diminished in the capacities required to participate in it. This formulation of violence assumes that two or more primary parties or groups enter into the social, despite a group or faction's unequal power in it. But what happens if the social between unequal groups is redefined or, as Giroux (2001a) suggested, reconfigured as a commercialized and privatized space, when it is not eliminated altogether? How can violence in public schools, or the society in which they exist, be understood if their basic *social* functions have been deterred, distorted, or destroyed?

Individual acts of violence become, or are largely functions of, the denial of social conditions and relationships in which students and citizens can engage in shared processes of meaning-making. This, in other words, suggests that individual acts of violence are often attributable to a less acknowledged but powerful form of violence: the structural violence associated with racial oppression, class and gender injustices, and processes of atomization that rob individuals and groups of the opportunities to participate collectively and justly in defining the terms and conditions of their existence, self-production, and social production. In this way, some acts of student violence might be acts resisting or opposing the dominant forces bearing down on them but which, nonetheless, reproduce the conditions of possibility for those acts. This is not to suggest that if every citizen were meaningfully engaged in school and social life, all violence would cease, but that the basic conditions of all physical manifestations of violence would be curtailed significantly. Further, this is not to suggest that citizens don't already make meaning, at least in the capacity of trying to make sense out of the social world they inhabit; this is something all individuals attempt to do with the means they have and in the contexts in which they exist. Meaning, however, is a social category. Meaning ceases to be produced when individuals are interrupted in sharing the sense they privately make of public matters. In these foundational terms, meaning is about purpose; it's about participating in processes that allow citizens to engage, on equal footing, a common, if not also contested, fate. Meaning-making is then fundamentally concerned with citizens having the tools and capacities to construct visions of future social relations. Citizens also need a social space in which they come together and construct a history from their separate pasts that brought them to their present condition and, as Hannah Arendt notes, propels them into the future. How could something be more violent than a whole way of life that demands individual citizens to take *private* responsibility for resolving such a *social* conundrum? This is exactly the condition that neoliberalism's cultural-economic project creates. It eliminates the social and commodifies the discourses that citizens use in the political space that both separates and relates them. This underpinning of violence, inhered in everyday life under neoliberalism, needs to be understood and contested if violence in schools is to be understood and contested.

J. Scott Staples (2000) insightfully explains that individual acts of violence are failed strategies that individuals engage to make meaning in a "broken world," a world of anomie, alienation, and existential insignificance. Staples, like Giroux, sees a broken world in which consumer goods and private desires drive most of social action and, consequently, give meaning to it. However, these two tendencies—the satisfying of private desires and meaning-making—countermand each other. Consumption is always and only a privatized affair; meaning-making is a social(ized) engagement. Individualized attempts to make meaning through violence fail because they fail to change the essential social conditions of a "broken world . . . lost to its deepest callings: the fundamental yearning for significance through engagement in the processes of reflection, creativity, compassion, and the gift of self to others" (p. 33). These processes are oddly out of place in a society and its schools in which "individualism, competition, . . . brutal self-interest," and consumerism are the guiding principles of public life and social action.

This brief inquiry into and reformulation of violence is necessary because it considers the centrality of violence in the social-cultural analyses of zero tolerance. It is also necessary because it demonstrates how neoliberalism makes zero tolerance, as an idea and practice, imaginable, let alone systemically functional. Furthermore, this look at violence demonstrates the deeper implications of the erasure of the social.

Without the social as a space in public schools or society where individuals can share in processes of meaning-making, violence is inherent as individuals are stripped of the opportunity to learn, to become more human(e). Violence is a physical and sometimes fatal consequence of the contemporary social failure of individuals to understand and relate to a common public existence. In turn, zero tolerance is violence because it excludes youth from processes of learning and prohibits teachers from participating in practices of reflection, creativity, compassion, and the gift of self to others, while reinforcing and rationalizing the conditions of neoliberalism. Adding these considerations of violence to a critical analysis of zero tolerance provides a definition that suggests it is a crucial threat to democracy: Zero tolerance is an official form of social and symbolic violence used to temporarily counteract the unofficial social and physical violence generated in the antidemocratic conditions under neoliberalism. Zero tolerance rationalizes the way of life under neoliberalism, and this undermines the possibility of meaningful democratic social relations.

Conclusion

The conclusions drawn about zero tolerance and violence are interpretative—purposefully so. How else can the disregard to constitutional rights that occurs more intensively as a result of zero tolerance be understood? What conditions, broadly conceived, could fail to respond democratically to the denial of educational opportunity, let alone to the large degree it occurs as a result of zero tolerance? What type of social and political order, and set of cultural practices could endorse the potential "civic death" (Wacquant, 2002) of youth of color by creating a direct link between schools and the criminal justice system? And what economic and political imperatives could so powerfully empty the democratizing feature of public schools by reframing and redefining their social and cultural contexts? Even if the term "zero tolerance" were stripped from our social-political, legal-educational lexicon, is it possible that its practice could occur under a different name or policy initiative (e.g., "excellent school environments," or "standardized schools and classrooms"), because its basic conditions of possibility and ideological power have not been transformed and opposed through processes of democratization? A public school that operates on conditions of fairness, cooperation, inclusion, and shared decision-making, instead of consumerism, competition, exclusion and individualism, would be hard pressed to even imagine the idea of zero tolerance, let alone create a credible need for it, by reproducing the conditions that spawned that need in the first place. The problem of zero tolerance is not only a problem of schools and youth, it is also and, indisputably, a problem *for* democracy.

CHAPTER 2

Suspending Citizenship

*The Social Contract, the Hidden Curriculum,
and the Not-So-Hidden Curriculum
of Zero Tolerance*

In the late winter and early spring of 1958, *Life* published a
series of articles and photographs comparing and contrasting
American and Russian schools and youth. The juxtaposition
was purposeful: Russia had recently and successfully launched
Sputnik, adding more grist to the nascent Cold War antagonisms. The images and discourses of this series of articles portrayed American schools as underperforming and inefficient,
and youth were cast at best as mediocre learners and in the
worst cases as uninterested and lazy. At first glance, these images
of youth and schools are not that dissimilar to those circulating
in contemporary media and policy circles about that state of
education. However, *Life's* articles were published in an entirely
different context, and they conveyed starkly different assumptions about what was needed to improve public schools and
academic achievement. These images and discourses were used
to mobilize public support for federal investment in public
schools in order to provide the requisite resources for American
schools and youth to compete with and surpass Russia in science and technology. The guiding assumption was that if money

and other public commitments were not devoted to improving
the learning contexts of students, America would suffer severe
setbacks both nationally and internationally by the threat of the
Red tide. By default, youth were conceived as critical elements
in the promotion of national security and the democratic fabric of society. Of course, there were contradictions in representing and investing in youth as such at this point in history, but
the fundamental social fact remained: Society believed that youth
could not achieve the academic and civic skills demanded by
a changing world if the public was not committed to investing
economically, politically, and socially in youth, public schools,
and the future.

On the morning of November 5, 2003, 17 plainclothed and
uniformed police officers took their posts to perform a drug-
raid—at Goose Creek High School in Stratford, South Carolina.
As 107 primarily African American students exited the buses and
entered the school at 6:40 a.m., police officers jumped out of
closets and from behind closed doors, brandished guns and unleashed a search-and-sniff dog. Officers slammed and locked doors
and, with the aid of school personnel, effectively blocked the
school's corridors. Students were forced frantically to the floor—
some by the barrel of a gun. Others were handcuffed as the
authorities performed their dubious search and seizure for 40
minutes. The event was so overwhelming, one student claimed,
"I thought it was a terrorist attack or something" (Mabrey, 2004,
p. 1). Far from it. No drugs, no weapons—not even cigarettes—
were found. What's more, according to the school's spokesperson,
it was just "coincidence" that the school's African-American
community was subjected to the raid as the arriving predominantly middle-class White students watched the disastrous operation unfold (McRoberts, 2004). Despite the trauma incurred by
the students at the behest of their principal's assumptions, CBS
reports that the school's administrator has "*built a solid reputation
as a first-class educator, one who runs a tight ship*. McCrackin regularly calls the police to bring in dogs to sniff backpacks and
lockers." He is also commended for having "installed a new
surveillance system—including 76 surveillance cameras—to re-

port students' every move." These disciplinary measures, it is presumed in "Ambush at Goose Creek," are a given—and therefore purportedly beneficial—because, along with armed police, they "have become a fixture in schools around the country—there to protect the students and to enforce the law." (italics added. Mabrey, 2004, p. 2)

_N_ ot only are these images separated by nearly 50 years, but they are also radically divergent in their assumptions about youth, educators, schools, and ultimately society. In the first image, public schools express an obligation to provide youth with the competencies needed to participate effectively in democratic society. Students were by no means innocent, then or now, but the ways they were valued and educated represented the future shape and efficacy of society. Moreover, the first image conveys a democratic desire to strengthen the civic and vocational functions of public schools by committing resources and energies to educate all students and prepare them to participate in governance, public life, and the general economic and political well-being of the nation. This is not to suggest that schools always and successfully meet this challenge, but to note that public discourses once supported such a vision of public education. The second image, however, exemplifies a different commitment to public education and a drastically altered conception of youth. It says less about serving all students and more about trying to stigmatize and exclude certain students. In this scenario, a first-class educator is defined by the capacity to run a tight ship, not by the provision of the contexts, relations, and resources that promote critical modes of learning and excellence in education. This is because, in this example, students are not viewed as promising symbols of the future; they are constructed, figuratively and literally, as dangers to the present. What this disturbing image suggests is that these and many educators of any rank are tacitly, if not explicitly, engaged in policing and enforcing the law instead of promoting safe and democratic school environments and relations. What's more, the practice of police raids and unleashing dogs on students blatantly contradicts the implicit and explicit role of public schools to graduate citizens capable of engaging in open, trusting, and critical, if not contested or contestable, social relationships.

The rise of zero tolerance policies is emblematic of this shift. Judith Browne (2003) argues that zero tolerance transfers certain students (if not schools) from the "slow track" to the "prison track." Browne is, of course, referencing the placement of students of color and class minorities in slower vocational tracks as opposed to academic or advanced placement programs. This is a crucial insight, and to broaden its terms is to understand zero tolerance in relation to the waning social contract of the welfare state as associated with the New Deal, the Great Society, the hidden curriculum, and citizenship.

The social contract was the narrative and tacit public agreement that guided public commitments to youth and schools. As the social contract and labor market was racialized in the United States, the forms and functions of schools were racialized, too. Hence, the partitioning of students in tracks classified as fast or slow, which can be understood by way of the broader logic of the hidden curriculum. If the social contract provided the resources and vocabularies to check the most damaging tendencies of the hidden curriculum, then changes made to the social contract provoke changes in its function and visibility. Consequently, the argument here is not that the social contract, in its American, minimalist version, is the best mechanism for protecting the democratic fabric of society. Rather, if the social contract is erased, the hidden curriculum has no reason to remain hidden, and there are no systemic public commitments to ensure that all students will receive the baseline competencies for the world of work and the work of citizenship.

This wider historical shift in the conception, prevalence, and relevance of the social contract is, in part, the basis for the redefinition of youth, education, and society with the rise of neoliberalism. Put differently, as the public is chided into believing social investments in public schools are ineffective, the public supports breaking, if not eliminating, the social contract between society and youth. Such a belief implies that at least certain youth are perceived as unworthy and constructed in ways that reinforce such an assumption. They are portrayed as and believed to be lazy, disruptive, dangerous, and criminal. This demonstrates that zero tolerance not only moves students of color from the slow track to the prison track, but it also institutionalizes neoliberalism's broader agenda of suspending citizenship.

To parse out the strong features of this shift and to provide a reference schema for the argument, refer to Table 2.1.

Table 2.1 The Relationships of Youth, Schools, and Society in Two Eras[1]

	1950–1980 The Liberal Social Contract and the Hidden Curriculum	1980 (1991)—The Carceral Pact and the Not-So-Hidden Curriculum
Economic Demands	Industrial/Post-Industrial Economy; Limited Social Welfare State—Remnant of The New Deal and Great Society Programs	Post-Industrial/Service-and Information-Based Economy; Corporate Welfare/Private Investment State[2]
Political Climate	Moderate—Moderately Conservative and Somewhat Public in Orientation	Ultra-conservative and Private/Individualized in Orientation
Role of Schooling	Public Good—Community centerpiece and social resource; prepare youth for higher education or work and provide basic skills for citizenship	Private Good—Consumer commodity[3] and testing center; train students in intensely competitive learning regimes and produce elite group of students for limited number of jobs in information-based economy
Education Policies	De-segregation (*Brown v. Board of Edu.* 1954); National Defense Education Act 1958 (to invest in science and mathematics education); Elementary and Secondary Education Act 1964 (to provide extra resources to communities and schools in need)	Goals 2000 (1994) (to increase standards, move towards standardization, promote school choice); No Child Left Behind (2002) (to use testing as a way to standardize curriculum and distribute/withhold funding, and to promote school choice and the charter school movement)

continued on next page

Table 2.1 (Continued)

	1950–1980 The Liberal Social Contract and the Hidden Curriculum	1980 (1991)—The Carceral Pact and the Not-So-Hidden Curriculum
General View of Youth	Future citizens and workers; a social responsibility and public investment	Future consumers or potential predators; public burden and private investment
Primary Mode(s) of Discipline and Subjectification	Discipline exercised by school officials; behavior management; students as members of classroom, school, and community environments	Discipline increasingly exercised by school and juvenile justice authorities; behavior containment; certain students as threats/predators to classroom and school environments

The Social Contract, Youth, and the Hidden Curriculum

From the 1950s to the 1980s, the social contract was a commitment by the state to protect its citizens. The social contract protected citizens through neighborhood groups, churches, the workplace, and schools from either the government or market forces undermining their civil liberties and life chances. The social contract also had the implicit function of reducing violence between citizens and between citizens and the state. It provided a public narrative in which citizens were responsible and by which they could act on common social terms.[4] This version of the social contract was enacted by Franklin Delano Roosevelt's New Deal programs in the 1930s and Lyndon Baines Johnson's Great Society initiatives of the 1960s. A central feature of both of these versions of the social contract was that society had a moral and political imperative to protect its most vulnerable segments from the vicissitudes of age, sickness, and economic hardship. This social contract became operative through the formation of social welfare and social security programs, a moderate health insurance provision, and later the Voting Rights Act and Title One entitlements that shored up budget shortfalls for areas of concentrated poverty, and limited efforts at school desegregation. The social contract associated with the welfare state was also enacted through social gains that prohibited abuse of youth, banned child labor, and required schooling with the goal being the successful reproduction of the social-political and economic order. That the social-political and economic order was to be reproduced in a society with a history of slavery, Jim Crow, and class and gender inequality, was reason enough for the allocation of basic but unequal civic and vocational skills—the hidden curriculum of public education (see Bourdieu and Passeron, 1977; Giroux, Penna, & Pinar, et al, 1981; Giroux & Purpel, 1983; Gress and Purpel, 1988).

The Social Contract

In spite of its damaged history, the social contract developed a foundation and set of terms for the state not only to safeguard individual freedoms, but also to provide social provisions and safety nets that enabled individual freedom—free of paralyzing social constraints. Put differently, the social contract, especially in its social welfare state articulation, can help provide the vocabularies, social relations, and material practices that guard against the translation of Thomas Hobbes's war of all against all into a war in which certain groups can possess a monopoly on violence and power, and accumulate—as a group—social, political, cultural, and economic resources under the guise of individual liberties and the rational pursuit of self-interests. Further, as David Theo Goldberg (2002) suggests, the social contract performs a narrative function in suggesting what provisions are made for what citizens and under what conditions, *while also providing the ideals by which citizens can narrate their roles in maintaining the social contract.* The narrative power of the social contract, and its actual materialization in state apparatus and intermediary institutions, cannot be underestimated, nor should it be underplayed.

As Pierre Bourdieu (1998) notes, the public institutions of healthcare, social welfare and social security, the legal-political infrastructure for labor protections and, importantly, the public and higher education system "are the trace, within the state, of the social struggles of the past" (p. 2). These institutions were and can still be the materialization of collective, if limited, efforts at protecting the well-being of society and the promise of democracy by guaranteeing that all citizens have at least minimum safeguards and resources. These materializations were, and are being limited, not necessarily by a lack of courage or initiative of past social struggles, but because the state—with its "right hand's" interests in protecting corporate and military power—blunted those efforts, as it institutionalized the struggles' more moderate demands at the expense of their more transformative goals.

This points to the productive dialectic between the social contract and the state: The traces of past social struggles allow citizens to recognize and value the social state, which implies being committed in word (story) and deed (collective action), allowing the social state to be renewed in contemporary struggles. If the social contract's materialization in the state is denied—that is, if the "left hand" of the state is cut off, symbolically through its stigmatization as inefficient and materially by being starved of both public commitment and investment—we are left with a state that increasingly promotes, without public intervention, a market society that is protected by forces of criminalization and militarization.[5] In this way, the social contract is not only an actual agreement made in a particular era and materialized in various social provisions; it is also a public story held in common, by and through which citizens articulate diverse interests in the maintenance of civil society. These socially responsible and protective assumptions guided the revisions that were made across the 20th century and were exemplified by the social welfare commitments legislated by the New Deal and some civil rights objectives incorporated into state policy with the Great Society. These and other social contract revisions widened rights, protections, and investments in youth.

The Social Contract and Youth

With the expansion of the social contract, practices and relations revolved more explicitly around notions of public and common good and youth as the subjects onto which visions of the future were projected. This is an important feature. Because of their age, youth have a precarious political life: They are prohibited from participating in the formal political process, and they have little authority to protect themselves or resist adult authority and the predations of market relations. Thus, the liberal, democratic social contract in the 20th century was a mechanism paramount in providing youth crucial social investments and ensuring their viability as citizens (and laborers). As Henry A. Giroux (2003a) states:

> [T]he liberal, democratic social contract occupied [during the 20th century] a defining feature of politics and was organized around a commitment which stipulated that all levels of government would assume a large measure of responsibility for providing the resources, social provisions, security and modes of education that simultaneously offered young people a future as it expanded the meaning and depth of a substantive democracy. In many respects, youth not only registered symbolically the importance of modernity's claim to progress, they also affirmed the importance of the liberal, democratic tradition of the social contract in which adult responsibility was expressed through a willingness to fight for the rights of children, enact reforms that invest in their future, and provide the educational conditions necessary for them to make use of the freedoms they have, while learning how to be critical and engaged citizens . . .

[D]emocracy was measured in accordance with the well-being of youth. . . . (pp. 174–175)

These social provisions were not free of contradiction (see Finkelstein, 2000). Nonetheless, the state and, by default, society expressed clear commitments to youth just before and across the 20th century. For instance, compulsory school laws were drafted in the early 1900s. This served multiple purposes:

- reduce street crime between competing ethnic groups in burgeoning cities; to inculcate a uniform set of values (see Noguera, 1995);

- fill the cultural deficits left by poverty;

- prepare youth bodies for routinized factory labor (Tyack & Cuban, 1995).

The double-edged consequence of these early objectives was the production of citizens and future workers. Though schools maintained strict discipline codes to fulfill these early objectives, students were provided the basic conditions in which they could learn civic values and practices—the codes of citizenship. For a short time, the progressive movement in education successfully incorporated the everyday lives of youth into school curricula and practices. Child labor was denounced and illegal by the early 1900s. *Brown v. Board of Education* (1954) banned segregated schools, although to no current practical effect. In 1975, *Goss v. Lopez* deemed educational opportunity a property interest, and thus a constitutional right for youth. These social gains made under the narrative of the social contract were not free of contradictory tendencies or forces. Nor is this list exhaustive. The point is that public discourses under the narrative power of the social contract constructed and provided for youth primarily as a social responsibility and a symbolic guarantee, "an affective investment in the future" of democratic public life (Grossberg, 2001, p. 133). The contradictory tendencies of the social contract—the simultaneous provision of baseline civic and vocational skills and unequal distribution of life chances along racial and gender lines—can be observed through the conceptualization of the hidden curriculum of schools.

The Hidden Curriculum

Scholars of various theoretical and political persuasions agree that public schools are powerful because they both explicitly teach students certain bodies of knowledge and socialize students in particular ways. But in their very structure and everyday relations, schools implicitly convey meanings and values about the function of education in the broader society. While the debates that have emerged around this issue are important historically, the conceptual tool used to identify and explain the relationships between the explicit and implicit functions of public education is central to understanding the aim and scope of this chapter.

The tool is the hidden curriculum. The hidden curriculum was defined as the characteristics of behavior or attitudes that are learned, but not explicitly taught, at school. These traits might be reinforced by the manifest curriculum's content but they are the unstated objectives of the visible curriculum. Giroux (2001b) redefined the hidden curriculum "as those unstated norms, values, and beliefs embedded in and transmitted to students through the underlying rules that structure the routines and social relationships in school and classroom life" (47). Unsatisfied with a merely descriptive definition, Giroux qualifies the hidden curriculum as "not simply . . . a vehicle of socialization but also as an agency of social control, one that functions to provide differential forms of schooling to different classes [and races] of students" (p. 47). Both conditions are the tacit messages conveyed in school structure and relations as well as the allocation of differential educational and social resources to different groups of students. These are crucial to identifying the full range of pedagogical relationships within which students are located.

The hidden curriculum works in some complex and very covert ways. Other ways are simpler and more overt or normal(ized). Although students are not tested on these tacit forms of education and socialization, per se, the impacts on achievement, development, and opportunities are profound. For example, as teachers interact differently with girls and boys, having different and often hierarchical conceptions of propriety and expectations for academic achievement, the "unstated" and tacit codes of schooling construct gendered identities and vest unequal amounts of power in each gender category. Because schools often favor docility, the attitudinal and behavioral characteristics of many girls who are generally socialized to be demure, polite, and quiet, are rewarded. In early schooling, girls may be treated more pleasantly by teachers, given smiles, kind words of encouragement and the like, rewarded by being invited more openly into the culture of the classroom and school. Alternately, boys are generally socialized to be rambunctious and aggressive. In subtle and sometimes not so subtle ways, boys are consequently punished for the gendered characteristics they bring to school. But this function of the hidden curriculum has been observed to flip later in school. Boys benefit, at least in traditional academic terms, from this toughening, as teachers subsequently put higher expectations on certain classes and races of boys in mathematics and the sciences because of their accumulated cultural capital and perceived confidence. The hidden curriculum, however, elides the ways by which girls and boys of lower classes and of color are deprived of similar expectations as a result of the structuring of divergent expectations into the organization of school curricula and more explicitly into the content of curricula. In both the structure and content of school interactions, boys and girls are provided differential forms of social and educational resources. While the process is not as simple (or simplified) as these examples would otherwise suggest, the hidden curriculum actively teaches boys and girls acceptable and rewarded or punished forms of behavior in school and the world. This produces valuations of each set of behaviors. While the manifest curriculum teaches specific skills, the hidden curriculum equips certain students with better tools for academic and social success.

There are other ways the hidden curriculum works to secure and enforce certain ideological interests and produce differential forms of educational and social opportunities. One of the most obvious ways the hidden curriculum differentially distributes educational and social opportunities via the nexus of race, class, and gender is through tracking (Darling-Hammond, 2000; Kozol, 1991; Oakes, 1999; Thompson, 2004). Academic, general, and business or vocational-technical programs are the most common tracks. Students cordoned in each area are exposed to educational and social opportunities to prepare them for future work, either in college, trade school or undervalued labor as they leave high school. The official learning that takes place in each area is obviously contingent upon the manifest curriculum; the unofficial learning that occurs is the result of the perceived and, by default, actual values attached to students in each of the tracks within the hierarchy of the school structure and broader community.

For example, the hidden curriculum operates through tracking mechanisms that disproportionately place working-class and African American students in vo-tech and other lower status programs of schools.[6] Not only are these students provided differential and devalued forms of education, but they are also, by default, unintentionally or intentionally, devalued. Oakes (1985, 1999; Oakes & Rogers, 2003) has demonstrated repeatedly how African-American and working-class students in lower curriculum tracks receive unqualified or less qualified teachers and inferior resources, and they are subsequently provided with educational and social opportunities much less valued than those offered to middle-class White students in higher-level tracks. This intraschool dynamic also exists on a higher level of abstraction: interschool and interdistrict.

Jean Anyon's (1980) pioneering study of the relationship between the "hidden curriculum of work" and "social class" documented how schools serving and constituted by different social classes of students produced relationships structured by codes and values that habituated students to relative social class position and occupational opportunities of their families and communities. For example, Anyon found that relationships in schools serving working-class students were defined by top-down modes of authority, a lack of ownership of classroom materials, the constitution of classroom activities, and student achievement, which was gauged primarily by how well students followed directions, not by critical or analytical thinking. In other words, students were equipped with the skills and dispositions to be obedient line workers or low-level employees. Alternately, Anyon found that schools serving affluent and elite students produced different relationships and fostered different modes of engagement. Students had more autonomy in movement throughout the classrooms and a greater sense of ownership of classroom materials as well as in classroom relationships. Student work was evaluated by creativity, the ability to integrate ideas and skills from different subject areas, and an emphasis on organizing and managing "complex systems," as early as upper-elementary school. In this case, students were prepared, intentionally or unintentionally, to fulfill subject positions in the creative and managerial classes. Jonathan Kozol (2005) and Paul Street (2005) document similar but intensified dynamics with the resegregation of public schools and "segregated pedagogies" (Street, 2005) of drill, grill, drill and grill, that disproportionately routinize and deaden the pedagogical relationships of poor working-class White schools and urban schools attended by primarily poor African American and Latino students.

Linda Darling-Hammond (2000, 2001) and others demonstrate how relationships of the hidden curriculum are supported and structured by the distribution of qualified teachers, not only within schools between curriculum tracks but also in how schools, marked by racial or class inequalities, generally receive underqualified or unqualified teachers (see also, Eskenazi, Eddins, & Beam, 2003). Again, students in these tracks are ostensibly impacted in ways that middle-class White students in other tracks and schools are not. Much like the world for which they are purportedly being prepared, working-class and African American students are subjected to routine classroom tasks in which compliance and obedience are rewarded at the expense of learning more critical ways of interacting in the school and broader world (see Delpit, 1995). Alternately, primarily middle-class, White students in academic tracks are believed to be more competent. Teachers engage these students in active discussions, expect higher levels of intellectual engagement, and encourage self-sufficiency and greater autonomy in thinking. Furthermore, the opportunities inherent in each track also provide students with differential access to academic and social skills. In other words, these students are provided the conditions in which the cultural tools of their class and racial locations are esteemed, encouraged, and rewarded or, if these forms of cultural capital are not rejected outright, their cultural tools are degraded by school relationships and marginalized in the social text of classrooms, "You can't use double negatives in *proper* speech." Or, "*We* demonstrate respect *this* way, Billy."

In its most extreme forms, the hidden curriculum works as a push-out mechanism for unwanted students. As underqualified or unqualified teachers, routinized curricula, substandard materials and school resources, and low expectations are combined in a volatile mixture and produce extreme forms of isolation and marginalization, working-class and African American students positioned in these relationships are more likely to read these characteristics of schools as metaphors for being unwanted, unrepresented, and unvalued both in school and the community. Simply, schools convey implicit and explicit messages about the expectations and values placed on African American and working-class students. Schools push out students by providing a choice between being unwanted and neglected or finding alternative places of belonging, and a sense of worth and self-efficacy. More precisely, there is the illusion of a difference between being unwanted, and choosing to drop out, paraded as a just division of academic labor. The statistics bear this out, as Latino and African American students "drop out at two to three times the rate of White students" (Cross, 2001, p. 7; see also Madaus & Clarke, 2001), despite the fact that education is a highly valued resource and much esteemed opportunity for individual and collective development in both communities.

Although the hidden curriculum promotes social relations and educational practices that countermand more radically democratic sensibilities, the social contract was a crucial concept and ideal that historically guided both the manifest and hidden curricula of schooling across the 20th century. Despite the differential investment in and distribution of resources to varied classes and races of students, public discourses argued that public schools should provide all students with at least the minimal capacities to function productively in both occupational and civic life. Though the politics of the traditional hidden curriculum is obviously a drawback to the democratization of educational opportunities and social life, the social contract entailed perceptions and involvement with youth as a valuable investment for the future. That is, the social contract provided the ideals, vocabularies, and broader social practices against which the excesses of the hidden curriculum could be measured and checked. This is not an argument for a return to some golden glory days when the hidden curriculum was less visible and more just, because it wasn't more just. At the very least, the hidden curriculum was accompanied by a social contract that offered a set of ideals to both expose and overcome the injustices promoted by it. The relationship between the traditional hidden curriculum and the social contract is a way to demonstrate the shift from society engaging schools as democratic public spheres that fulfilled economic imperatives to society's use of schools as sites to suspend citizenship through profiling and punishing students. Invoking the social contract thus highlights how the faint dialectic between producing future workers for the labor market and developing future citizens for civic life has been all but obliterated. The legislated practices of zero tolerance explicitly institutionalize the latent and oppressive features of the once hidden curriculum in a political culture that progressively values neither workers nor citizens, but consumers and criminals (Bauman, 2001 [1998]). Without the guiding narratives of and investments in the social contract, public schools are increasingly engaged in criminalization and militarization instead of democratization.

The Not-So-Hidden Agenda of Neoliberalism Comes to School

In the first image presented at the beginning of this chapter, the ideals of the social contract informed the arguments and assumptions about schools and youth. The concern was not so much with the outright limiting of educational opportunity for some students through laws and practices like zero tolerance, but the quality of educational opportunity itself, and whether it promoted forms of learning beneficial to national security, academic excellence, and a student's capability of being an informed and engaged citizen. The second image does not convey a similar picture of public schools and the role of youth in society. Plainly, the use of urban schools as venues for new branches of police forces, testing grounds for new security technologies, centers for massive test-making companies, and holding facilities for students about to be criminalized and decitizenized was unthinkable when public schools were considered public assets and held accountable through *social* responsibility, for ensuring that students would be prepared to meet the challenges of mind, citizenship, and the economy. This is not to say that public schools are not still public in the sense that public revenues support them; most students are admitted regardless of race or class and, when time is available, community members can involve themselves in school affairs. Rather, this suggests that public schools are forced to follow the ideals and codes of a different sort of contract—the corporate-commercial agreement and the neoliberal carceral pact. As a result, public commitment, social forces, and the broadly defined types of learning promoted in schools are translated from a public and political nature to a privatized and criminalized-militarized character.

A short overview of neoliberalism is necessary in order to elaborate on the codes that inform contemporary impulses that contravene the public mission of schools and those of substantive citizenship. Zero tolerance is arguably the most powerful of these tendencies. It is a legitimating factor for the not-so-hidden agenda of neoliberalism's mission to suspend citizenship. It is also racially bifurcated, like the traditional hidden curriculum, but with radically different consequences.

The Ideals and Codes of Neoliberalism

Neoliberalism is the economic philosophy and cultural project that ascended to prominence, most notably with the Reagan presidency, and continues to inform much of social, political, and economic life. This economic philosophy claims that the only problems which need to be solved are those of the market. The free market—left to its own rapacious interests—will resolve all other problems of social and political organization (Friedman, 2002). This means that the government's regulatory responsibilities in the economy and investment in public institutions must be curtailed as much as possible. This is a socially devastating process that parades under the euphemism of deregulation. Deregulation also implied the incursion of market interests on public institutions when government disinvestment threatened their reproductive capacities and thus social stability. Hence, the newfound popularity of increasing educational quality and, ironically, efficiency throws public schools into choice, charter or privatization schemes, and subjects them to harsh testing regimes as a condition for funding. Schools are coerced into partnerships with corporations for curriculum materials, computer technologies, and vending machines to shore up budget shortfalls due to "deregulation" (Molnar, 2005).[7]

Neoliberalism has a more explicit cultural project that is produced on material and symbolic levels. As Robert McChesney (1998) points out, the cultural project of neoliberalism has become powerful because of the defunding, privatization, or elimination of a range of public institutions and spaces responsible for providing social forums for citizens to disseminate information and debate public issues. Public libraries persistently face budget difficulties. Public space in communities has been sold to corporations or made ill-conducive to social gatherings. Ten large conglomerates have devoured public airwaves in the United States, leaving television, radio, and the internet to be commodified by commercial interests, the ultimate effect being the gross limitation of public debate and commercialization of public life.

On the other side of these material shifts are stories that prevail in these recently privatized and commodified venues. It is now commonsense that individuals are responsible for their (allegedly) self-produced fate; the strongest and the smartest survive. Big government is wasteful, except when used to expand and protect corporate interest. Corporations can be socially responsible, taking the place of public oversight of social problems. Consumerism is the civic duty par excellence, as President Bush verified when he told citizens to express their patriotism by shopping in the days after 9/11. This is the new private-commercial contract of neoliberalism in which the social actors who can participate in the new market order, instead of civic order, are the ones who get their just desserts. Citizenship is not suspended entirely, it is simply translated from civic to commercial practices.

What happens to the other social actors who have histories of class, gender, and racial subjugation, recent unemployment or illnesses that are unaccounted for in quarterly profit margins? Social conservative ideology, in connivance with neoliberal initiatives, has created the myth that social and political disparities around the categories of race, class, and gender are the results of failed individual responsibility, cultural deprivation and, occasionally, biological inferiority. In other words, those individuals who have not benefited from the seriality of White, middle-class male social, political, and economic opportunities, only have themselves to blame. These social actors, who are written out of neoliberalism's contract, can be criminalized, effectively suspending citizenship. Hence, the proliferation of drug, curfew, and other quality of life laws that are enforced with three strikes and mandatory minimum sentencing policies, and the turn of criminal justice from rehabilitation to incarceration over the last twenty years (Cole, 1999; Davis, 1998; Parenti, 1999). In 1991, the United States had 710,000 prisoners (Marable, 2001), whereas by 2004 that number surpassed 2 million, approximately tripling in just over a decade. The number of people under some form of correctional supervision—in jail, on parole or probation, or under house arrest—now tops 6 million. It is important to note that African Americans and Latinos make up approximately 25% of the national population, but account for 63% of the incarcerated population. Women of color are now the fastest growing segment of the prison population.

In the most general terms, social conservative ideology, coupled with neoliberalism's cultural-economic project, has rendered public institutions and their concomitant social support ineffectual, claiming that market priorities override the common good. Citizenship is measured by one's consumptive value. Individuals have only themselves to blame or celebrate for their lot in the new market order. And for those written out of the private-commercial compact of neoliberalism, the carceral pact now provides for them. This project impacts public schools in different ways, and these are important for understanding the function of zero tolerance in the not-so-hidden curriculum of schools under neoliberalism.

The Not-So-Hidden Curriculum

In the simplest terms, the not-so-hidden curriculum of schools under neoliberalism limits or eliminates citizenship by translating its basic role from civic duty to consumer responsibility and transforming the spaces in which agency is exercised. Public schools are the ostensible targets on which neoliberalism can work its market magic—an alchemy of individual responsibility, punishment, and consumerism. This is what Stan Karp (2004) means when he suggests that progressives have had to shift from arguing over the quality of public schools to struggling to defend the existence of public schools, especially with the accountability-punishment program instituted by President Bush's No Child Left Behind (2002). Intense, high-stakes, testing-funding programs are only one mechanism by which market imperatives transform the manifest and hidden curricula of public schools. But testing is only one facet of the not-so-hidden curriculum of schools under neoliberalism, school choice is another. These two separate but related political-economic forces give wider legitimacy to the law and practices of zero tolerance because they construct some students as burdens on current fiscal priorities, not investments in the future.

This emphasis here on testing is not concerned with whether or not tests can be effective measurement tools in the classroom when partnered with other methods of evaluation. The concern here is how high-stakes tests *are being used*, and according to what logic, under current educational policy. While the tests promoted by No Child Left Behind (NCLB) are intended to indicate which students have or have not learned, the primary hidden purpose is to subvert public support of public schools vis-à-vis funding contingent upon the test results and annual yearly progress. In other words, the tests are not instructional tools; they are devices used to punish schools when they fail to both meet achievement criteria over which they have little to no say and to compete with well-funded schools.

Although the testing scheme promoted by NCLB has an academic veneer, it really operates on the logic and language of the market. Excellence is defined in narrow terms; it's the image of excellence that matters. As demonstrated by the Houston Miracle, whether or not schools find ways to retain and accommodate marginalized and at-risk students, or engage students and the broader community in democratic modes of learning and governance, it is ancillary as to whether or not they produce high test scores. Also, accountability is subverted or translated into strict market terms. Accountability is a metaphor used to suggest that schools are individually responsible for their performance, and that performance is not conditioned by broader demographics and resource allocation. What's more, public schools then become client test centers for massive test development corporations and the many companies cashing in on test preparation materials. Under these conditions, and when no other tools are used to measure a school's success, testing cannot be anything but an *individualized* undertaking. In this way, certain schools are written out of public support from the start (i.e., they are individually responsible). With such high stakes placed on performance, schools are encouraged to look at certain students *as risks*, instead of being faced with risks that schools should help mitigate. The predominance of testing in schools promoted by NCLB is matched by another market ploy: choice.

Because NCLB endorses the practice of choice, a school's marketability is a guiding concern of administrations and teachers. If a school fails to convey an image that suggests they are serious about learning, parents can choose another school. If schools have students identified as dangerous, parents can send their children to another school. The primary mechanism by which schools market an image of academic achievement is through test scores and annual percentage increases which are publicized. Another strategy is to create a positive image through the types of students they promote and the groups of students they retain. This is no small matter because schools receive per-pupil funding, primarily from the relative value of taxable property (and state income taxes and gambling). Thus, in poor rural areas where family farms and industries have been devastated and poor urban areas where manufacturing has been eviscerated, school districts have a paucity of economic resources. However, homeowners in these areas typically pay a higher percentage of taxes on their property than homeowners in suburbia to cover shortfalls. That White, middle-class parents choose schools and neighborhoods with mostly White, middle-class youth is not a coincidence (see Johnson & Shapiro, 2003). Schools and communities are racialized landscapes where poor students and students of color are treated as if they contaminate those landscapes. There must be an exit route for White and middle-class parents who have the resources to flee the school system and a push-out device for unwanted students when parents find it more difficult to leave. NCLB provides the mechanisms for both of these antidemocratic practices. However, because urban schools and some suburban ones are resegregated by default of segregated communities (Kozol, 2005; Orfield & Eaton, 1997), the inordinate punishing of African American youth through zero tolerance is not so much a mechanism to encourage choice as much as it is a tool to rationalize the exclusion of students of color from public education and the continued underfunding of districts strapped by class inequalities and racial injustices. Thus, students and families from wealthier White backgrounds have their civic interests and responsibilities in education translated into competitive and consumptive ones, while other students, primarily of color, have their civic rights quite literally suspended. This is the not-so-hidden curriculum under neoliberalism and the consequences of the erasure of the social contract.

Of course, zero tolerance has its own logic, but it was formulated and is practiced amidst transformed institutional arrangements that encourage individualization, intense competition for scarce (educational) resources, privatization of public goods, and consumerism. It is important to review the general features of schools under zero tolerance and specific examples of the practice of zero tolerance, before I consider the lessons taught about citizenship and schools by the not-so-hidden curriculum under neoliberalism.

The Not-So-Hidden Curriculum and Zero Tolerance

When zero tolerance is understood within the context of neoliberalism, its individualization of social risks, and privatization and commercialization of public life, the not-so-hidden curriculum can be provisionally redefined or defined as:

the symbolic forces, cultural practices and material conditions in public schools that not only provide differential access to social and educational resources to different races, classes and genders of students, but also explicitly structure the school's social relations in ways that teach all students the value of certain groups of students by way of their disproportionate (temporary or permanent) exclusion from school life.

Reviewing the changing image of schools and intensified forms of student profiling and punishment can draw out the not-so-hidden curriculum. Specific examples of school policies and practices are helpful here, too. The racialization of the not-so-hidden curriculum demonstrates how it works on the colorline. The politics of school security personnel sheds light on how the social space of school is transformed. Lastly, returning to the role of NCLB and resource shortages also provides insight as to why the not-so-hidden curriculum of zero tolerance is so easily promoted.

The Changing Image of Schools and Surveillance of Students

Schools have been described recently as "learning prisons" (Beger, 2002). This applies to how they look and how they operate. No longer are schools conceived as tranquil red-brick buildings of the three R's and latent socialization. Schools are now dressed in elaborate snow fences and security devices and personnel. As demonstrated by the second image, some schools are also blanketed by random, intense drug sweeps and sting operations. What's more, the framing power of the punitive testing schemes working on schools cannot be overlooked for the ways it disciplines student, teacher, and administrator perspectives on school life.[8] Consider the following additions to and transformations of the school image:

- Over 1000 schools deploy drug-sniffing dogs in police sweeps.

- Some schools have even purchased their own search-and-sniff dogs.

- Schools ranging from remote locations in the Mojave Desert to urban settings such as St. Louis and Los Angeles are adorned by intimidating snow and barbed wire fencing systems.

- Schools have electronic-locking entry doors, and parents have to gain permission for entry and go through sign-in rituals before meeting with school staff or their children, as if they were being prepared to navigate correctional systems.

- Covert and overt cameras capture school life for closed-circuit television systems (CCTV).

Beyond these modifications, metal detectors and biometric scanning devices have become popular commodities for school systems and a boom industry for high-tech security firms.

Elissa Gootman (2004) presents a seemingly ambiguous case from the Bronx, reporting on the efforts of a Bronx high school principal in improving his school's environment. John F. Kennedy High School was reported to be plagued with vandalism, violence against administrators, and objects tossed from windows. As Gootman reports, the current principal Rotunno has been instrumental in making remarkable changes in the school. Tests scores on the New York State Regent Exam increased in the year Rotunno has been principal, and teachers feel much safer. But the question is at what costs do temporary test score increases and teacher comfort come? According to Rotunno, he proudly adheres to a quality of life policing model taken from the criminal justice strategies of the former authoritarian Mayor Giuliani.[9] Purportedly as a result of this hard-nosed strategy of "weeding out" students, the " 'school system's version of petty criminals—the chronic hall-walkers and the persistently disruptive' " (C14), Rotunno said he was paid the greatest compliment: that the school's homecoming game in the fall felt like a suburban environment. But this school isn't quite Mayberry, and it is disingenuous to report positively on the compliment without critiquing the political and economic relations that give the comparison such saliency. Nor are the other tactics being used to bring order to the school suggestive of most suburban environs, and this is where the costs shouldered by the students are most readily seen. In fact, the school added 50 police officers, and students are corralled in random stop-and-frisk points as they move throughout the school during the day, replete with hand-held and free-standing metal detectors.

Drug sweeps are becoming fairly typical features of school environments and occur in both urban and suburban districts. In the spring of 2004, Narragansett High School, a relatively White, middle-class school in Rhode Island, unleashed its first of many proposed drug sweeps. Hurst (2004) reports that the first raid found four different drug positive scent sites, but no drugs. However, one student was suspended for three days, simply because the police chief believed that the student's locker smelled like marijuana. While it appears that there is no profound threat to school life in Narragansett High School, the administration remains steadfast on random drug sweeps because, as the school superintendent claims, it is important to address " 'the addiction issue before it becomes a legal issue' " (Hurst, 2004). Since the drug issue is, a priori, a legal issue and also a legitimate concern for constructive intervention, it is difficult to glean from this report that the school is sincerely interested in the addiction issue, especially as nothing indicates that the suspended student was referred to counseling. Nonetheless, the classrooms at Narragansett High School will continue to be stymied by lockdown procedures and other modalities of the pedagogy of panic when the school performs drug sweeps.

But the framing power of the testing regime adds a definite albeit subtle disciplining ambience to the school. From administrators to teachers, the language alone that surrounds the current testing, or accountability, climate are felt, and alter the ways professionals relate to students. Underachievement on tests puts schools on probation. This of course is perceived by teachers as a form of punishment. If a school fails to produce adequate yearly progress over three years, the school will face state "takeover," a term readily bandied about by teachers and administrators with whom I have worked. As teachers and administrators rightfully perceive themselves to be subjected to surveillance and punishment (recall these are the key functions of zero tolerance), they are deterred not only in exercising and modeling critical forms of teaching and citizenship, but are encouraged to relate to students who might present both academic and social challenges—identifiable risk factors—as risks and threats. Pauline Lipman's (2004) observation that schools most frequently on probation are schools marked by racial inequalities is telling; these schools also have the highest rates of exclusion. Whether or not some teachers perceive the behaviors of students of color through the racist lens of pejorative stereotypes (Akom, 2001; Skiba, 2000) is now ancillary to the fact that they work with students under the framing mechanisms and conditions of surveillance and punishment promoted officially by accountability schemes and zero tolerance. The not-so-hidden curriculum is a little more explicit. Citizenship is the last lesson when performance, school probation, and other forms of punishment are the order of the day.

Some individual examples of school exclusions that have recently occurred are suggestive of these changes made to both the physical environment and social relations of schools by zero tolerance and accountability. Students have been excluded through "snap suspensions" for as little as rolling their eyes at teachers (Dunbar & Villarruel, 2002, p. 96). A seven-year-old in Louisiana was given in-school suspension and sent home according to the school's zero tolerance policy, as he allegedly "disrupted" class by saying the word "gay." When another student asked about his parents, he told the student that his mom was "gay," meaning, in his words, "when a girl likes a girl" (Moller, 2003, p. 01). In accordance with local zero tolerance policies, some Seattle schools have gone as far as punishing students for snowball fights and sometimes for just touching the snow around a school, what one reporter sarcastically calls "snow criminalization" (Fulbright, 2004). Student clothing is also criminalized under some school policies, demonstrated by the misdemeanor given to a young Toledo girl for refusing to cover her midriff (Rimer, 2004). In the fall of 2003, R. J. Epstein (2003) reported that a Wisconsin student was suspended for a rap CD he produced at home, and on which he claimed he would "beat [the principal's] ass down" if he didn't leave the town. Regardless that the CD lyric was part of a larger creative production and the student was a member of the school's honors program, the student awaited expulsion hearings at the time of this report, because his lyric was considered to be the equivalent of "making a bomb threat" (on line, 2003). Similar to this incident, there are increasing violations of school zero tolerance policies vis-à-vis content on student homepages in recent years. Jennifer Sughrue (2003) studied an incident in Pennsylvania where a student was suspended for three days for commentary on his website. The incident was litigated, and the court ruled in favor of the school. As Sughrue reports, the court "agree[d] that the pages had created a disruption when the teacher who was the object of much of the Web pages' [sic] ridicule was unable to perform her duties satisfactorily as a result" (p. 253).

The drug sweeps and potentially unreasonable searches of students have successfully removed students from school. A high school student in Virginia was suspended for five days for having two Tylenol in her backpack. The Tylenol tablets were found during a drug sweep when the girl was attending gym class and her bag was left unattended in the locker room (Scaife, 2004). A fifteen-year-old in Louisiana was expelled for having Advil in her purse (Brumble, 2003). Despite the fact that the Advil were found as a result of a teacher searching the girl's purse for cigarettes (the Advil were found on a false pretext, in other words) and the state law does not mandate expulsion for such an offense, the school's administration expelled the girl for one year. While the student in the following example was not excluded from school, the framing power of zero tolerance's not-so-hidden curriculum of punishment and suspension of citizenship on administrator or teacher perceptions of students could not be clearer. In February 2004, South Haven High School in Michigan learned that its assistant principal had intentionally planted marijuana in a student's locker, simply because, as the *Detroit News* (2004) reports, the troubled administrator wanted this student expelled.

There is no dispute over what the not-so-hidden curriculum in the South Haven incident teaches students and conveys to the broader community: If certain students aren't caught breaking some obtusely defined rule when they are being policed relentlessly, some educators will simply abuse their authority and attempt themselves to implicate unwanted students—this is the push-out function on speed. Whether or not these educators are exposed for committing such an egregious breech of ethics and law is beside the point. There are social relations, a political climate and cultural practices in place that encourage an educator to imagine stinging unsuspecting and apparently undesirable kids. In this way, violations of student rights are devastating. Randall Beger (2002) is correct when he claims: "Ironically, children are unsafe in public schools today not because of exposure to drugs and violence, but because they have lost their constitutional protections under the Fourth Amendment" (p. 127). Thus, not only are youth personally unsafe, they are also politically threatened in both figurative and real terms. Because of their age, students have little autonomy is contesting violations of their Fourth Amendment rights. More politically despairing, "because the Fourth Amendment is a subjective protection" (Blankenau & Leeper, 2003, p. 582), the not-so-hidden curriculum explicitly and erroneously teaches public school students that a purportedly democratic government and its representative institutions can obliterate constitutional rights whenever its dominant factions find it advantageous to their self-interests to do such. These are central lessons about citizenship taught to students (and the broader society) by the not-so-hidden curriculum.[10]

What makes certain infringements on student rights particularly dangerous is that although young students might not be afforded the autonomy or respect to contest such infringements, these violations increasingly direct more and more students to the criminal justice system. This is a debilitating paradox, and it assuredly impacts some students more so than others, both in the short-term and the long-term. As in the broader world of law enforcement, the students most susceptible to impingements on their rights are students of color and the poor (Cole, 1999).[11]

The Not-So-Hidden Curriculum is Not-So-Color Blind

Browne (2003, 2005), of the Advancement Project, demonstrates that the not-so-hidden curriculum is, quite disproportionately, an unequal opportunity criminalizer, a form of "carceral affirmative action" (Wacquant, 2002). In making the link between the "old track," which led to work, vocational or college education, and the "jailhouse track," which directs primarily African-American students to the juvenile and criminal justice system (Browne, 2003, p. 9), Browne begins to unravel the racialized consequences of the not-so-hidden curriculum. In her survey of Palm Beach County schools, Browne found that African Americans constituted the disproportionate amount of suspensions and expulsions, and school-based arrests. African American students were 30% of Palm Beach's enrollment, but 65% of school-based arrests (p. 19). Offenses categorized as miscellaneous, simple assault, crimes against property and other crimes against property resulted in 85% of the arrests (p. 58), miscellaneous being primarily the codifier for defiance. Weapons and drug violations, of which weapons possession is the only violation endorsed by the GFSA 1994, resulted in a combined total of 15% of the arrests (no weapons violations culminated in arrest) (p. 58). Moreover, Browne found similar patterns replicated in Baltimore County schools. Unfortunately, these trends are not endemic to Palm Beach County or Baltimore County schools.[12]

In other words, African American students are being expelled and arrested in vast disproportion to White students for offenses that previously would have been handled within the classroom or school and in most instances resulted in suspensions. These trends beg unfortunate questions: Are African American students more violent and disruptive than White students? Can differences in behaviors between

African American students and White students account for the vast disparity between African American exclusion and White exclusion under zero tolerance?

In his extensive review of research, Russell Skiba (2000) found that there is nothing to suggest that African American students are more violent or disruptive than other students. Ironically, he notes that students of all colors perceived that teachers interacted unfairly with students of color and poorer students in their schools. African American students are not more violent than their White counterparts but, in actuality, schools elicit and encourage different behaviors from each set of students—the hidden curriculum at its best. This only answers the first question. Differences in—or, I should say, differences in teacher perception and understanding of—student behavior play a crucial part in the disciplining of students. It has been noted that teachers of White, European American female status simply but dangerously misread and misperceive the communication styles and patterns of African American students (Noguera, 2001; Robbins, 2005; Skiba, 2000). These teachers assume that students should be quiet, polite and respectful in their communicative patterns; the generally more (inter) active communication styles of African American youth purportedly frighten (read: threaten the authority of) "teachers who are prone to accepting [and promoting] stereotypes of adolescent African-American males as threatening or dangerous" (Skiba, p. 12). Thus, teachers discipline and push-out African American youth in greater numbers than White youth. This is the penultimate function of the hidden curriculum: the differential distribution of educational opportunity and life chances to different classes and races of students.

Disappointingly, legal and quasi-legal functionaries perform much of the dirty work of the not-so-hidden curriculum, further abdicating teachers and schools of responsibility of educating students for democratic public life and cloaking these abbreviations of students' life chances in legal as opposed to educational and political terms (e.g., zero tolerance as opposed to public accountability and social responsibility).

Enforcing the Not-So-Hidden Curriculum—The Politics of Security Personnel

Security personnel are now regular features in public schools in the United States. Police have not only gained an increased presence in schools, but have also attained increasing control over the lives of stu-

dents. Public schools in Chicago, Los Angeles, New York, and Philadelphia all maintain their own police departments or contract school
security with city police departments (Browne, 2003; Mukharjee &
Karpatkin, 2007). As a result of the DARE program, most school districts have a school police officer, and this relationship between the
school and its police officer has intensified since the events of 9/11. In
addition to this standard school-police liaison, some schools hire undercover cops who perform a range of duties from stinging students for
drugs, fights, weapons violations and verbal threats (see Beger, 2002), to
producing a snitch culture in the school that directs students to 1-800
anonymous reporting systems through which they can perform the
same functions as the official "21 Jump Streeters." The not-so-hidden
curriculum has also upped the ante on other visible security mechanisms, school resource officers.

School resource officers are "the fastest growing area of law enforcement [with a] membership quickly approaching 10,000," the website
for the National Association for School Resource Officers (NASRO)
proudly announces.[13] NASRO's stated mission is to educate, counsel
and protect school communities. This adds a particularly new twist to
the function of police officers in schools, as it seems to me that a
teacher's historic role was to educate, counsel and protect. NASRO's
foundational concept is what it calls the "TRIAD," the hybridization of
"Law Enforcement Officer-Teacher-Counselor." Misunderstanding the
implied goals of the not-so-hidden curriculum is very difficult, especially in a post-9/11 political climate.

As schools are defunded because of outlays required by the War
of Terror, diminishing values of taxable property, and the testing-
punishment demands of NCLB, schools still receive funds to purchase
security equipment and personnel. NASRO has not let the lucrative
security market of the post-9/11 landscape evade it. In fact, NASRO
pressured congress to include a stipulation in the Homeland Security
Act, "The Education Homeland Security Act," which permits the government to provide funds for school resource officers and high-end
security technologies such as iris detection units, digital closed-circuit
television systems and biometric devices, whether or not the government can provide funding for academic materials. On February 10,
2003, the executive director of NASRO, Curt Lavarello (2003), sent out
a letter that unabashedly played on the politics of fear, claiming that
education budget cuts left schools "unprepared for dealing with terrorist

threats like suicide bombers or attacks with chemical, biological and other weapons of mass destruction" (p. 1). Whether or not the government responded directly to this inflated call, it earmarked $350 million for schools to purchase security technologies (Casella, 2003c), while the Bush administration left its self-heralded NCLB act underfunded by as much as $6 billion dollars in the same year. However, it is not just the presence of security personnel that is troubling; their behaviors are equally reprehensible.

School resource officers have harassed and intimidated minority students in Florida. Browne (2003, p. 28) reports that a "school police officer flicked the Puerto Rican flag medallion [a] student wore around his neck, and made a derogatory remark." Other students informed Browne that Latinos are "assumed to be gang members," and they are profiled and harassed in related measure. It gets much worse in this regard. Girls in New York City public schools, for example, are not only often frisked by male police officers, which is a blatant violation of the law, but they are also wanded by male police officers for unnecessary periods of time (Mukharjee and Karpatkin, 2007). Fifty-three percent of students surveyed in New York City public schools have been verbally harassed or intimidated by police officers with names like " 'baby Rikers,' " (a reference to the penal colony off of New York City) or told, during security operations, " 'That girl has no ass' " (p. 16). Nearly one-third of the students surveyed by the American Civil Liberties Union (ACLU) reported that they were touched inappropriately by security officers (p. 16). Moreover, school resource officers can skirt Miranda rights in some instances. Like school administrators, school resource officers are not considered law enforcement officials, at least when their agency has a primary mission other than to enforce the law (Rubin, 2004). In this way, one can imagine the hair splitting that can occur as a result of NASRO's triad concept, because the triad is not first and foremost a way to enforce the law, but primarily a way to integrate the responsibilities but apparently not the skills of police, teachers, and counselors. In turn, the evidence retrieved by school resource officers can be used for pressing criminal charges, skirting due process.

Couple the wide, discriminatory authority of school-based police officers and school resource officers with intractable racial inequalities between schools, and the not-so-hidden curriculum becomes clearer. Pushing-out of African American students is no longer a social and political practice, but a legally structured practice—a legislative fiat. As a result of zero tolerance and fiscal acumen, test scores are boosted by booting both marginalized students and students who need extra resources. School resource officers are "protecting the school," "protecting teachers from intimidating students," "saving the school from potential drugs," "promoting a safe and clean school image," and "eliminating the criminal elements"—all claims appeased or justified by the practice of zero tolerance. New York City Mayor Michael Bloomberg used rhetoric reminiscent of the Reconstruction-era South when he stated, in reference to proverbially disruptive minority students, "How about those they prey on?" (Herszenhorn, 2003). The use of this metaphor implies how he perceives these students.

The Not-So-Hidden Curriculum, Language, and Resource Allocation

Because of the intense accountability-punishment practices endorsed by NCLB and zero tolerance, this language promotes and justifies exclusion policies in two ways: One, testing has always been a racialized educational tool. The use of anything from interest area tests and vocational aptitude tests to IQ tests is a crucial mechanism by which the traditional hidden curriculum operated. Based on the allegedly objective results of the tests, students are channeled into particular tracks and provided differential educational access, resources, and opportunities. So, especially in those schools that have small African American and other minority populations, retrograde signifiers of African Americans influence teacher perceptions of student behaviors. Subsequently, they have zero tolerance for those "predatory" students who might not perform well on the mandatory tests on which their evaluations and school funding are contingent (see Wright, Weekes, & McGlaughlin 2000). Expressed differently, the intense pressures put on schools create classroom environments in which quick responses to student defiance are the most expedient solutions of ensuring curricula is covered expeditiously and that students are well-prepared to take the tests. Interestingly, California, Florida, Kentucky, Illinois, Michigan and Texas are states that have engaged intense testing programs over the past few years, even before NCLB. These are the states with some of the most severe zero tolerance policies and highest rates of suspension and expulsion for students of color. With vigorous pressure to perform well on mandatory tests, throwaway terms such as dangerous, defiant, insubordinate, disruptive, and criminal that are so readily bandied about, quite simply encourage teachers to resort to zero tolerance (Zweifler & DeBeers, 2002, p. 209).

Two, the metaphorical and virtual disinvestment in schools attended predominantly by minority populations can be effected through the testing-punishing device endorsed by the NCLB. And for urban schools already disadvantaged by dilapidated infrastructures, underqualified teachers and sub-par resources, this is an eminent threat. How can urban schools, dealing with severe resource shortages, work with students who have more intensive demands than the "traditional" student? Urban schools across the country are experiencing extraordinary levels of suspensions and expulsions, beginning as early as kindergarten. For example, "In the 2000–2001 school year, 90,559 children were suspended from school around [Connecticut], up from 57,626 two years earlier" (Gordon, 2003, p. 14CN.1). While these are state-wide figures for Connecticut, a state official unabashedly claims that the rate of exclusion " 'has to do with kids who are very undisciplined, especially at the urban schools, where the children haven't received discipline at home' " (Gordon, 2001). On this level, it is clear that urban students are perceived—because it's not a characteristic endemic to particular racial groups—to be undisciplined. This descriptor is a little more polite than superpredator, but again, the urban African American and Hispanic student and school is undisciplined in relation to what can be assumed to be a suburban, White, middle-class student and school. It would seem that as schools have been sites of social and moral regulation, students perceived to be undisciplined would be provided greater opportunity for social and moral development. But the issue goes deeper than political charges. Darling-Hammond (2000) and Kozol (2005) demonstrate, in terms of the provision of adequate physical structures, qualified teachers, and quality resources, how tracks exist between schools. Urban schools are expected to perform commensurately to their suburban counterparts on fewer and fewer resources, and as schools are threatened further by low test scores, the exclusion of students of color is a predictable outcome. If certain students need extra support, whether it is staff, education materials, or time, these are prohibitive factors when teachers need to cover "benchmarks," meet "standards," and complete "test prep" exercises on strict timelines to be as best prepared as possible. Defiance and disruption, let alone actual danger, promote a more disparaging structure of feeling for schools, where pejorative stereotypes of students of color are circumscribed by state threats of defunding and takeover.

This struggle for resources, particularly as public school funding is hedged against test performance, is very real and it demonstrates how the not-so-hidden curriculum demands legitimation. An academic official for Toledo public schools recognizes how the drain on resources encourages schools to push-out students, zero tolerance providing the precise justification for this response. Cotner claims, " 'For students who did not fit the mold—whatever that may be—there were many more options [in the past] . . . In some cases, those students who found it impossible to sit for five hours in a classroom could function very well in a labor environment' " (see Rimer, 2004, p. 1.1). Although students might not have found it completely impossible to sit in school in the past, Cotner sheds light on what happens to youth when the social contract no longer matters. As Sara Rimer rightfully observes, "those students, with far fewer options, remain in school, but the school district has fewer resources to handle difficult students" (p. 1.1). Consequently, schools find it challenging to meet the needs of most students, let alone those who demand greater resources of any kind, and they subsequently resort to pushing-out kids vis-a-vis zero tolerance. A crucial difference between students excluded from schools in the past and those currently provided zero tolerance, however, is that today's students have neither the economic or social support systems that were available in the past—viable job opportunities without a high school or college education and a social safety net.

The struggle over resources, then, is a struggle over what groups of students can, will, and should gain access to active citizenship, in whatever form it might be exercised as the social contract is rewritten as the carceral pact for increasing numbers of youth of color. Without viable occupational opportunities and alternative forms of public education and support, where else can excluded students turn? The question then is, what type of society is being produced by the types of citizenship promoted by the practices of zero tolerance and the codes of the not-so-hidden curriculum.

The Hidden and Not-So-Hidden Curriculum Compared

The hidden curriculum and the not-so-hidden curriculum should be understood in relation to each other: The hidden curriculum still exists; the not-so-hidden curriculum is simply superimposed on it. Furthermore, neither forms of these curricula produce democratic social relations in school. Again, the hidden and not-so-hidden curriculum are used as tools to demonstrate the broader historical turn from the social contract to the private-corporate contract and carceral pact, how this turn impacts schools and youth and, importantly, the function of zero tolerance within the wider goals of neoliberalism—one of which being the suspension of citizenship.

As Giroux (2001b) notes, the hidden curriculum is "those unstated norms, values, and beliefs embedded in and transmitted to students through the underlying rules that structure the routines and social relationships in school and classroom life" (p. 47). The differential access to educational and social resources along classed, gendered, and racialized lines that emerges from these "unstated norms, values, and beliefs" can be (and was) observed to be a "rational(ized)" consequence of the role schools played in a particular period. The hidden curriculum was and is the fabric of school and classroom relations in a society in which schools are used to produce different classes of students for a hierarchicalized and competitive labor market. One of the operative terms in this definition of the hidden curriculum is classes. When the economic functions of public schools are countered by interest in their public and civic functions, students are interpellated into social classes, and the terms of the liberal social contract by which the hidden curriculum can be criticized revolve around equalizing the opportunities that groups can access and accumulate through the process of schooling. A consequence of this relationship is that public schools are struggled over as democratic public spheres in which social groups vie not only for the democratization of political power but also the equalization of access to and mobility in the broader economy.

However, as the language of the liberal social contract is supplanted by the individualized and privatized terms and logic of neoliberalism, the hidden curriculum is also privatized, and its disproportionate provision of education as a social resource to different classes and races of students is recast as a matter of personal shortcomings, cultural depravity, and purported biological inferiority. This is the not-so-hidden curriculum of public schools when the liberal social contract is erased, consumerism drives the mission of formal schooling, and public schools serve radically altered economic interests in which a broad and stable industrial labor market is replaced by an everchanging and limited information and service based economy. Instead of different classes of students being the cause and effect of competitive and iniquitous social and economic relations, individuals with allegedly private shortcomings or gifts are recast as winners and losers, instead of as competing social classes. In part, this consequence is attributable to the use of intense testing programs and reduced funding as mechanisms by which elite groups of students are produced to fulfill limited vacancies in a reconfigured labor market and emasculated civic duties in a political climate in which the realm of the social has been evacuated. As a result, the not-so-hidden curriculum not only reflects but is also constitutive of the cultural logic of neoliberalism in the broader society: Individuals (or winners and losers) exist in social, political, and economic relations in which the discourses of the self, consumerism, or criminality are the primary frames by which one can approach, interpret, comprehend, and intervene in the world.

Whereas the hidden curriculum exists as the fabric of school and classroom relations—the unstated, tacit norms and values of competitive social relations—the not-so-hidden curriculum is an explicit lesson, an overt attempt at teaching varied groups of students and the broader public differential lessons about an individualized and privatized social and economic world. In order for the not-so-hidden curriculum to become operative and legitimate, students who are excluded from the imaginary equal playing field of testing, funding, and school choice must be redefined and recategorized. New stories must be told about that redefinition and recategorization. Zero tolerance is the guiding metaphor, legal recourse, and social practice that legitimates the not-so-hidden curriculum of public schools in the age of the erasure of the social contract. It privatizes issues of unequal access to schools as social resources. It punishes individuals for the consequences of social disinvestment in certain schools and youth, and, consequently, it provides the practices and terms by which stories can be told to legitimate the criminalization of racial and class minority students. Their inclusion in schools and the broader society as civic agents is no longer considered a public commitment and social value, but a private problem and social threat. Simply but devastatingly, the not-so-hidden curriculum uses zero tolerance to redefine the civic function of public schools in new historical conditions, without altering the fundamental structure of schools that was produced under previous historical conditions and public commitments. In other words, zero tolerance expels hope for a democratic future by suspending the civic capacities and opportunities of students who could play a critical role in promoting a democratic future.

In this way, more than ever, citizenship is about who has the power to not only name themselves and "challenge the power structure by attempting to challenge some of the social relations that give rise to it" (Mayo, 2003, p. 8), but also the particular social relations they would like to create and in which they want to participate.

Conclusion

It should be clear that the traditional hidden curriculum, particularly as it relies on tracking and questionable measures of student value in a school, has produced forms of alienation for students and disintegration of school communities. The hidden curriculum provides the official structure in, by, and through which the symbolic and real violence of devaluation and exclusion inflicted on racial and class minorities is sanctioned, normalized, and legitimated. Students are separated from their peers, put in classes with unqualified and underqualified teachers, given watered-downed curricula, provided teacher-centered and demeaning classroom relationships, and thus have many academic and social needs unmet. In turn, this ostensibly leads many students to be disenchanted and disengaged from the educational experience and, deprived of the skills of effective citizenship, left with few resources to contest the processes of devaluation and exclusion with which they are confronted. What's more, the structure of the hidden curriculum provides the frame through which teachers' beliefs and behaviors are harnessed to support the systemic disinvestment of students marginalized by color and class. Furthermore, as schools face increasing shortages of resources, teachers have more pressure put on their classroom time by an intense testing scheme. Exclusion becomes a quick and easy fix made legal by the mandate of zero tolerance and normalized by the practice of zero tolerance and "accountability." Thus, my contention throughout has not been to suggest that keeping students in school by returning to a gentler hidden curriculum is a viable way of constructing and maintaining safe learning environments. The traditional hidden curriculum, which operated in a dialogic relationship to the broader narration of and commitment to the liberal social contract, is unmoored from its relationship to the liberal social contract and something else obviously happens in schools and to their democratic mission. It should also be clear that the not-so-hidden curriculum of the erased social contract is even more devastating to students' life chances, in addition to threatening—if not eliminating—the preconditions for all students to learn. This is where the consequences for the possibility of citizenship are most deeply registered.

A primary concern implied throughout this investigation is not that students don't already exercise forms of agency—progressive, regressive, oppositional, resistant or reproductive—but that the investments students make in school life and the shape and efficacy of their agency is inseparable from both the symbolic forces working on them, in and outside of schools, and the structure of the school relations in which they are placed. The subjectivities that students internalize and by which they exercise agency are not determined as much as they are conditioned and limited by the identifications they make in school life and the symbolic and real resources with which they are provided, all of which are contingent upon the shape and force of public commitments. Quite simply, while some students might not identify as easily as others with the culture of their school, the vast majority of students participate in ways that the structure and content of classroom and school relations provide and permit. The practices and consequences of zero tolerance suggest that fundamentally punitive views of youth and deracinated forms of citizenship are being developed and reinforced as a result of the shift from the liberal social contract to the private, corporate contract and carceral pact.

If students are immersed in a school environment that privileges open communication, interactive and cooperative learning, and the ideals of trust, respect, equality, and responsibility, then it is tautological that the physical structure, cultural practices, and social relations of the school would support these interests and students' involvement in the definition, redefinition, and maintenance of these values. Students would not be monitored incessantly but engaged as active, positive, and productive members of a school community. As members of a larger and common good, students would be provided the resources and conditions to perform a critical role "in formation of the values that regulate the living of [people] together: which is necessary from the standpoint of both the general social welfare and the full development of human beings as individuals" (Dewey, 1994, pp. 264–265). In other words, students would learn what it means to be a participant and a citizen. In this way, students would be perceived and engaged in the production of democratic public life by way of reproducing the conditions and relations central to the formation and operation of civic agency.

Alternately, if students are surrounded by hidden cameras, CCTVs, undercover cops, school resource officers, search-and-sniff dogs, metal detectors, biometric scanning devices and are involved in relentlessly individualizing and competitive testing regimes, they are learning that they are, indeed, suspects and agents or animals in Hobbes's war of all against all in the scramble for scarce educational opportunities and social resources. Teachers are not immune to the effects of these forms of subjectification. Coupled with sedimented assumptions about race, class, and criminality, and the contemporary media onslaughts of stereotypical, retrograde images of race and crime, teachers and administrators are encouraged to be suspicious of students. The forms of authority and types of citizenship afforded to and engaged by teachers are inseparable from both preexisting perceptions of students and the broader environmental cues and symbolic forces that construct and reinforce differential beliefs about race and class. These are hardly the conditions on which the democratization of school and community life can be built, and the relative silence in the media about these changes and, as in the case of "Ambush at Goose Creek," the celebration of surveillance technologies imply a crisis. Schools are not so much the cause but the mechanism, by which the crisis is reproduced.

The crisis is the erasing of the social contract, the idea(l) that all citizens be provided a modicum of resources (time being one of them), and the conditions in which they can participate in the social contract when forms of exclusion and domination threaten the democratic well-being of society. Although it has existed in damaged ways, the social contract implies a relationship between state and civil society. Individuals and groups are provided protection from the war of all against all, and the legalized, normalized war of one group against another. The social contract helps to provide a narrative in which public participants and civic agents reproduce the conditions for the narration of the social contract and broaden its commitments. But to a certain degree, the inverse holds true. The production and relevance of citizenship implies a certain definition of the social contract, and citizens must be provided with and involved in the production of relations in which they can narrate the social contract in light of altered historical conditions. Consequently, if the social contract no longer matters, or is no longer maintained, reconstructed, recast, and renarrated, civic agents and citizens no longer matter. Being deprived of the vocabularies and material conditions, people have little impetus to translate private problems and interests into social issues and commitments.

This is the broader social and political crisis in which schools are now engaged: The "Law of the land," as Sen. Dorgan (1994) refers to GFSA 1994, currently is to suspend citizenship through the cultural-economic logic of neoliberalism and the exclusionary power of zero tolerance in schools. This is a foundational lesson. This objective is assuredly manifest in the failed sting operation in the second image that opened the chapter and reinforced by the silence that surrounds the fabricated naturalness of the event and others like it. The implications for society are threatening and send a shocking message that schools have become more effective at eliminating the prospects of citizenship rather than enhancing the conditions fundamental to the construction and process of democratization.

Thus, the choice is clear, but by no means simple. Either teachers and administrators work with students and their communities as citizens involved in the construction of the public good, or they reproduce and exacerbate the erasure of the social contract and replace it with the carceral pact. This is where the not-so-hidden curriculum becomes operative: As the democratic function of public schools is eliminated, the not-so-hidden curriculum conveys and reinforces the legally sanctioned disinvestment in certain groups of students and their inordinate exclusion from schools as democratic public spheres.

Because the not-so-hidden curriculum is visible, it would seem that it would be easier to contest than the hidden curriculum. Again, without discourses and public stories to support public schools and maintain commitments to all students, little affective investment is created and mobilized in the societal beliefs and values that make such stories operative, especially if available resources are devoted to other interests, for instance, the security industry, culture of fear, and the ongoing militarization of society. This is the choice being made and it is the greatest, most frequent threat to student safety, citizenship, and democratic public life.

CHAPTER 3

Occupying Education

Zero Tolerance and the Militarization of Schooling

"[S]pace is by its very nature full of power and symbolism, a complex web of relations of domination and subordination, of solidarity and cooperation."

—Massey, 1994, p. 265

"The way we arrange ourselves in space has much to do with relationships, whether in the short term or over rather longer periods. In particular it reflects the roles we play in those relationships."

—Lawson, 2001, p. 133

"Some times come unexpected, when we are not looking, and they stun us, perhaps for ever after."

—Miller, 2001, p. 273

" 'We know the process . . . We know what to take off, what shoes will set off the metal detectors. But you do feel like a prisoner.' "

—Medina, 2002, p. A25

The quote above offers powerful insights into one of the lessons learned under zero tolerance. The qualification made with "but . . ." indicates a slippage between her perceived role as a public school student and the subjectivity created by the predominance of carceral codes conveyed by the social text of the school and wider society. In other words, "but . . ." demonstrates inherent contradictions

87

students must resolve as a consequence of the changing language of space-time in schools under the law and policy and ideology of zero tolerance. The word "but" also signals that despite being able to predict what personal belonging will trigger what security device, and acquiescing to other messages such as "schooling is good" and "these security measures are for *your* safety," this student still "feel[s] like a prisoner." The word consequently suggests that no countermessage offsets students constructed as criminals; nor are there broader counter-discourses that erase the oppressive languages of agency promoted by the space-time of zero tolerance. Ultimately, this student's insight suggests that a dangerous translation of the space of schooling has occurred. If these changes to school space (e.g., metal detectors, police officers, automatic locking doors, JROTC programs and their military personnel, etc.), were simply minor appendages to schools, their effects wouldn't penetrate so deeply—to the body. But because the criminalization and militarization of school space are processes, they implicate people and security tools in hierarchical social relationships. One might thus assume that urban schools—with their comparatively more intensive security and military measures and practices—have effectively become prisons, or boot camps, and support relationships appropriate to carceral and military institutions. The spatial-temporal codes of urban schools are so powerful and seamless that moments of reflection to think that schools are like prisons are prohibited. For many students, they are left with simply feeling and responding to the social text of the school like prisoners or cadets. This contemporary feature of urban schools comes with a profound consequence: Students and teachers lose the normative language capable of critiquing the construction of schools as prisons or military feeder systems.

In this chapter, I explore the criminalization and militarization of school space-time and the production of school space, temporal codes, and relationships conducive to a flourishing security industry, and the ongoing militarization of society. In order to better understand the relationships between space-time, agency, and democratization, and how contemporary school security practices transform and undermine them, these observations are interpreted according to Doreen Massey's (1994) theorization of space-time as mutually constitutive categories of social action created and defined by social relationships. In other words, space-time is socially constructed. Its meaning and impacts can be understood by looking at the social relationships that simultaneously produce, and are produced, by space-time.

Selling Security and Making War(riors)

The burgeoning security industry and the ongoing militarization of U.S. society must be addressed in order to clearly understand how the ideology and practice of zero tolerance participates in the transformation, if not complete subversion, of school space-time.[1] This is because the security industry interests are not unrelated to the militarization of society and because both agendas intensively penetrated U.S. public schools—at the same time as, or in the years since, zero tolerance was legislated (See Casella, 2001; Giroux, 2004; Lutz and Bartlett, 1995; Lutz, 2002). Schools now contract with private corporations and local police departments to install, maintain, and monitor surveillance equipment and safety measures, while the military gains increasing access to and visibility in schools through JROTC programs, recruitment officers, and the "Troops-to-Teachers" program. (Troops-to-Teachers is a federal plan, first implemented in 1994 and renewed with a vengeance by No Child Left Behind in 2002. It seeks to fill teacher shortages in poor and urban public school districts by providing incentives to retiring military officials to become teachers in those districts.) Moreover, the Department of Defense underwrites the purchase and use of military hardware and information-tracking systems in local police departments (Haggerty & Ericson, 1999; Kraska, 1999). The information databases are used in coordination with urban schools to track potentially violent students, allowing an invisible and powerful method of surveillance and discipline. Importantly, the objectives of the security industry and the military are not only complementary—the latter picking up where the former leaves off—they also underpin antidemocratic conceptions of authority and discipline by altering the spatial and temporal codes of schools. As a result, these codes of the security-prison-military-industrial complex prepare youth and, by extension, society for either a prison order or social order defined by a perpetual state of war. The security industry and militarization of schools operates more intensively on larger, poorer, darker urban schools and targets students of color and poor students in other schools. Operating in tandem with the ideology of zero tolerance, the security industry and process of militarization not only transform school space-time, they also racialize it in new ways.

Selling Safety, Making Danger

The security industry has found and cultivated a boom market in public schools. Some of the devices the industry unloads on school systems, in some instances costing upwards of $50 million, include, but are not necessarily limited to hand-held and freestanding metal detectors, electronically locking doors, student and teacher identification badges, motion-sensitive lights, and hidden cameras. Closed circuit television systems are sometimes directed to local police departments. These systems also include, biometric scanning and iris recognition mechanisms, video cameras and GPS locator systems on school buses, and the presence of police and military personnel. These devices are then partnered with strategies of random and daily metal- detector checks, closed lunches, school visitor sign-in routines, drug sweeps and blitz operations, random drug tests of participants in extracurricular activities, and the dissemination of disciplinary and student information to local police departments. Due to the capital invested in existing security devices and increasing technological sophistication, it is sound business protocol for the industry to tap this nascent market, especially with legitimation conferred by the culture of fear and War of Terror.

Like any other industry, the security industry has a vested interest in making school administrations and, ultimately, tax payers believe they need more security. Ronnie Casella (2003c) notes how numerous security program training guides and industry advertisements show compliant, if not happy, individuals being frisked or passing through metal detectors, or concoct danger scenarios, alerting readers and school administrators to hotbeds of disruption and danger that lurk in their classrooms, hallways, and on school grounds. In the security industry trade journal *American School and University*, Mike Kennedy (2004) plugs a school safety strategy called Crime Prevention through Environmental Design (CPTED), demonstrating how the industry has a clear understanding of the pedagogical and social implications of the ordering of school space. Under the persuasive guise of allowing school administrations to "choose building layouts and features that promote desirable behavior," Kennedy offers a school layout that resembles a correctional facility more than a learning environment. Kennedy explains that:

CPTED encourages strategies such as minimizing the number of buildings on a campus; limiting the number of entrances to buildings; ensuring that administrative offices have clear sightlines of the main entry, parking lots and play areas; and establishing boundaries between a school and adjacent properties. (2004, para. 5)

Of course, school administrations should plan for contingencies and design school environments in ways that promote safety. This is not the issue. The question is for what professed reasons and to what ultimate effects would a school empty its environment of spatial forms that promote sociality, movement, and openness both within its structure and between the outside world?

The reasons for these school designs are explicit in Kennedy's article, which reads more like an advertisement for the security industry than an essay. Danger and crime are inevitable unless they sharpen their safety measures. One suggested safety measure is for schools to reduce their publicness by "limiting public accessibility" (Kennedy, 2004, para. 10). As Kennedy suggests, if schools foolishly open themselves to the public after normal hours, separate entrances should be made for the spaces used, "so that the rest of the building can be *locked down and secure*" [italics added] (para. 11). Kennedy adds that this measure should be coupled with security devices. School grounds should be extensively lighted with timed and motion detector systems to "ward off trespass-ers." Schools should employ resource officers, install cameras, use "wire-less technology" for administrators and teachers, and have functioning and monitored metal detectors. All of these devices are touted as mecha-nisms that schools need to promote safety. Kennedy states, as an alleged universal fact, that "police presence can make a community feel safer, and a school community is no exception" (para. 16).[2] Nonetheless, these reasons are mostly self-evident thanks to the rampant culture of fear and the ideology of zero tolerance.

The question of what potential consequences these measures produce is less obvious. One might idealistically yet naively say that the result is increased student safety, more desirable behaviors, and the like. This is not necessarily the case because research indicates no strong correlation between increased security measures and decreased rates of undesirable student behavior. In fact, available research suggests that these measures might increase undesirable and sometimes violent student behaviors (Skiba, 2000). This is less obviously related to the question of what other institutions have layouts similar to those of CPTED? The obvious answer is the correctional model, which prohibits free and unsupervised movement between buildings, limits the number of entrances to or thoroughfares within it, provides for administrator observation of the grounds or streaming video surveillance to their offices, and, clearly demarcates itself from the surrounding public—a primary stigmatizing function of carceral institutions. In prisons, in spite of intensive surveillance and attempts to reduce social intercourse and limit movement, inmates find ways to sidestep, resist, or simply transgress these environmental impositions. Likewise, if adequately pushed by school relations and broader conditions or if excluded from relationships that allow them to participate positively in the school community, students will find ways to "beat the system."

Whether or not this is the hidden agenda of the security industry, the latent consequences of creating lockdown school space fulfill the industry's market prerogatives. If school safety needs are not actual and identifiable, then the sterilizing of school relationships by security technologies will produce a false need. In other words, the security industry builds its market by constructing environments in which certain potential risks become actual dangers—because social mechanisms for promoting safety are supplanted by adversarial relationships, fear, closed and monitored school spaces, or multimillion dollar security equipment.

What's more, purchasing high-tech security devices is subjected to the pressures of the security industry and to the structure of the culture of fear. Elaborate security systems are dependent on the market and the prevalence of these devices in other public institutions. That is, one, while technology becomes more efficient, allowing for security devices to become more sophisticated and be produced more inexpensively, and as more players enter the market, the price of security technologies decreases. As one cheerleader for the industry explains:

> As society continues to change and become more safety conscious, biometrics will also gain a strong foothold in the commerce, governmental and public arenas—*making school applications seem much less unusual and intrusive . . . which seems like a small price to pay in order to foster a safer learning environment.* [emphasis added.] (Goldberg, 2003, p. 19).[3]

Critical to this rationalization of biometric security technologies is the myth that schools are patently unsafe (because certain students are inherently dangerous); the criminalization of society is not only "good" but also inevitable—the natural teleology of society as it becomes more complex and increasing security and surveillance technology becomes both *more powerful and less visible* (or more powerful because it is less visible and increasingly accepted); and schools cannot be made safe by more educational, open and democratic measures that allow students and their communities to be involved as productive participants instead of suspects. These are not simple rhetorical charges but observations of complex social relationships developing between students and schools.

The security industry drains resources from poor schools. For all public schools, public monies, particularly federal funds, are scarce or made scarce by many tax cuts, the punitive testing-punishment scheme, and the increasing costs of perpetual war. Thus, poor urban public schools are particularly strapped, because their additional funds are procured from taxes based on low, urban property values. Instead of finding ways to distribute existing funds for educational resources such as competent teachers, books, computers, and infrastructure, poor urban public schools are wheedled into spending limited funds on expensive security devices.

Ronnie Casella (2003c) notes that Chicago public schools "spent about $35 million during the 2000–2001 school year on security" alone (p. 84). This is all the more remarkable because Chicago public schools have a history of being underfunded and under-resourced in terms of facilities, staff, and curriculum materials. They have also reported sharp increases in student exclusion over the last ten years (see Lipman, 2002, 2004; Gordon, Piana, & Keleher, 2001; Street, 2005). This misallocation of resources, from curriculum materials and staffing to security measures in 2000–2001 is not a fluke. Chicago invested more than $54 million on school security for the 2003–2004 school year (Olszewski, 2003). Dell'Angela & Cholo (2004) report that although Chicago public schools "eliminated an estimated 1600" positions between staff, teacher, and teacher aides for the 2004–2005 school year, it allocated "$20 million for a new computerized student-tracking system" and added "10 new officers—a crisis team to work in the district's most troubled schools" (p. 1). Based on a "typical salary of $43,000," the $20 million spent on security and tracking technology translates into approximately 465 teaching positions.

The educational influence of the security industry is not endemic to Chicago public schools. In the winter of 2003, New York City public schools planned to add probation officers, establish a school safety hotline, open four off-site suspension centers, and increase the number of schools using metal detectors (see Herszenhorn, 2003). This in addition to its force of 4,108 security agents as of 2004, a gauntlet of metal detectors, and repeated attempts to link police department databases with schools to compile and track student and school crime data (Herszenhorn, 2004).[4]

Serving the metro-Atlanta area, the DeKalb County School System spent $8.9 million on camera upgrades in its 140 schools in the fall of 2003, increasing the number of cameras from an average of 16 to 32 cameras per school and using digital instead of video technology. Allegedly plagued by the inconvenience of rewinding videotapes to review school incidents, DeKalb opted for digital technology. With a couple of keystrokes, administrators and officers would not have to worry about changing tapes. If these changes and situations regarding the degree to which surveillance is an accepted part of daily school life are not compelling enough, then this should provoke a moment of pause: The officers of DeKalb County school system's Department of Public Safety can monitor all the district's 4,000 plus security cameras on "four large plasma screens" from the comfort of their "headquarters" (Sansbury, 2003).

The sweeping use of security technology in DeKalb County schools has been matched, if not trumped. The trade journal *Satellite News* (2004) reports that the San Francisco Unified School District contracted with California-based Satellite Security Systems (S3), "a provider of asset tracking and control for . . . government organizations," to install what is called "GlobalGuard and Virtual Perimeter" technology on 220 of its buses. This Global Positioning Satellite (GPS) technology will be used to track school bus routes, alerting a communications center "if a school bus *suddenly* deviates from its normal route" [italics added.] (p. 1), as if sudden bus detours are frequent and probable happenings. This technology also charts bus driver performance. But further, this technology could be coupled with card-swipe technology that would record and transmit to databases a range of student data as students board busses. If S3 and the writer of this trade journal article advertisement can imagine the likelihood of a bus being hijacked by either the bus driver, a student, or a terrorist and create a plausible case for a school system's dumping of millions of dollars into the technology, it seems equally as likely that one can imagine a dangerous underside to its safe veneer.[5,6,7]

The security industry has a rational interest in canvassing all schools. But, again, because the industry prides itself on security, dangers have to be fabricated. This is seen in the divergent security measures of urban and suburban schools, small and larger schools, poor and wealthy school systems, and the local and regional politics that emerge from these relationships. Nearly 25% of all public schools had a daily police presence in the school year 1999–2000 (U.S. Department of Education, 2002, p. 71).[8] Nonetheless, daily police presence is not evenly distributed across the nation's public schools when school size, percent of students qualifying for free lunch (a class category), and community type (largely a racial indicator in our segregated society) are considered. Slightly more than 23% of public schools, with less than 15% of students qualifying for free lunch, had a daily police presence. Slightly more than 33% of schools with 75–100% of students qualifying for free lunch had a daily police presence in 1999–2000. Almost 38% of central city schools had a daily police presence, yet only 14% of rural or small town schools had a daily police presence. Similar disparities were found with other school security measures such as random metal detector checks. Twice as many urban schools as rural and small town schools used random metal detector checks. Schools with large percentages of poor students were more likely to have daily metal detector checks than schools with smaller percentages of poor students. Drug sweeps were the only school security measure for which these disparities were reversed; rural and small town schools had twice as many drug sweeps as urban schools, and video surveillance was used in relatively equal amounts between types of school settings, differing only in level of schooling (e.g., elementary, secondary, or combined).[9]

These broad trends suggest that the industry criminalizes larger, poorer, and darker schools disproportionately more than smaller, wealthier, and "whiter" ones. Because of the actual criminalization of urban school students and judging from the frequent media coverage of dangerous urban school space, it would seem logical that darker, urban schools are inherently more dangerous than their suburban counterparts. In their study of school violence and segregation, David Eitle and Tamela

McNulty Eitle (2003) demonstrate that rates of official and self-reported violence are *not* significantly higher in poorer, predominantly Black school districts than in wealthier, White school districts. Instead of finding a strain in poorer and darker districts, Eitle and Eitle find that reported acts of violence were higher, not between segregated districts, but within districts and individual schools where racial and class inequalities are magnified.[10] They do not argue that integrated districts inherently produce violence because of racial and class diversity. They report that integrated districts have higher rates of reported violence because racial injustice and class inequalities are exacerbated. Thus, many acts of violence in integrated schools are the symptoms of subtler and officialized forms of violence exercised, first by a social system that produces gross class inequality conjoined with racial oppression, and second by teachers and administrators who control oppressive school structures that provoke animosities (see also Parker & Stovall, 2004; Watts & Erevelles, 2004).

What does this indicate about the latent impacts of the security industry on school relationships, student subjectivity, and ultimately, school space? Historical, racial misconceptions have not been corrected; they have been translated from those based on alleged biological inferiority to those that circumscribe African American youth as more dangerous, pathological, and criminal than White youth. The security industry not only reinforces this myth but also creates the threat via countereducational and antidemocratic conditions and relationships. In other words, the tools of the security industry—the tricks of the trade— encourage school relationships and subjectivities that translate societal stereotypes into probable school dangers allegedly perpetrated by racial minorities. Security measures, coupled with the ideology of zero tolerance, literally permit school professionals and stakeholders to see minorities as violent, criminal threats. In light of this, the old, educational psychology adage, catch 'em when they're being good, is no longer simply problematic, it is now impossible. The security industry reproduces its interests and convinces schools they can be made safer by intensifying politically, socially, and educationally unsafe teacher-student relationships. When they are not engaged in disruptive behavior, students must nonetheless be identified as disruptive and potentially violent because the security industry and the culture of fear orders the visual field—school environment—on those terms.

In terms of the definition of urban and suburban school space, the security industry not only taps preexisting inequalities, it also amplifies those inequalities. The security industry helps itself when it helps translate intraschool and interschool relationships from the language of racial injustice and class inequality to that of fear and criminality.[11]

Making War(riors)

The process of militarization must not be seen primarily as simply gearing up for a particular battle or, in the current context, numerous battles. Nor should militarization be confused with militarism, which points specifically to an ideology that can be reified as the system of beliefs belonging to one or a few factions in society. Alternately, Catherine Lutz (2002) defines militarization:

> [as the long] process involv[ing] an intensification of the labor and resources allocated to military purposes, *including the shaping of other institutions in synchrony with military goals.* Militarization is simultaneously a discursive process, involving a shift in general societal beliefs and values in ways necessary to legitimate the use of force, [and] the organization of large standing armies and their leaders. . . . (italics added. p. 723)

Public schools are one such institution shaped in line with military goals both in longer and shorter historical views. In the longer view, schools were enlisted from 1958–on, largely due to Eisenhower's response to Sputnik—the National Defense Education Act—to promote excellence in science and mathematics for the purposes of producing military technology capable of competing with Cold War rivals. Preexisting this impact of the military on education is the predominance of military might and technological triumph at the expense of social movements such as labor, women's rights, and race struggles in history curricula. History curricula are also in large measure responsible for promoting a national myth defined against the backdrop of the Revolutionary War—the use of force as the event, par excellence, of U.S. independence (see Aronowitz, 2003, pp. 46–48). Further, the forms of authority and discipline that predominated in public schools throughout the 20th century were not only analogous to those found in industrial management but also to those found in the military (e.g., strict hierarchies of command and obedience, corporal punishment, emphases on lining up single file, standing tall, sitting straight, and the like). In the shorter view, the military has gained increasing prominence in the social text of public schools through JROTC programs, fundraisers and other school events (Reinolds, 2004). Recruitment officers, and assemblies framed ostensibly as patriotic events, celebrate the military's prowess—as if patriotism can only be defined and exercised through the filter of jingoism. And currently, student-tracking technologies and linking school information systems with police databases, as evidenced in New York City public schools, are the indirect result of the government's policy of turning the military toward internal enemies from the late 1980s to the present, demonstrated, in one way, by the military underwriting grants for information collection technologies for local police departments (Haggerty & Ericson, 1999; Kraska, 1999). The impacts of militarization on school relationships all occur within the broader pedagogical force of an overabundance of "images of soldiers in recruitment ads that blast across the popular culture landscape through both the [exorbitant] annual recruitment budget and Hollywood fare from the *The Sands of Iwo Jima* to *Black Hawk Down*" (Lutz, 2002, p. 724; Boggs & Pollard, 2007).

In 1992, the JROTC received a new boost and was implemented extensively in public schools across the United States. At a time when funding and public sentiment for the military was flagging, the JROTC was "meant to cultivate a public image for the military as efficacious, reliable, and concerned" (Lutz & Bartlett, 1995, pp. 9–10). The JROTC's objectives were also deeper and potentially more significant than this public relations' function. The JROTC penetrated schools when the first wave of panics about school violence swept the nation. As a result, the JROTC was not only framed as a mechanism to launder the military's image; it was also a tool used purportedly in the service of enlisting "troubled youth." Not coincidentally, as undisciplined kids were and are frequently assumed to be students of color and other minorities, the JROTC primarily penetrated darker, poorer schools (see Berlowitz & Long, 2003). Proponents of the JROTC claim that it "helps minorities" by "straightening them out" and enticing them to join the armed forces. In a recent story, one reporter casually documented that the

JROTC ". . . offers a quick route into the military or simply a way to build confidence and leadership skills," or even a "sense of belonging" (Diamond, 2004; Smith, 2004), leaving the former consequence uncriticized and the latter as seemingly the most effective measure a school can take to boost student self-esteem and leadership, and to provide a community context for some students, particularly students of color (see Brown, 2003).

Considering the influence of the security industry and zero tolerance on urban youth of color, a corrosive racial subtext is operative with JROTC. Not only were urban and poor rural schools originally targeted by the JROTC, but they continue to support or are pressured to support JROTC programs. In 1992, Department of Defense expenditures on the JROTC were $76 million. By 2002, the total DOD spending on JROTC reached $243 million, doubling the number of operating programs from 1,500 to 3,000 (the current cap that Congress is attempting to lift) in the same period; JROTC enrollment climbed, during the same period, from 300,000 to 500,000 cadets. These expenditures contribute to the increasing numbers of minority youth who later join the military, despite JROTC claims that the program is about just about everything except recruiting.[12] Lutz and Bartlett note that as of 1995, "45% of cadets completing JROTC enter[ed] some branch of the service, a rate much higher than the general student population," whereas more than 50% of JROTC cadets joined the military post-high school after 2000. With nearly 500,000 students on a national scale enlisted in the JROTC, and recruitment targets falling short in the last five years, the military has a vested interest in making the JROTC attractive. The Combined Arms Center reports that as of 2001, JROTC cadets were more than five times as likely as the general student population to join the military, a disproportionate number of whom were African American or Latino (Corbett & Coumbe, 2001). Approximately 8% of high school graduates from the general school population enlist upon graduation. In Chicago alone, Claire Schaeffer-Duffy (2003) reports that not only are Chicago public schools 91% non-White and 85% poor, but also "[f]orty-four of the city's 93 high schools have the JROTC program." The JROTC wishes to increase the enlistment rate from 37% to 55% in Chicago public schools. This racial dynamic is visible in all urban public schools attended by disproportionate numbers of poor students of color. Consider the following: twenty-two of Detroit's 39 public high schools have JROTC programs; nearby middle-to-upper-middle class, predominantly White schools systems, like Bloomfield Hills or Novi, have zero JROTC programs. Ten of Philadelphia's 45 public high schools host JROTC programs; nearby, wealthy and White Haverford, Ardmore, and Wynnewood school systems do not have JROTC programs. These racial dynamics explain why 50% of JROTC cadets are African American or Latino on a national level even though their combined representation in the national population is approximately 27%. This is not accidental. In fact, a recent JROTC assessment details repeatedly how the Department of Defense "needs" to increase JROTC programming to the point of "1 in 5 educationally and economically disadvantaged schools" by 2011, suggesting nowhere in the report that even 1 in 100 suburban (read: White and affluent) schools should develop JROTC programming (Expect More, 2006).

The intrusion of the JROTC on schools must not be seen solely in terms of the students who are entrapped by the institution. The JROTC must also be understood by way of the visibility of military officials and military practices in public schools and the pedagogical functions such visibility implies. For instance, with the JROTC come official military personnel and "cadets" fully clad in fatigues on training days. The cadets march around school grounds to the barking of orders, and parade throughout the school day in their uniforms—all with the inherent and purposeful effect of showcasing these students and their newfound self-esteem and discipline. The tacit message here is these students are in but not of the school. It is the military—not the school system—that is transforming the lives of these students. All things being equal, these practices are relatively innocuous, if not inane. But things are not equal, especially when the relationship between images of the military, civic action, and peaceful opposition in the broader cultural field of the United States is considered.

Despite the current military debacles in Iraq and Afghanistan and state-sanctioned travesties committed by military personnel in prisons, images of military certitude, strength, and sanctity perpetually pervade our mediascape. In the last presidential debate season, presidential candidates did not debate issues of policy or the intellectual and moral rigors of the presidency. Rather, Sentator John Kerry and President Bush had contests over who could thump his chest harder. A year and a half out from the 2008 presidential elections, Republican candidates began to compete to see who could unload the most belligerent rhetoric concerning foreign policy. All this while antiwar protests continue to be cast as sacrilegious and treasonous. The use of public schools as official public sites to house and display the military bestows additional prestige and legitimation on the military; this use also naturalizes societal beliefs and values that privilege belligerence and bravado over brains, or boots over brains as one Bush-Cheney campaign poster suggested, obedience over opposition and, ultimately, physical force over political finesse. These broader pedagogical functions of the JROTC are nonetheless the ideals impaled on the curricula JROTC cadets learn, an observation that Lutz & Bartlett (1995) made years ago. Simply, the JROTC program helps execute an officialized frontal assault by military values, objectives, and practices on primarily urban public schools, while pulling disproportionate numbers of poor children of color into its arena of battle.

The military spreads it tentacles into the education realm through education policy and midcareer teacher hiring plans. One of which is plainly called Troops-to-Teachers and, more recently, another called Spouses-to-Teachers. With President Bush's education act, No Child Left Behind, schools, with some exceptions, must now open student records to military recruiters. Student information was previously off-limits to any outside agency, with the exception of university representatives and potential employers for the students. Nonetheless, NCLB promotes the military in another related way. Touted as a program to "recruit quality teachers for low-income families throughout America," the Troops-to-Teachers (TTT) program was devised in 1994 and renewed in 2002 by NCLB, which continued to enlist the Department of Education for oversight and funding of the program, and the Department of Defense for the operation of it until at least 2006 (DANTES, 2007a). As of November 2007, 10,649 former troops had been employed as teachers in over 3,000 districts participating in the TTT plan (DANTES, 2007b).[13] This is not to say that these teachers are incompetent. However, it is a trend to think about as traditionally trained teachers come under public fire. Some reporters imply that if one is capable of successfully directing a band of thugs for years, then one should be perceived, a priori, as capable of leading a school of impressionable youth (see Levenson, 2004). Nonetheless, it is telling that we subsidize soldiers—83% of whom are White males—to teach in poor urban and rural schools instead of investing in the citizens who live in those communities, know the social needs and values of the communities, and could more effectively reach students if they were provided the opportunities and resources to be trained as teachers. Just think of TTT's motto: "Proud to Serve Again," as if these former military people are preparing for battle instead of teaching.

This explicit military infiltration of schools happened during a time when schools were put under the gun of accountability and increased calls for public schools to adopt military school models. Professor Smreker of Vanderbilt University claims in *USA Today* that the military school system " 'is the finest [school] system in the world' " (Schouten, 2004), the remainder of the article suggesting that public schools should adopt its model if they desire to achieve excellence. Even after the despicable crimes at Abu Ghraib were publicized, *USA Today* ran an editorial that reiterated this claim, exclaiming in its title "Pentagon could teach public schools some lessons" (*USA Today*, 2004)— as if the lessons the American public has to learn again about military power are not enough and kids must be subjected to further military regimentation in public schools. It goes without saying, however, that this is one of the penultimate objectives of militarization: to offer up, and insist on, the military as the quintessential model for organizing purposeful and meaningful social action in public-cultural institutions and, by extension, society.

These policy initiatives and calls are misleading on another level. To suggest that schools could learn much from the military, in terms of standardization, achievement, excellence, and helping minority youth, deceptively papers over the many ways that public schools are already in connivance with the military. One specific way public schools are forced into relationships that share much with the military is the accountability-punishment scheme. Although the scheme has its moorings in terribly narrow strands of behaviorist psychology and psychometrics (not to mention neoliberal economic cost-benefit models), the codes of the system are not dissimilar from those supposedly demonstrating educational excellence in military schools: Curriculum is standardized when schools can afford the process; authority refigured or simply emboldened on the side of domination, as increasing constraints on time and other resources encourage top-down models of command and obedience (Lipman, 2004;

Saltman, 2007); and the language pervading policy discourse and schools increasingly takes the form of war talk—takeovers, sanctions. Calls for public schools to emulate military schools justify government subsidies for retired military personnel entering the teaching or administrative ranks. These observations do not simply show how the military progressively penetrates formal education, they demonstrate how deep societal beliefs in the military are rooted, especially when preexisting military codes in schools go unnoticed, or actively ignored as the military unloads more of its educational arsenal on formal learning arenas.[14]

But as with most school practices and relationships, one would be irresponsible to present these transformations as phenomena unrelated to the educational force of the broader culture. The lessons learned in this wider domain do not dissipate when students enter the school. Nor are students baptized in bellicosity solely by the military bunkering in public schools. A General Accounting Office (2003) report shows that the Pentagon spent $591 million on advertising alone in 2002 (p. 2). This does not include the cost of actual recruiting and, now, video game production. The total annual recruiting budget now tops $4 billion (p. 1). The Army uses part of these expenditures to operate its own video game production studio. The *Official Army Video Game* simulates attack scenes in sandstorms, night settings, and blown-out buildings resembling those found in Iraq and Afghanistan. Scores of video games simulate assault missions on Cuba, and reformat fights that occurred in Viet Nam, or settings that resemble it. Many others replay the horrors of World War II, or simply envision new battles. I am not suggesting that these video games have a one-to-one correspondence with student propensities to fight or promote violence in school. Yet, the broader cultural field is predominated by incessant Hollywood blockbusters replaying and rewriting wars and terrorist attacks. Reports and outward claims pervade newscasts and crime dramas, suggesting that the United States is involved in a never ending war. The prevalence of physical violence in everyday life (Boggs & Pollard, 2007), video games, and other forms of leisure and entertainment emulate the military, and simply give a playful and safe façade to the profound existential gravity of perpetual preparation for battle, auguring visions and conditioning subjectivities predisposed to militaristic agendas that support any war that could be imagined (see Provenzo, 2003). It is important to keep in mind how the prevalence of combative relationships and their narratives secure social identities that can be recruited for the wars already waged in or by the United States: the War of Terror, War on Homelessness, War on Drugs, War on the Poor, and the alleged cultural wars. Because of the broader educational force of a militarized culture and society, youth have fewer resources to question the JROTC or recruitment officers. The overdetermination of military codes in most spheres of society, especially schools, simply enlists the tacit or active support of youth for the military as an exercise in patriotism and a new form of citizenship as youth are barred from other modes of civic action in a commercialized criminalizing society.

I have been reluctant throughout this inquiry to address the ideology of zero tolerance and the spatial-temporal impacts of the security industry and militarization on school space-time. In line with Massey's theorization of space-time, I identified the symbols pervading the social text of schools, the forces that promote them, and the relationships that mediate them.

The Space-Time of Zero Tolerance

If we think of space-time as political categories that social relationships create or define, then definite geometries and lines of power can be seen to be produced by the corrosive mix of zero tolerance and the related forces of the security industry and process of militarization. Within these shapes and rhythms of power, framed by the wider privatizing and individualizing logic of neoliberalism, teacher-student interactions are underpinned by new definitions of authority, discipline, responsibility, and agency. The relationships promoted by zero tolerance, the security industry, and militarization are inherently pedagogical because they are not only full of power and symbolism, but also transmit power, rely on certain conceptions of the past or redefine it, and divvy up authority, social challenges, and responsibility into individualized, commodified, criminalized, or militarized parts. They consequently position student bodies within social relationships that engage them affectively and cognitively, laying the foundations on which social relationships and identities will be based and mobilized. Individually, these mechanisms share a common target (e.g., youth in schools) and logic (e.g., the removal of authority and discipline from democratic relation-

Table 3.1 Relationships Between Zero Tolerance, the Security Industry, and Militarization

	Symbols	Rationale	Consequences	Conceptions of Agency	Spatial-temporal Definition
Zero Tolerance	Teachers and schools present themselves as sites of domination	Target individuals students and incidents; scare through spectacle of exclusion	Redefines teacher school authority and responsibility as authoritarian; position youth as threats; exclude students defined as threats	Students: agency is fearful and compliant Teachers and other professionals: antidemocratic, forceful and acritical, reactive but unresponsive	Space is constituted by relationships based on fear and power acting on schools, not by schools and teachers, and students—society engaging youth as proactive participants in democratic relationships.
Security Industry	Police and security officers, dogs, cameras, metal detectors, biometric scanning devices, identification badges, drug sweeps, electronic locking doors, satellite surveillance	Make schools "safer"; perpetually redefine safety and threats posed to it	Redefines student-teacher interaction and teacher authority and responsibility by privatizing authority and commodifying safety	Students: compliant, passively resigned, or oppositional to symbols and practices that position them as criminals Teachers: acquiescent to prerogatives of security industry	Time operates on battle codes; quick, individual responses to emergency situations.

continued on next page

Table 3.1 Continued

Symbols	Rationale	Consequences	Conceptions of Agency	Spatial-temporal Definition
Militarization Military personnel, uniforms, social authority, drill routines, acceptable forms of community, authority and obedience	Primary: Absorb troubled youth Secondary: Frame the military as model for positive and acceptable social relationships	Shift social responsibilities for school challenges from the school, community and, ultimately, society to the military	Students: Obedient and acritical future subjects of legitimate violence Officials: dominative and authoritarian	

ships between youth and teachers). Collectively, their latent consequences reinforce the other's strong and blatant tendencies.

Zero tolerance completely atomizes authority and discipline. It
allows perceived disruptions or actual school violence to be translated
into adversarial relationships between school officials and individual
students This position leads to the ultimate objective of excluding or
eliminating the student and isolated behavior under the belief that the
social processes that founded the incident can be elided or will simply
dissipate.[15] Zero tolerance bolsters a pedagogical space in which teachers and students learn to ignore the social, political, and economic roots
(routes?) and processes that lead to and provoke disruptive school interactions. But zero tolerance has a definable temporality. As tolerance
implies a degree of reflection on the past (e.g., the formative processes,
relations, and conditions that might provoke a behavior that is perceived
to be "disruptive"), projection on the future and patience within a
current relation of difference, "zero" tolerance in large part signals an
absence of reflection, projection, and patience. Zero tolerance erases the
past, aborts conceptions of the future, and narrows the social frame of
reference to the repetition of the conditions that underpin the present.
How can teachers most effectively punish a student now? How will
excluding a student now help a teacher reach the most pressing and
immediate test standard? How will excluding a student absolve teachers
and society of the responsibility for past social, political, and economic
relationships that produced the disruptive unwanted behavior?

Zero tolerance informs notions of quick-time, "emergency time"
(Giroux, 2003a), if it denotes any time at all, because it blunts the
ethical edge of tolerance by unmooring professional beliefs about their
own behaviors, students, and the conditions of possibility for their
classroom relations. In this way, zero tolerance is used to rationalize
conditions of inequality and injustice by providing the legal and discursive framework through which these conditions can be refracted. Equally
and importantly, zero tolerance trains student bodies to respond viscer-
ally to incidents of perceived contention. Instead of helping build literate social practices that engage moments of difference, dissent and
danger in ways that protect or encourage democratic social relationships, behaviors are perceived merely as contentious, incompliant
or dangerous.

Perceived contentions or moments of disruption are always open
to redefinition; this is where the security industry produces petulant

effects on school space. These effects are produced through the symbols of the industry (cameras, metal detectors, police officers, dogs) and the school relationships the security industry defines. The ultimate effect is that safety is defined as a commodity where certain students can only be seen as potential threats. This is purposeful because, otherwise, the security industry would be unable to rationalize its necessity and schools would be incapable of justifying multi-million dollar investments. Further, because of wireless, digital, and satellite technologies, school space-time is transformed from something produced primarily by face-to-face situations into relationships in which teachers and students are virtually factored out of the process of making safety because a virtual tool does it for them. As Julie Webber (2004) elaborates, this consequence of abstracting responsibility and control is coupled with the disintegration of structures that allow students to develop a sense of self- and social-efficacy by knowing what their rebellion could be directed against. Instead, she notes, students and teachers have "virtual structures." Because students are unsure about how they can define competent and critical senses of self and community, it can be said that teachers and other authority figures, too, are unsure of the conditions of their authority and responsibility and how to exercise it. There is, however, an additional consequence of the security industry as it operates within or in relation to the guiding framework of zero tolerance. When safety is reified as a commodity, schools can never have enough safety. Schools can only be made "safer," when the security industry organizes the visual field and orients teachers in ways that permit a persistent redefinition of what "safer" means, what devices promote the next level of safety, and who is seen as a threat. In literal terms, the security industry privatizes the consequences of unequal school-society relationships and commercializes faulty mechanisms for promoting socially, politically, economically, and educationally safe school relationships—that is, space. This, too, reinforces the consequences of zero tolerance. Teacher and student subjectivity is continuously positioned as incapable of contesting and transforming undesirable school and societal relationships because teachers are thought to be incompetent. Teachers are deprived of the resources to engage those relationships, and students are framed explicitly as perpetrators of potentially dangerous school incidents. The security industry underpins subjectivities that practice and imagine only privatized, individualized, and commercialized social relationships. The effect is the criminalization of school space and the production of temporal logics defined by emergency conditions or the strict cadence of the military time.

The militarization of school settings induces similar effects on school space-time and subjectivity. Operating on well-embedded cultural beliefs in the military, the JROTC, recruiting programs, and the emulation of military codes in accountability practices and authoritarian teacher-student relationships, as well as antidemocratic models of authority and discipline are privileged as the most effective ways to create a sense of community, boost student self-esteem, and bring about educational excellence. The same narratives of teacher and student roles promoted by the security industry and zero tolerance are told, if only by different characters, in the process of militarization. Authority resides solely in officials. Discipline is simply obedience, not one's commitment to shared power and gover- nance of classrooms and schools. Discipline is unhinged from moral authority and the guiding power of communities to structure conditions that encourage community members to engage in behaviors that benefit the common good. With the military as the guiding model, difference— whatever it may be—must be jettisoned entirely for a definition of appropriate and uniform(ed) social interaction. Furthermore, the spatial- temporal codes installed by militarization share much in common with zero tolerance. Official force and rapid individualized responses to, or annihilation of, moments of ambiguity or challenge are the solutions par excellence to social and political relationships. Students are cast as the elements that need to be changed, not the local, regional, and national politics that produce the conditions of anomie to which they are rel- egated. Ultimately, the space-time of zero tolerance, especially in urban public schools, is comprised of relationships that encourage subjectivities capable of engaging correctionalized and militarized relationships instead of processes of democratization.

Conclusion: Making Space and Time for Democracy

The security industry and militarization operate in complete synchrony. Their combined impact on school and social relationships transfigure school space-time and the pedagogical conditions in which student sub- jectivity is produced. In large part, the security industry, and explicit modes of militarization, could not carry their specific forms of authority and legitimation if zero tolerance did not institutionalize a legal discursive framework in which students are continuously defined as threats and if zero tolerance ideology did not rationalize adversarial, quick battle responses as the most effective way of dealing with social antagonisms. Taken together within broad social commitments to the production of fear, insecurity, and official violence enacted by the state, military, and the entertainment industry, zero tolerance encourages social relationships that create spaces and temporal definitions antithetical to democratization.

Democratization is not an ideology. Democratization is a *process* that ostensibly needs supporting ideologies. This is a purposeful distinction because democracy can be defined and appropriated by factions that promote social relationships with contents that are anything but democratic. To suggest that democracy and its supporting ideology is the goal of social relationships, then formal representative democracy exists alongside gross economic inequalities and the mass abrogation of civil liberties perpetrated by the government without public oversight. This suggests, as Difazio (2003) notes, that participatory democracy cannot be operative unless economic inequalities are reduced, if not entirely obliterated, because economic inequalities are correlated with both spatial and temporal inequalities, which limit citizen capacities to participate in shared governance and power.

The spaces in which citizens are located carry the symbolic representation of historical processes and relationships of inequality and exclusion. The spaces in which citizens act imply greater and lesser degrees of access to social and political resources. But spaces inhabited by citizens, whether they are social strata locations (e.g., woman, man, African American, business person, middle class, etc.), or geographic locations (e.g., the city, a ghetto, a gated community, etc.), imply greater and lesser degrees of access to *the time needed to participate in civic action* instead of time simply used to recuperate basic life necessities. Space and time are categories that people create and define. They are categories that citizens inherit. These, in turn, condition the mechanisms and modes by which citizens participate in political affairs—or not.

As a process, democratization requires an intensification of the labor and resources allocated to democratic purposes, *including the shaping of institutions in synchrony with democratic goals.*[16] Democratization is simultaneously a discursive process, involving a shift in general societal beliefs and values necessary to legitimate the use of dialogue, debate, contestation, and consensus, and a set of material practices involving organization of the economic and cultural fields in ways that promote equitable access to both symbolic and material resources fundamental to mass democratic participation. In this way, democratization requires that new narratives of U.S. and global history be told, particularly those that provide insight to institutions and agencies that have acted on the side of justice and peaceful opposition instead of oppression and the legitimate use of force. Importantly, democratization implies that these existing narratives receive official hearings and forms of witnessing.

Narratives of democratization not only face a predominance of militaristic and individualistic conceptions of the past and future, but also the force of a corporatized cultural field, and an increasingly privatized public realm that are not, ironically, hostile to modes of social action that question their authority and demonstrate the arbitrariness of their official power. Thus, democratization demands the transfer of labor and resources that confer legitimation on democratic social relations and practices. Public schools are indeed such an institution capable of authorizing democratic social relationships and practices. Otherwise, public schools would not be under such heated and sustained attack by individualistic neoliberal forces promoting privatization, accountability, zero tolerance, and militarization.

Think of the participatory forms demanded of citizens, youth included, if contemporary education debates were not concerned with promoting excellence as defined in strict market terms of accountability and efficiency, but with public schools as sites of common struggle and investment fundamental to reproducing and questioning social and political relationships acting in the name of democratization. Questions of the causes and consequences of education would revolve less around how individual students and schools perform better on less resources, than on how society provides the material conditions and symbolic frames by which schools are better utilized in making citizens capable of successful civic participation and involvement in the economic realm. Specifically concerning the issues in this chapter, citizens—students, parents, community members, teachers, administrators, and state officials—would be less interested with what new security devices might prevent or how it would catch an individual student violating a school's disciplinary code, than with the set of relationships and range of practices that are effective in ensuring that the conditions that underpin such behavior are resolved.

Processes of democratization entail different spatial relations and temporal codes than those of zero tolerance, the security industry and militarization because, again, space and its particular temporal codes are inherently pedagogical. Space is constructed by social relationships that create subject positions and guide citizens in how those positions are taken up, by whom, under what conditions, for what purposes, and to what effects. Accordingly, time is a central component, and it is pedagogical as it defines the rhythms of social practices and how these are related, dialectically, to the spaces in which they are engaged, and the access citizens have to temporal codes that either reinforce or disrupt conceptions of the past, explanations of the present, and visions of the future.

Democratization requires social relationships that create spaces capable of supporting notions of time that offer moments of reflection and projection, consensus and critique, stasis and transformation. This is what Cornelius Castoriadis (1991) and Giroux (2003c) mean when they suggest that public time is the defining frame through which and the temporal logic by which citizens can question the past in light of the present. Public time is needed to build a critical democratic culture that "provides the knowledge, skills, and social practices that encourage an opportunity for resistance and a proliferation of [democratic] discourses" that connect "social responsibility and social transformation" (Giroux, p. 9). Time that operates on narrow, individualized terms of accountability, zero tolerance, and battle is simply antithetical to a public time that functions on wider, social(ized) notions of public commitment and responsibility, patience, and critical engagement, and judgment.

In closing, although using public schools for purposes of democratization seems relatively, if not wildly utopian, acquiescing to the use of public schools as sites in which social exclusions are officialized is not only a cynical and antidemocratic social process, but also, fundamentally, a pedagogical, or political, relationship. This antidemocratic use of schools is pedagogical because it positions students and teachers in spatial-temporal relationships that produce social identities, rationalize unequal social and economic forces, and cast visions of future social relationships conducive to a criminalized and militarized social order. It is a political relationship because we, as a society, are currently making choices to allocate resources for the purpose of promoting social relationships that rely on exclusion and participate in the militarization of public life. Quite possibly, if the space and time of public schooling is indicative of democratization, students will think and feel like citizens instead of feeling like prisoners. They will be seen and taught as citizens. Alternately, teachers will be predisposed to fulfill the role of citizen-educators, instead of prison wardens or military officials.

Zero Tolerance in a Color-blind Era, or How the Consumer Society Wastes and Disposes of People of Color

Introduction

*C*learly, zero tolerance disproportionately targets students of color, particularly African American students, by promoting racial injustice through exclusion and limiting life opportunities. Zero tolerance threatens the fabric and possibility of democracy. The underlying features of this threat are incomprehensible outside of what sociologist Howard Winant (2004) calls the "new racial politics:" a "reformed version" of White supremacy in which "racial inequality can live on, still battening on all sorts of stereotypes and fears, still resorting to exclusionism and scapegoating when politically necessary, still invoking the supposed superiority of 'mainstream' (aka white) values, [while] cheerfully maintaining that equality has largely been achieved" (pp. xiii–xiv). A formidable component of the new racial politics is the ideology or myth of colorblindness (Aziz, 2002; Barlow, 2003; Bonilla-Silva, 2001, 2003a, 2003b; Brown, Carnoy, Currie, Duster, Oppenheimer, Schultz, Wellman, 2003; Doane, 2003; Giroux, 2003c; Goldberg, 2002; Guinier & Torres, 2003; Lipsitz, 1998; Williams, 1998). In general terms, the ideology of color blindness claims that race and its concomitant inequalities can and will exist in the alleged absence of racism. Color-blind ideology claims that racial inequalities exist because of the behaviors of African Americans. According to the ideology of color blindness, racism and racial inequality are simply private problems to be shouldered by individuals. The racialized practice of zero tolerance, however, creates an apparent paradox: If U.S. society is color blind, how does zero tolerance, as it is practiced according to varying definitions, invariably impact youth and people of color?[1] This is only an apparent paradox because color blindness and zero tolerance are forms of racial exclusion that operate on a similar politics of vision, a set of visual practices, or ways of (not) seeing, around which individuals and groups organize, and by which responses are mobilized, in reference to social relationships that have emerged in conditions of racial injustice and class inequality. Although it is important to detail the emergence of color blindness and the ground it shares with zero tolerance, it is also important to address them in relation to the cultural-economic project of neoliberalism, which makes use of these forms of exclusion and renders them normal.[2] More precisely, zero tolerance and color blindness are different ideologies and practices that dominate the contemporary political climate on race. They are fundamentally interrelated in terms of how they justify and enact the social exclusion of populations deemed disposable by the private investment state and consumer society of neoliberalism.[3]

The Racial Consequences of Zero Tolerance

Zero tolerance in the United States intensifies the symbolic disinvestment in urban public schools and students of color. It reinforces patterns of material disinvestment. By providing a racialized and institutionalized frame through which student behaviors and school relationships can be profiled, zero tolerance helps reinforce deeply etched stereotypes of youth of color as dangerous and criminal. It diverts exorbitant funds and energies from educational resources and public responsibility for urban public schools to the security industry, the military, police departments, and the criminal justice system. The not-so-hidden message of zero tolerance is that citizenship, if not agency itself, for poor youth of color must be suspended entirely. For others, zero tolerance translates citizenship in schools and society into catatonic modes of compliance and conformity. This only after students have failed to give in to a faithful devotion to the testing-punishment scheme and a willingness to embody the competitive, consumerist codes imposed on schools. These general implications of zero tolerance come with specific punishments and social consequences.

School exclusions, suspensions and expulsions have rapidly and consistently risen, especially for youth of color, since zero tolerance was legislated. Annual suspension rates increased to over 3 million in each of the years since 1997, up from 1.7 million in 1974 (Bay Area School Reform Collaborative, 2003 [2001]; Fuentes, 2003). Expulsions have topped 1 million since 1997. Students of color bear the brunt of school exclusions. African Americans constitute 32% of students suspended yet they represent only 17% of the student population. Nationwide, schools suspend African American students "at roughly 2.3 times the rate of whites" (Brooks, Schiraldi, & Ziedenberg, 2000), though this rate varies wildly in certain school districts. Although national rates of exclusion approximate their representative percentage of the school population, Latinos are also subjected to highly disproportionate exclusions from various school contexts. In other instances, Latino students might be "under-counted in school discipline data, because they are counted as white or " 'other,' " suggesting that their rates of exclusion, on a national level, is not so proportionate (Richart, Brooks, & Soler, 2003, p. 8; see also Gordon et al., 2000). Some statistics of specific local and state rates of exclusion bear repeating. Expulsions in Chicago jumped from approximately 10 in 1994 to over 1000 by the year 2000; 63% of these expulsions were given to African American students who account for approximately 50% of the Chicago public schools (CPS) population— a rate of disproportionality of 1.26. During the same period White students were expelled at a rate of 8% yet were 9.1% of CPS's student population—a rate of disproportionality of 0.8 (Gordon et al., 2000; Chicago Public Schools, 2004). In Michigan, 66% of students expelled in the school year 1999–2000 were African American, although they were only 28% of the statewide student population. A similar disproportionality was found in Michigan for suspensions, producing a rate of disproportionality in suspension or expulsion of approximately 2.5 for African American students and 0.83 for White students (Michigan Public Policy Initiative, 2003). Connecticut doled out 90,559 suspensions in the school year 2000–2001, up from 57,626 in the school

year 1998–1999; most of these suspensions were attributed to, and
blamed on, undisciplined students in Connecticut's urban schools (undisciplined and urban can be read as operative code words for "of
color") (Gordon, 2003). Public schools in California, Florida, Kentucky,
Maryland, New York, South Carolina, and Texas produce severe rates of
disproportionate exclusion for students of color (see Browne, 2003;
Eskenazi, et al., 2003; Richart, et al., 2003).

Two observations beset these disproportionate rates of exclusion.
One, violent crime committed by youth has decreased steadily over the
last 15 years (Snyder, 2003), and violent crime in schools has decreased
generally since its peak in 1992. Rates of school violence began to drop
before schools adopted zero tolerance and after the legislation of the
Gun-Free Schools Act of 1994. In 2003, the National Center for Education Statistics reported that the rate of students who claimed they
were victims of crime dropped from 10% in 1995 to 6% in 2001
(DeVoe et al., 2003). Furthermore, youth are "more than forty times
more likely to be the victims of homicide away from school than at
school" (Gagnon & Leone, 2002, p. 101). Students have a one-in-two-
million chance of being killed at school and a one-in-a-million chance
of "dying or committing suicide on school grounds" (Brooks et al.,
2000). These general findings of decreased violent crime in schools was
found again in 2006 by the National Center for Education Statistics
(U.S. Department of Education, 2006, pp. 82–83, 194–195, 297). Two,
nearly 80% of zero tolerance exclusions are meted out for offenses that
are unaccounted for in federal law; more than 60% of zero tolerance
exclusions are given for offenses that are nonviolent (Harvard Civil
Rights Project, 2000; Browne, 2003, 2005; Fuentes, 2003).

But this sampling is only evidence of the *punishment*. Educators
and concerned citizens should also be interested in eliminating the
disparate *consequences* of exclusion experienced by wealthier, white students and poorer and darker students. Although many schools fail to
provide, if not require, alternative education placements, wealthier students procure extracurricular services, such as tutoring, test preparation,
or counseling, far more easily than African American and poor White
students when they are excluded from school, because they have the
requisite resources to travel to, and pay for, those services (See Casella,
2003a; Stone-Palmquist, 2004). As detailed in chapter 1, this disparity,
founded in issues of class, says nothing of the comparatively large num-

ber of students of color who are often directed to overcrowded detention facilities, while White students are rarely directed to the criminal
justice system or have the option of attending a less crowded private
facility. Furthermore, school exclusion for students of color removes
them from potentially more positive school and community relationships, and pits them in social settings rife with criminalized behavior
(e.g., gangs, older youth and adults who have already been, or are in the
midst of being, educated by the criminal justice system, unofficialized
economies, etc.), when they are not funneled directly into the criminal
justice system. This process unequally targets students of color, setting
them up to be punished, and then sent spiraling into the criminal
justice system. At this point, formative family and broader community
relationships are disrupted, not only fragmenting families and civically
disabling individuals, but also politically disarming their communities
(Cole, 1999; Marable, 2001, 2004a).

The consequences of zero tolerance are homologous to the symbolic, discursive, historical exclusion of African Americans promoted by
the ideology and practice of color blindness. In turn, deep and related
social functions of zero tolerance and color blindness cannot be understood outside of the specific society that uses and makes sense of them.
The questions that need to be addressed are as follows:

- What is color blindness, and how is it a form of exclusion?

- What is the relationship between color blindness and zero
  tolerance?

- What types of social and political visions do they construct
  and promote?

Colorblindness and Zero Tolerance, or the Vision/Practice of Exclusion

Color blindness and zero tolerance are related in the sense that they
emerged from and maintain similar historical contexts. They operate, in
greater and lesser degrees, around the category of race. Color-blind
ideology emerged slowly in the 1970s after the moderate social and
political achievements of the Civil Rights Movement in the 1960s.

Since the resurgence of social conservatism and economic liberalism in the 1980s, it has played a central role in constructing and maintaining dominant worldviews on race, racism, and racial inequality. Zero tolerance the ideology, alternately, emerged from wide-ranging social and criminal justice policies. Get-tough-on-crime initiatives, enacted primarily in response to urban problems in the 1970s (see Wilson, 1985 [1975]), underwent significant revisions and extensions throughout the 1980s and 1990s. However, color blindness and zero tolerance are also interrelated in more direct and dangerous ways. Color blindness has become a way for Whites of most classes to *see* race and ignore the existence of racism—a way to erase public recognition and witnessing of the history of racism and its persisting consequences under new historical conditions.[4] Zero tolerance was and is a way to *treat* individuals marked by oppressive conditions of racism by punishing them for the manifest symptoms of racial inequality in schools and society. Color blindness and zero tolerance can perform mutually reinforcing forms of exclusion—symbolic and figurative in the former, social and literal in the latter. To understand how color blindness and zero tolerance perform these exclusions, the visual field and the politics of vision produced by colorblindness and zero tolerance also must be addressed.

What is Colorblindness?

Color blindness is a peculiar phenomenon, if not an outright contradiction of terms, that has both animated and stymied public discourse on race and racism, most prominently over the last twenty years. Color blindness asserts at once that race and racial inequality exist and racism is dead, except for the willful or pathological acts of individuals who commit hate crimes (Goldberg, 1997), or in the beliefs of radical groups that are always "elsewhere" (van Dijk, 2002). This is not to suggest that individual acts of racism are inane, but that they operate within structures and processes of racial power, inequality, and exclusion—to make short-lived spectacles of racist acts often conceals the structure of racism and who benefits from color blindness's insistence on the end of racism. Color blindness supplants the causes of racism with the symptoms, structural relationships with individual behavior, public accountability with private responsibility, and state implication with the abdication of the state. In other words, color blindness attempts to erase, from public discourse and decision-making, the social relationships and economic conditions that make individual acts of racism possible in the first place. But because race is the operative category and racial inequality the symptom of the structure and practice of racism (Memmi, 2000), color blindness is in all practical terms an impossibility—until the structures, conditions, and relationships that support racism on any level and under any guise are eliminated. Color blindness is also rendered impossible simply by way of its vociferous insistence on the absence of what it always refers and reproduces: race. In particular, the social, cultural and biological valuations that have been socially and politically ascribed to varying degrees of color are at issue.

To say color blindness is an impossibility, however, is not the same as recognizing that the practice of color blindness carries racial power, while it justifies the conditions that reproduce the very same power. Color blindness is a myth and functions ideologically: It positions social actors, provides rationalizations for those positions, and refers, in this case, by way of omission, to a structure or system that gives meaning to the asymmetrical ordering of those social positions. In this way, color blindness can be understood as a racial ideology (Doane, 2003, p. 13; see Bonilla-Silva, 2001, 2003a, 2003b), a set of terms and racialized "meaning[s] [enacted] in the service of power" (Bonilla-Silva, 2001, p. 137; see also, Guinier & Torres, 2003).

What color blindness consequently demonstrates is not the end of racism, but a renaming and reworking of its preexisting forms and modes of practice in altered historical conditions (see Giroux, 2003c). Previous forms of racism, most notably Jim Crow and slavery, were easier to identify. There was a direct, visible fit between racial discourse and racial oppression, public policy and law, and private exploits. In the most general terms, Jim Crow racism had an explicitly racial discourse that stigmatized and inferiorized African Americans by circulating and playing variably on pseudoscientific explanations of biological inferiority and alleged cultural deficits. These rationales were used to justify and maintain legally segregated schools and neighborhoods, a dual class structure in which African Americans were denied the labor protections given to unionized or unionizing Whites, the denial of social welfare provisions to African American families, and the partial enfranchisement of African Americans, that is, the denial of full citizenship, among many other patterns of social isolation, public denial, economic disinvestment and wealth disaccumulation (see Barlow, 2003; Brown et al., 2003).

Racism in this era was freewheeling: Whites had social, legal, and political support to flaunt their power's conditions of possibility. To a large
degree, violent displays of power were a precondition for protecting
and enforcing it, as demonstrated by the mass lynchings that occurred
throughout the South and the systemic police brutality inflicted on
African Americans in northern cities throughout much of the 20th
century. As Steve Martinot (2003) explains, "gratuitous violence"—
symbolic or physical—performed and still performs a primary function
in creating and policing racial boundaries by completing the circuitry
of a vicious cycle of "paranoia," "fear," and "violence," each modality
legitimating the other and aligning working class and upper class whites
alike in a common enterprise of white supremacy (see also, Winant,
1997). Martinot argues these modalities of white power "are intimately
interlinked and inseparable within the white supremacist framework;
racial violence is the expression of allegiance, allegiance to whiteness is
the expression of a paranoia, and paranoia is the expression of a gratuitous violence" (p. 131).

But the White supremacist framework of Jim Crow racism was
significantly questioned and contested by the Civil Rights Movement
across the 1950s and 1960s, and was moderately transformed by the
partial institutionalization of their demands in the civil rights' legislation of the mid-1960s. Voting rights were achieved; African Americans
were given, albeit means-tested, access to social welfare provisions. Public
school desegregation was temporarily regulated and enforced more
stringently; and affirmative action permitted relatively increased access
to higher education and the subsequent entrance of some African
Americans into law and medicine. Employment opportunities in government offices were opened to African Americans. However, demands,
such as reparations for 300 years of slavery and 100 years of disenfranchisement, support for and full control over cultural institutions, and
autonomy in community policing, were obviously excluded. Because of
these gaps, the conditions on which the civil rights' moderate demands
were institutionalized and the preexisting structure of racism remained,
but with a new discourse on race and racial inequality in public cir-
culation. This allowed the appropriation and convolution of Martin
Luther King Jr.'s dream for people to be judged by the "content of their
character," not the "color of their skin" (see Ansell, 1997; Aziz, 2002;
Brown et al., 2003; Giroux, 2003c): Hence color blindness. It must be

noted, however, that the limits put on civil rights legislation were, and are, not as indicative of failures of the Civil Rights Movement as much as indicative of racist structures built into state and civil society.

Color blindness continues to be effective in mobilizing anti-Black and antistate commitments for a number of reasons. The most apparent is that, with the institutionalization of civil rights legislation, the state, which in theory is democratic, was recast as a supporter of Black interests, not the liberal ideal of individualism or "abstract equality" (Bonilla-Silva, 2001) vouchsafed in the civic religion of the United States. In the abstract, liberal democracy historically worked for all Whites across the 20th century because its basic terms were tailored to their interests. Whites from all class locations were never denied the basic right of citizenship. However, once the terms of citizenship were expanded in principle and practice to include African Americans, the state was represented as giving "special treatment" to "lazy" and "criminal" "blacks," and "unfairly" discriminating against "whites."

There is another formative reason why civil rights legislation was undermined and its language appropriated and rearticulated. The dominant structure of power in the United States was challenged under both intense interrogation and fierce resistance in the late 1960s and early 1970s. The U.S. power structure witnessed advances made by the Women's Liberation, Anti-War, and Labor Movements in questioning the structure of dominant White male power (See Aronowitz, 2003; Parenti, 1999). This while middle-, lower-middle-, and working-class Whites began to feel the downward pangs of economic insecurity brought on by a deep recession, demographic changes with increasing numbers of Latino and Asian immigrants, and a nascent globalizing, neoliberal economy (see Barlow, 2003). Thus, on the one hand, civil rights legislation lost much of the economic support and regulatory mechanisms needed for proper implementation and oversight to the ongoing Vietnam conflict and the decreased revenues of a flagging national economy. On the other, Whites were instructed to see minorities as threats to their jobs, jobs that were, and continue to be, scarcified by the neoliberal global economy. This form of stigmatization soon shifted, throughout the late 1970s and, most prominently, during Reagan's first campaign and subsequent two terms (see Delgado, 2002), to minorities being a lazy, deviant, and otherwise criminal group that was wasting "hardworking" whites' "hard-earned" tax dollars. Consequently, color blindness, in Martin Luther's King Jr.'s conception, was emptied of its material bearings and used to claim that the Civil Rights Movement succeeded—simply by default of partial institutionalization—while Whites could say their comparatively better economic standing and access to social and political resources were the results of initiative, individual responsibility, and good morals. Collectively, Whites discounted the sum total of historical patterns of accumulation and disaccumulation along racial lines, and the manifestations of a system in which structures still tilted, in reduced measure, the social, political, and economic opportunities in their direction.

Even though these factors and conditions were critical to the rise of color blindness as the hijacking of relatively successful civil rights discourse, Martinot (2003) again offers a different perspective, one that supports these material and structural elements rather than downplays or erases them. Martinot argues that civil rights legislation did not significantly alter the racialized structure of politics and power, but it questioned the dominant ethos—and was perceived and portrayed as an assault on normalized White privilege. In other words, until the Civil Rights Movement organized sustained opposition to the Jim Crow system of U.S. apartheid and the drafting of civil rights legislation, Whites were never forced to reflect on and share their "monopoly" on citizenship. As Martinot convincingly demonstrates, contrary to what the civil rights backlash has argued and used to bolster the politics of color blindness, civil rights did not ask to revoke White rights, opportunities, and resources; it simply asked the establishment to expand them and share them. Simply, the Civil Rights Movement and legislation questioned the ethos of the racial state and racist culture conceived, from inception, according to the normative codes of whiteness (Goldberg, 2002).

The ideology of color blindness was and is necessarily articulated and reproduced at multiple levels of politics and society. Color blindness is articulated by the state, in the capacity that it must—in keeping with its post-civil rights whitewashed façade and its historic dressing of liberal neutrality—simultaneously craft policy and express commitments that are free of explicit racial language or support for Black or minority causes. Color blindness ignores preexisting, intensifying, race-based inequalities. Color blindness is articulated at the level of intermediary institutions, such as schools, finance institutions, and corporations. For instance, as the dissenting opinion of Supreme Court Justice O'Connor suggests in the University of Michigan affirmative action case concerning law school admissions, *Grutter v. Bollinger,* 2003, universities have a constitutional right to consider diversity in admissions processes, at least in graduate school. One might see this as support for the use of color in admissions processes and that universities would readily find ways to ensure that race or color be central considerations. But, with spiraling tuition rates and decreasing student aid, diversity becomes a catchword for any sort of difference (e.g., ethnic, gender or, potentially, ideological).[5] Diversity becomes a method of flattening the varying histories of difference, eliding the fact that the majority of potential African American students are strapped from the start by the often-conjoined historic structure of racism and class inequality. Color blindness is also articulated by and through culture. For example, the densely corporatized media benefits from the spectacle of race as the parading of Black athletes and seasonal hip hop sensations garner vast profits. However, the codes of color blindness prevail, since race-as-commodity is stripped of its historical, social, and political trappings in favor of a profit-driven, consumer friendly aesthetic of exoticism or an empty multiculturalism that allows Whites to watch race while believing they are uninvolved in its social production (see Denzin, 2002; Gray, 1997). Lastly, color blindness is articulated and reproduced at the level of social interaction. For instance, studies show that a majority of suburban Whites explain their segregated neighborhoods as a result of choice, hard work, or the manifestation of cultural difference—of wanting to be with one's own kind. This is what Eduardo Bonilla-Silva (2001, p. 141) calls the "biologization of culture" that occurs in coordination with color-blind ideology: the ascription of a fictive biological teleology to fundamentally historical, cultural, social, and political relationships (see also Johnson & Shapiro, 2003). Nonetheless, segregated and unequal spheres of increasingly atomized social interaction provide the context in which and content by which color blindness can persistently be reproduced in very practical and pervasive ways, because its practitioners are free from being held publicly accountable to the contradictions between the ideology of color blindness and the benefits they receive from its practice (see Robbins, 2004).

Consider the following pervasive contradictions between color-blind ideology and the racial structure of opportunity that hides behind it:

- Although color blindness attributes African-American unemployment to lazy individuals who simply don't try hard enough,
  "one in nine African Americans cannot find employment"
  (Muhammed, Davis, Lui, & Leondar-Wright, 2004).

- Unemployment rates for African Americans in some urban areas
  are as high as 50% and, of course, this says nothing about whether
  the jobs would pay a living wage if they were available.

- On average, African American unemployment is twice the rate
  of Whites unemployment. Color blindness asserts that poverty is
  a function of flawed character.

- African Americans, however, are subjected to poverty at a rate
  of nearly 23%, while Whites experience poverty at a rate of 10%
  (U.S. Census Bureau, 2003).

While any rate of poverty should be morally and politically
condemnable, the fact that a significant percentage of Whites and a
greater number of African Americans are subjected to poverty suggests that it is at once a structural and racial (or racist?) problem. With
color blindness, one is left to assume that the structural moorings of
poverty are either biological markers or cultural factors inherent in
individual African Americans (see Herrnstein & Murray, 1994). Color
blindness played at least a peripheral role in Clinton's welfare reform.
Welfare was said to be an impediment to people of color, especially
the income-earning capacities of women of color. It denied them the
ability to take rightful, equal responsibility for their lot in the brave
new world. Welfare rolls have shrunk by more than 50% in the ten
years since the reform was passed—meaning that former recipients are
employed, or they opted out of their temporary welfare benefits and
sought economic remuneration through other means—but poverty
rates have stayed the same, if not increased, for African Americans (see
Deparle, 2004). Again, individualism and liberal neutrality, wrapped up
in color-blind discourse, translates a social provision that was intended
to benefit society into "special treatment" of African Americans. Color
blindness also cites lack of education as a reason for unemployability
and lack of social mobility. For instance, a prominent color blindness
spokesperson and English professor claims:

> There comes a point, during any previously reviled group's
> climb to the top, where that group can reach the same level as
> the ruling group only if the safety net is withdrawn. Sometimes
> a group must refashion its entire self-concept in order to move
> ahead. (McWhorter, 2003, p. 25)

This author is specifically referencing affirmative action, and more generally the social state, when he suggests the removal of the safety net.
However, education, a linchpin in the climb to the top, is a function
of wealth, not the other way around. The safety net was built, however
tenuously, to shore up the disparate gaps in income experienced by
people of color so they could access higher education and exercise their
initiative in jobs that could be used in strategies of wealth creation and
accumulation. As of 2001, however, the median household net worth of
African Americans was $19,000, while for whites it was $121,000
(Muhammed et al., 2004, p. 8), median family incomes were $33,525
and $58,270 (p. 7), respectively, in a time when college tuition increased
rapidly and affirmative action programs continue to be attacked. These
are hardly the conditions in which individuals of reviled groups could
make gains on the ruling group.[6]

Although this sketch of color blindness is overly schematic, its
conditions of emergence and mechanisms of reproduction should be
clear. This overview does not interrogate the practice of color blindness
itself and what it means in a state, society, and dominant culture racially
conceived and ordered, and racially reconceived and reordered by way
of figurative and literal forms of racial omission or expulsion.

Colorblindness, Zero Tolerance, and the Politics of Vision

Color blindness refers to vision and the practice of not seeing, and to
color and the various social and material valuations that have been put
on it. Because color blindness refers to the social production and race
valuation, it also refers to the structures and relationships in which these
processes occur. Alternately, zero tolerance refers directly and literally to
an affective state, a condition of (dis)comfort, frustration, or anger.
In legal, social, and cultural terms, it refers to a law and policy,
an ideology, and a practice that occurs in conditions of inequality.

Indirectly, it provides a discursive and emotive frame through which school professionals and criminal justice authorities see, or read, social relationships and respond to their manifest symptoms. Like the ideology of color blindness, it guides vision while bringing into existence new ones. To see how color blindness and zero tolerance are ideologically consonant and effectively identical, the concept of the visual field must first be understood.

Judith Butler (1993) explains that the visual field is an arbitrary frame imposed on the social world. It guides practices of seeing according to a range of conditioned meanings and their subsequent possible readings. Social actors see things, but they understand and interpret things by way of the relationships in which those things exist and the meanings socially ascribed to and produced by those relationships. The field of visibility acts as a filter through which things, individuals, and relationships are distilled in the service of power. Because meaning is socially produced through the modality of culture, it is subject to culture's hierarchical ordering of meanings and the relationships in which meaning is made from preexisting unequal conditions of possibility. There is a dialectic of visual interpretation here. Although individuals exercise a degree of agency in "seeing" and "interpreting" social actors and events in the visual field, some of that seeing and interpreting is done "in advance" (p. 16) by the predominating educational forces of the culture from which social actors borrow the requisite tools for meaningful and purposeful vision, interpretation, and subsequent social action. But what happens when the field of visibility is "racially saturated" (p. 15)? More precisely, how do people see and interpret social relationships and events, because, in large measure, a "racist schemata" (p. 17) is built into a "racist culture" (Goldberg, 1993) and at once organizes and reproduces the images of race that saturate the field of visibility? Until the asymmetrical relationships of racial power and disparate, dehumanizing valuations ascribed to skin color are eliminated (see Myers, 2003), social actors—White and Black alike—will always see, read, interpret, and respond to other social actors vis-à-vis the color-coded filter of a racist schemata (see also Williams, 1998). This creates a paradox for the practice of colorblindness, but suggests much about the types of vision color blindness encourages.

The principle paradox of color blindness is that practitioners vociferously insist on the irrelevance of color. This does not translate into collective social, political, and economic insistence on eliminating racial inequality. Instead, color blindness elides the structures of racial inequality. Color blindness is not possible when the visual field is teeming with representations of race; the processes and relationships producing racial representations can only be ignored by the practice of color blindness. Thus, color blindness supports a short, if not eviscerated, historical vision because it masks the formative processes of economic disaccumulation and cumulative forms of social stigmatization that disadvantage people of color. Consequently, color blindness promotes a distorted vision of the present, in the sense that it does not do away with race, but re-imagines, or re-images, it in different terms and under new social and material conditions. In the increasingly atomized and privatized social relationships that have emerged under neoliberalism, color is primarily recognized and reproduced not to be dominated, but to be dismissed, at least as a political category (Guinier & Torres, 2003), because it calls into being collective social identities, not individualized ones. Color blindness thus promotes normative visions of future social relationships.

Due to the social unacceptability of publicly seeing or witnessing whiteness, it is lifted to a new level of normativity. Color blindness pushes whiteness outside of the public field of vision and realm of discourse, rendering it incontestable because it is placed outside self- and social critique. Thus, whiteness is returned to its status as the assumed bearer and measuring stick of all value. Because of the aggressive assertion that color is irrelevant as a social and political marker, color blindness, to paraphrase one of Goldberg's (2002, p. 231) many insights, devalues blackness.[7] However, color blindness devalues blackness not necessarily by material and symbolic domination, but, in this case, by symbolic exclusion. Under color-blind ideology, race can only be presented and appropriated as a nonpolitical category or market commodity, denuded of its substantive history and modes of production. Color blindness sees a "racially saturated field of visibility" (Butler, 1993, p. 15) and casts future relationships in it not in the imagery of the Jim Crow system of racial domination by inclusion, but according to the racist schemata of racial domination through expulsion. It renders inaccessible—disposes of—the history of race and thus the productive appropriations of it by racialized groups (e.g., resistance, opposition, transformation). But as symbolic degradation is part and parcel of political and economic degradation, color blindness as symbolic exclusion from the public mind is part and parcel of social exclusion from the public body.

This is where the vision(s) of zero tolerance become dangerously operative, picking up where colorblindness leaves off. From the vantage point of law, the vision of zero tolerance is subjected to the same codes of neutrality inhered in color blindness. The law itself says nothing about race, but the consequences of its practice demonstrate the false neutrality of its rationale when it is exercised in a racially ordered, visual field. This is because zero tolerance references behaviors assumed to be endemic to and perpetrated by a certain race and class of students. This consequently guides ways of seeing those students and the relationships they inhabit. This can be witnessed, for example, in the commentary of a school official in a *New York Times* article, "City Applies Police Strategy to its Most Troubled Schools" (Saulny, 2004). The official states: "If you concentrate on the small things, you send an unequivocal message that order is the order of the day" (p. A25). By small things, this official is referring to "Do restrooms have toilet paper? Does the school tolerate graffiti? Are the windows kept clean?" (p. A25).[8] No mention is made of concentrating on larger things like competent and caring teachers, small classes, an inviting school environment, or critical and democratic modes of experience, learning, and citizenship. With zero tolerance fixing and narrowing the social vision of school professionals on small things, one can rightfully assume that racial inequality and the disparate funding this troubled school ostensibly receives (otherwise, it would not, in part, be so troubled), and the effects on students of both conscious and unwitting demeaning, devaluing, professional behaviors (not to mention the complex histories of these racial dynamics), all fall outside of this vision of order-making. Even in the punitive testing environment, one has a difficult time finding a well-dressed, suburban White public school getting away with promoting such a heartless, morally bankrupt, and dehumanizing vision. To the contrary, these schools produce order by seeing and imagining into existence larger things. They provide encouragement, and they promote inclusion in primarily educational, not carceral, relationships. Though in increasingly limited ways, due in part to the high-stakes testing-punishing scheme, better funded suburban schools focus on learning, and order emerges; urban public schools focus on order and punishment and exclusion follow.

Implied in this example are the multiple impacts of zero tolerance on vision. Historical vision is reduced to the frame of an incident, not the relationships and conditions that produced it. Future vision is trimmed to the horizon of repeated and repeatable nows, in the sense that practices of seeing are directed to the next small thing. Most powerfully, the social vision promoted by these professionals, and legitimated by zero tolerance, is trained, from the outset, on seeing and constructing students of color in these schools as always and already dangerous.[9] All professionals need to do to recuperate and reproduce this authoritarian system of order-making is focus on the small things students allegedly have done, or could potentially do. The social fixation on small things cannot fit into its narrow field of vision the vast historical and contemporary injustices repeatedly done to students. The most prominent is the social fact that they are seen, educated, and thus constructed, as dangerous, if not socially and politically disposable. The vision of zero tolerance already sees its objects; it merely has to find a threat that can be pinned on them. The past and the future are both inconceivable according to this vision, because the practice of seeing small things fails to reach behind or beyond the present.

Consequently, color blindness and zero tolerance, while operating on different registers, are mutually constitutive forms of exclusion. Color blindness is a tacit attempt to maintain racial categories and hierarchies of power, while overtly allowing dominant, White social actors to blind themselves to the racist social processes and structures that produce racial power. Zero tolerance, parading under the mystifying codes of individualism and neutrality of color blindness, and egged on by the politics of fear, consistently and disproportionately excludes students of color from formative school and social settings. The racist practices and racial consequences of zero tolerance are thus rendered as the normal response to troubling students of color, because color blindness mutes any claims of institutional racism. It is otherwise difficult for poor students of color, and their parents, to muster the private resources to prove that exclusion is race-based. Because the past is largely factored out of the decision-making process, students of color can only be seen as troubling—they are no longer seen as students troubl*ed* by oppressive conditions marked by racism and class inequality. The argument is not that color blindness and zero tolerance are identical, but that they effect nearly identical consequences: exclusion. But what type of society and mode of social organization could make common sense of these related forms of exclusion? What functions are these forms of exclusion serving?

Neoliberalism's Consumer Society and
How It Disposes of Its Waste

A subtext throughout the study has been that changes in the state and civil society due to neoliberalism have effected changes in how youth and adults of color are treated, the practice of zero tolerance being just one example. An investigation of the society created by neoliberalism indicates how the forms of exclusion promoted by color blindness and zero tolerance are normalized and to what dangerous function they are being put.

The ideology of neoliberalism argues that the social state is useless and, by default, the private investment and police state is useful and necessary:[10] Free markets and the privatization of public goods are efficient and effective strategies for social organization. Slick and rugged individuals, acting in their atomized, rational self-interests in struggles over scarcified social, political, and economic resources, are the epitome of civic virtue. Social problems, in all of their historical, political, and cultural complexity, are reducible to the inhuman(e) and illusory data of profit formulae (see Bourdieu, 2003). As the neoliberal fundamentalist and architect Milton Friedman (2002 [1962]) explains: "The basic problem of social organization is how to co-ordinate the economic activities of large numbers of people" (p. 12), and there are two ways of coordinating these activities: "coercion" through "the technique of the army and the modern totalitarian state;" and "the voluntary co-operation of individuals—the technique of the market place" (p. 13).[11]

Two defining facets of the neoliberal agenda offer insight to the normalization and function of the related forms of exclusion promoted by zero tolerance and color blindness. Namely, what type of society and what type of agents are needed to reproduce the cultural politics of neoliberalism and the social exclusions that it produces, and what agents are redundant?

The Consumer Society

Zygmunt Bauman (2004a, p. 123; 2001 [1998]) argues that contemporary society under the rule of neoliberalism is a "consumer society" or, in President Bush's atypically honest locution, an "ownership society." What separates contemporary society from its previous form, the modern "producer society," is that it engages its members first "in their capacity as consumers." As Bauman further notes:

> "The way present-day society shapes up its members is dictated first and foremost by the need to play the role of the consumer, and the norm our society holds up to its members is that of the *ability* and willingness to play it." (italics added. 2001 [1998], p. 24)

To refer to an obvious example of this shift, think of President George W. Bush's admonition from the rubble of the World Trade Center: "Americans must get back to work, go shopping, going to the theatre [sic], to help this country. . . ."[12] However, the role of citizens is not the only thing that has changed with the rise of the consumer society.

In the shift from the producer to consumer mode of society, the character of the state has also changed. In the producer society, the state was obviously concerned with the market, but it was also concerned with producers—workers and citizens who fulfilled the duties of labor and, if time was available, citizenship. The state had a vested interest in ensuring that industry had a steady, willing, able, and sometimes waiting pool of healthy producers. The state demonstrated this interest by investing in programs like social welfare and institutions such as public schools. In the consumer or ownership society, however, the state primarily supports not the public good, but private interests. Hence the private investment and police state that supports policies and programs that promote the privatization of schools, healthcare, social security, and the elimination of social welfare. What results is a state that protects its valued consumers and private investors from disabled consumers, citizens who have been disadvantaged historically by the oppressive social and political relationships of racism and class inequality. In coordination with the consumer society and its engagement of members as consumers, the state is engaged less as a conduit for social organization and reproduction than as a broker and a police officer, channeling the flow of capital into private interests and punishing disabled consumers.

The norm of the consumer society has become operative for a number of reasons. One, the economic base has shifted markedly in the last 20 to 30 years. Due to rapid technological progress, fewer hands are required to produce a significantly greater volume of consumer products, and fewer minds are needed in high-skill information industries. Thus, many former industrial workers are, to quote Bauman (2004a), "redundant" which means "supernumerary, unneeded, of no use" (p. 12). The driving force of consumer society is consequently not a vast, capable pool of workers and civically engaged citizens, but individual consumers who devour masses of disposable goods. Little mention is made of unemployment statistics, which range from estimates of approximately 8 million to 14 million. The numbers, of course, diverge along racial lines (Yates, 2004, p. 36–37). The boom industry of employment agencies represent approximately 4 million temporary workers, employed precariously by fiat and denied benefits (Magdoff & Magdoff, 2004, p. 27). Lack of a living wage for millions of citizens compound the issues. Instead, sales are reported and newscasts celebrate a big-box retailer's latest slashing of prices, which implies slashing wages and labor. The message for citizen-consumers is that they need to shop to stave off economic crisis and exercise their patriotism. The tacit message is that consumers can more easily perform their rituals and quickly take advantage of the opportunity—until another big-box follows suit and cuts its prices. In other instances, media consumers learn of the latest consumer scam instead of state and corporate philandering and fraud, as if one's being cheated on a disposable good is tantamount to or greater than scores of workers losing their livelihoods or pensions.[13] Hence, traditional workers are quite literally out of the game, and consumers are in. Large numbers of workers reduce profits—willing and able consumers increase them (Bauman, 2001 [1998], pp. 64–65).

Two, with state support of neoliberalism's free trade agenda, the cutting of social welfare provisions, and the diminishing efficacy of unions, tenuously employed producers have the cloud of corporate exodus and job loss hanging over their heads. Corporations do not need workers in any permanent sense. Corporations simply leave when they have usurped the locale's natural resources. If workers or local citizens—who forgot that they are to be consumers—make demands on corporations to improve labor conditions and take responsibility for impacts on the community, they flee to another area, here or abroad, that is, at least, temporarily hospitable to their needs.

Three, and equally important, the consumer society of neoliberalism not only produces changes in the economic realm, but also reforms society at the level of cultural politics by fundamentally reshaping primary spheres of social interaction and common concern. The media is densely corporatized and hostile to the public interest (McChesney & Nichols, 2002), providing an endless stream of celebrity gossip, Darwinian reality shows, advertising, and political debate shows that function more like firing squads than dialogue forums. Public spaces are increasingly commercialized, subjected to intensive surveillance and militarization (Giroux, 2004a), simultaneously interpellating citizens as consumers and possible victims of potential threats. Public services continue to be privatized. Social welfare is virtually eliminated, shredding the compact of the Great Society. The chasm between the upper-classes and the disemployed lower classes and groups of color becomes larger and larger (see Delgado, 2002; Deparle, 2004). Thus, it is no surprise that the most reviled groups of the consumer society are youth of color and the elderly, the former scapegoated as dangerous, the latter burdensome. And, public education is persistently whittled away by market-based initiatives, leaving students with teachers-turned-salespeople or teachers-turned-prison guards. Citizens are left with few social venues that provide noncommodified public and democratic languages and experiences. The cultural politics of consumer society promote highly competitive and individualistic languages and modes of social interaction in which, as John Comaroff and Jean Comaroff (2000) point out: "The personal [has become] the only politics there is, the only politics with a tangible referent or emotional valence" (p. 305). As a society of consumers, it cannot be any other way because consumption is always a private affair. This is so, of course, only for those who are privileged, valued shoppers.

The Underside of the Consumer Society

These fundamental changes made by neoliberalism, trotted about deceptively in the liberating language of deregulation, have been anything but liberating or deregulating. It is well-documented that the average American workers are working longer, and, even though they are urged to consume more and more, they do so with less and less money and time. The free market might have lifted all boats, but it exacerbates the economic and social distance between the rich and poor (Navarro, 2004).

The state is hardly smaller with deregulation. Just think of the magnitude of the U.S. military, with the Department of Defense's annual budget topping $700 billion in 2006, over 10 times federal expenditures on P–12 education. President Clinton added 300,000 police officers to the streets of America during his tenure, doubling in eight years a prison population that took more than 150 years to produce. Witness the preponderance of intelligence agencies before and after 9/11, the burgeoning Department of Homeland Security, and the continued technological intermeshing and structural symbiosis of the military and other public and intermediary institutions.

The shifts from producer to consumer society, social to private investment, and police state are consequently not exercises in deregulation, but as Stuart Hall (1997) notes, shifts "from one mode of regulation to another." The alleged deregulation of the economic realm "require[d] and is complemented by re-regulation in others" such as culture and politics. Re-regulation, to cite Hall again, has come to revolve around "questions concerning sexuality, morality, *crime, violence, standards of public conduct and behaviour . . .*" (italics added. Hall, p. 230). As in the producer mode of society, where social anxieties were leveled not at the dominant but the less-dominant producers, these relatively recently promoted anxieties have become catchwords in discourses and policies, targeting not able consumers but disabled consumers. In other words, those who are deprived the requisite economic and valued forms of cultural capital in the producer society are now denied social provisions by the private investment state of the consumer society. Criminalization and exclusion have become principle modes of regulation.

In a segregated society such as the United States, reregulation has had devastating impacts on people of color. These can be seen in general terms. For instance, although suburban areas and gated communities inhabited predominantly by Whites are strategically linked to semiviable jobs, decent hospitals, good schools and shopping centers, deindustrialized and deconsumerized urban areas inhabited by people of color are strategically linked to prisons.[14] These conditions position suburban Whites of most classes within the boundaries of insecure employment, minimal incarceration, and enfranchisement, whereas urban people of color and, in particular African Americans, are relegated to a vicious cycle of structural racism, what Marable (2004a) calls the "unholy trinity" of "mass unemployment, mass incarceration [and, subsequently], mass disenfranchisement." Consider these observations in statistical terms: One in 20 Whites is under- or unemployed (Muhammed et al., 2004), and 1 in 60 Whites is incarcerated (The Sentencing Project, 2004a). Conversely, 1 in 9 African Americans cannot find employment (Muhammed et al., 2004), while 1 in 8 African Americans is imprisoned (The Sentencing Project, 2004a). Of the 2.2 million Americans in federal, state, or local prisons, the largest incarceration figure in the world (U.S. Department of Justice, 2004; The Sentencing Project, 2004b), approximately 50% of them are African American, although they constitute only 12.7% of the general population.[15]

This unholy trinity of structural racism, however, is not the product of divine intervention. It is the underside of consumer society composed of a volatile admixture of social, political, and legal forces that circumscribe groups of citizens who have been disabled and made socially and economically redundant by neoliberal state and social transformations, in their capacities as consumers in officialized markets and as laborers. The admixture of forces is as follows:

- economically strained and socially fragmented communities;

- structurally and practically depoliticized groups resulting from lack of economic power, and shattered, quite often state occupied communities;

- social marginalization resulting from pervasive stigmatization, harassment, and police brutality, despite colorblindness's insistence on its absence;[16,17]

- punitive drug and quality of life laws, including zero tolerance that have been popular criminal justice strategies.

Saying that this admixture operates in deindustrialized and deconsumerized cities is not a theoretical abstraction or flippant use of rhetorical categories. Young African American males face a 33% chance of being incarcerated, while young White males have a 5% chance (The Sentencing Project, 2004a), Black unemployment is 10.8% on average, but varying wildly between low double digits and upwards of 50% in some urban areas such as Harlem (Muhammed et al., 2004, p. 1; Marable, 2004a), while White unemployment is 5.2% on average, and, in the terms of the consumer society, there are "three times as many bars in poor neighborhoods as in rich ones, and four times as many supermarkets in White neighborhoods as in Black ones" (Epstein, H., 2003, p. 80). The combination of incarceration and unemployment fragments communities. Incarceration not only often strips the incarcerated of voting rights, it also removes able-bodied and intelligent young people from their homes and social settings, decimating formative, productive social relationships (see Brown et al., 2003; Brown, Russo, & Hunter, 2002; Cole, 1999). Unemployment contributes to this fragmentation in two ways: (1) It de-structures time and reduces economic power, making it difficult to construct individual and collective goals (See Bauman, 2002), because available time and money are devoted primarily to basic biological needs, and it leaves unemployed, deconsumerized individuals sitting targets for police harassment and agents in unofficialized economies. (2) Whether or not urban people of color were systemically and gainfully employed indicates nothing about the lack of official venues in which their consumer capacities can be exercised. They are structurally incapacitated as official consumers.

The concentration of African Americans in deindustrialized and deconsumerized urban cores does not simply facilitate the alchemy of these forces; it is a precondition of them. As Loic Wacquant (2002) demonstrates, the "hyperghetto," existing symbiotically with the prison-industrial complex, is the structural-spatial form of "ethnoracial domination" (p. 48). The hyperghetto's roots, as Wacquant points out, are founded in the ghetto of the producer era where Blacks were cordoned and stigmatized in urban areas to provide a cheap industrial labor source; Jim Crow lasting from 1865–1965, and slavery. Each form of ethnoracial domination was produced and maintained, by both explicit state policy (see again Brown et al., 2003) and de facto patterns of White privilege and opportunity (e.g., White flight to suburban areas and the hoarding of social, political, and economic resources), for the "conjoined" purposes of "extraction of labor and social ostracization" (p. 44). However, with the subsequent exodus of manufacturing industries from cities, first, with the White flight of 1950s and 1960s, and, second, with neoliberal economic deregulation and the advent of the information and service-based economy, extraction of cheap urban labor is no longer a necessary component in ethnoracial domination—thus, social ostracization and political exclusion have become the principle modes of racial domination and regulation, superimposing carceral modes of containment, punishment, and regulation on the deindustrialized ghetto: "stigma" (e.g., "Cities are dangerous."), "constraint" (e.g., little opportunity for temporary or permanent movement outside of the ghetto), "territorial confinement" (e.g., ghettoes are hemmed in by a caustic combination of beltways, toxic dumps, tourism districts, and various forms of surveillance, allowing for the easy demarcation of

urban enclaves of color)[18], and "institutional encasement" (e.g., a punishing mixture of police, courts, a harsh child welfare system, etc.)
(Wacquant p. 50; see also Goldberg, 1993; Roberts, 2003).

There are clear markers of this domination, showing how it evolved
coterminous with the rise of consumer society and color-blind ideology. The economic recession of the late 1970s and its impacts on the
industrial cores of cities were met in the 1980s not by Reagan administration support of social welfare, the public good, and incentives for
corporate investment in urban areas, but with social welfare cuts and
Draconian crime laws, birthed in good measure by his dubious War on
Drugs. Although unemployment in urban areas increased and wages for
African Americans stagnated and decreased relative to Whites throughout the 1980s (Williams, R. M., 1993), Reagan's Omnibus Budget
Reconciliation Act of 1981 began the first in a series of social spending
cuts, resulting in the draining of:

> billions . . . from social security, unemployment insurance, food
> stamps, housing assistance, aid for families with dependent chil-
> dren, employment training, nutrition programs for children,
> low-income energy assistance, vocational education, the job
> corps, and compensatory education for the disadvantaged.
> (Robinson, 1993, p. 75)

When dominant politicians and the media began to make claims of
reverse discrimination, coupled ironically with claims of racial equality
and a need for color blindness, the racial contours of these policy
changes made under the euphimistic deregulation became clear. The
economy shifted to more knowledge-intensive, high-tech industries,
and African Americans were the primary victims of social spending
cuts. Having been employed in fairly well paying manufacturing jobs,
by default they were denied entrance to the higher-end jobs of the new
economy, deprived of both the requisite training and social support to
pay for preparation in the new industries.

Simultaneously, the War on Drugs was launched, inaugurating
mandatory minimum sentencing in 1986 for drug possession and traf-
ficking violations, and zero tolerance came into vogue. Zero tolerance
became not only the catchword in the drug wars, but also synonymous

with other get-tough initiatives such as quality of life policing implemented by police departments in New York, Philadelphia, Los Angeles, Chicago, and other large cities. Zero tolerance came to be used for social behaviors as inane as sleeping in public, loitering, and breaking curfew laws enacted in certain areas of cities. Between 1981 and 1988, the prison population nearly doubled, jumping from 369,930 to 627,600 (U.S. Department of Justice, 1995). Unsurprisingly, the racial composition of prisons also changed with these "racially targeted 'law-and-order' policies" (Wacquant, 2002, p. 56): "Between 1979 and 1990, the number of Blacks as a percentage of all persons admitted to state and federal prisons increased from 39 to 53 percent" (Human Rights Watch, 2000).

Much of this racial exclusion promoted in the color-blind consumer society continued under President H. W. Bush and intensified under President Clinton. Before President H. W. Bush left office, he passed a program focused on urban areas derogatorily named "Weed and Seed." City governments received funding to weed urban areas of classes deemed invasive to reurbanization schemes (See Davis, 1993). His administration also laid the groundwork for zero tolerance with the passing of the Gun-Free School Zones Act of 1990. In 1994, the first Clinton administration passed the Violent Crime Control and Law Enforcement Act of 1994 (VCCLEA). Part of this legislation was the three strikes policy that provided the permanent incarceration of repeat offenders. Some states like California drafted their own versions, allowing permanent encarceration of offenders even if their third crime was nonviolent, and regardless of the amount of time that passed between the second and third offenses.[19] The bill also provided for varying sentencing for violations involving the more recreational and expensive, suburban powder cocaine and cheaper, urban crack cocaine, an average sentence of 55.6 months (4.5 years) for the former, 103.5 months (roughly 9 years) for the latter (Human Rights Watch, 2002). What's more, the zero tolerance component of the bill allowed for the eviction of residents from subsidized housing if someone in possession of drugs visited their residence, even if the residents had no social or familial relationship with the individual (Brown, Russo, & Hunter, 2002).[20] VCCLEA also directly tied the drug war to education (see Blumenson & Nilsen, 2002); the law prohibited sentenced drug offenders from receiving Pell Grants. The Souder Amendment of 1998 added to this punitive law the denial of "federal grants, federally-subsidized loans, and work-study funds to college students who have been convicted of *any* drug offense—felon or misdemeanor, sale or possession, heroin or marijuana (but not rape, robbery, or murder)" (Blumenson & Nilsen, 2002, p. 10).[21]

To add insult to injury, the Clinton-sponsored Personal Responsibility and Work Opportunity Reconciliation Act of 1996 (PRWORA), marketed deceptively as welfare reform, virtually eliminated welfare by deregulating its administration to states and making its provision temporary (Temporary Assistance for Needy Families). PRWORA also required individual work contributions without the provision of childcare (Workfare), and threatened permanent exclusion from the system if the recipient tested positive for drug use or was arrested for drug possession (see Hardisty & Williams, 2002; Polakow, 2000). Some states refuse additional funds for children born while a family is receiving TANF or for children born out-of-wedlock. Others, now under President G. W. Bush's cajoling, are looking at plans to make heterosexual marriage one of the preconditions for additional assistance, all this while eligible partners for women of color, particularly urban African American women, are scarce due to wickedly high rates of incarceration. Needless to say, in economically eviscerated cities, the attack on social welfare is virtually an attack on poor African Americans, pushing them further out of the social purview of the public and social state and deeper into grips of the police state.

The sum total of these social and criminal justice policy shifts of the easy-going, color-blind and consumer-friendly 1990s was the incarceration of intolerable numbers of poor people of color, and the redistribution of public monies to the prison-industrial complex. In fact, "the United States locked up nearly as many people during that decade as it did during the previous 150 years combined" (Justice Policy Institute, 2004, Online). In 1990, there were 773,919 people incarcerated in federal, state, or local prisons. By 1994, the number increased to 1,053,738 (U.S. Department of Justice, 1995). By 2000, the end of the "liberal" President Clinton's second term, 2 million people had been incarcerated and, by midyear 2003, 2.2 million were incarcerated (U.S. Department of Justice, 2004)—more than 50% of whom are African Americans. Further, as many as "one-third of all prisoners were unemployed at the time of their arrests, and others averaged less than $20,000 annual incomes in the year prior to their incarceration" (Marable, 2004b).

Stated differently, the prison population doubled in six short years after VCCLEA and four years after PRWORA, *all while violent crime rates steadily decreased during the same period* (United Health Foundation, 2003). This suggests that public resources and social energies are being devoted to incarcerating poor people of color for nonviolent social behaviors, which are typically the manifest symptoms of deeper social problems. This is truly compelling, or should be, as it costs, on average, $35,000 to $40,000 per year to house an inmate, while only an average of $7,000 is spent per year on public school students (Johnson, 2002). Furthermore, corrections officer salaries typically rival, if not sometimes surpass, those of many public school teachers (see Bureau of Labor Statistics, 2004a; Bureau of Labor Statistics, 2004b). And recall, at this point, how the exclusion of students of color from schools follows similar rates of increase over the same period (1994–2000), similar rates of racial disproportionality and similar geographic lines (i.e., urban public schools), and rates of school violence were decreasing before the widespread initiation of zero tolerance. For these reasons, zero tolerance in public schools must be seen, not as a relatively autonomous phenomenon that emerged solely in response to real or imagined school violence, but as *a central component in completing the circuitry of a wider social system of racial subordination and exclusion.*[22] Evidence of this can be seen in the relationships between race, incarceration, and higher education.

The Justice Policy Institute (2002a) notes that, between 1980 and 2000, spending on corrections increased six times that of higher education. In strict dollar amounts, spending was $20 billion on corrections and only $10.7 billion on higher education. Substantial rises in the incarceration of racialized minorities, particularly African Americans, were also witnessed. Between 1980 and 2000, there were three times as many African Americans incarcerated as were admitted to universities. California is a despairing example of these trends. Between 1984 and 1994, California built 19 prisons and only one new state university (Berube, 2000). In California, African American males constitute 43% of the third-strike prisoners alone, though they only make up 7% of California's population (Cole, 1999, p. 148). Regardless of the method of incarceration in California, there are nearly five times more African American males in corrections than in higher education and three times more white males in universities than in the corrections system (Berube). The combined total of these factors shows that 39,400 African Americans were added to California's corrections system, while their enrollment in higher education decreased by 3752 between 1980 and 2000 (Justice Policy Institute, 2002a). So, to Marable's unholy trinity of mass unemployment, mass incarceration, and mass disenfranchisement, add the denial of education to African Americans to square off the vectors of structural racism—or the disposal system for wasted lives (Bauman, 2004a).

A Telling Example of the Consumer Society, Color Blindness, and Zero Tolerance

An argument made by the vice-chair of U.S. Commission on Civil Rights in the *Los Angeles Times* provides an object lesson in the relationships between the consumer society and private investment state, the combined use and function of color blindness and zero tolerance, and how they act in concert in attempts to dispose of people of color as "flawed consumers" (Bauman, 2001[1999]; 2004), all in the supposed interests of equality and "battening on all sorts of stereotypes and fears" (Winant, 2004, p. xiii). This argument plays on the commonsense of neoliberal ideology and needs to be thrown into relief; and, what will be seen to be simply an evil argument is made by, nonetheless and how ironically, a member of the U.S. Commission on Civil Rights, showing how color blindness operates on codes and produces racial relationships that, while being "color-blind," might be more pernicious than the visible ones of the past.

Despite the evidence provided in this study and many others that demonstrates the systemic and obvious zero tolerance displayed to people of color and African Americans in particular, U.S. Commission on Civil Rights vice-chair Abigail Thernstrom (2003) argues that "inner city" students have somehow missed out on zero tolerance. She makes this subargument within a larger one, claiming that noncharter urban public schools are causal factors in the racial gaps of educational achievement:

> [Inner-city kids] need schools where there is zero tolerance for violence, erratic or tardy attendance, *inappropriate* dress, late or incomplete homework, *incivility* toward staff and other students, *messy* desks and halls, trash on the floor and other signs of *disorder* (italics added. p. B17).

Notice the language she uses. It is strategically crafted to avoid overt racial reference and epithets. It is color-blind in and of itself, but the statement is not devised from a historical vacuum. It also is not projected into a race-free social text and visual field in which fear and symbolic affronts to dominant White sensibilities don't carry profound weight. Inner-city youth, she claims, practice incivility. This, remember, is a gross stereotype disinterred from the early Jim Crow era, when segregation of schools was deemed necessary until Blacks were civilized enough to attend White schools. The use of this stereotype is found further back, in slavery: A justification for slavery purported that, unlike Native Americans who, according to Thomas Jefferson, had the potential to be civilized, Africans were not civilizable, thus validating their subhuman status as slaves. Inner-city youth wear inappropriate clothes, Thernstrom claims, presumably because they wear baggy pants and leave their shirts untucked, much like suburban White youth who don't have to wear school uniforms and borrow from hip-hop fashions that originate in the inner city. But what does dress have to do with educational achievement? It seems, at least in this case, to serve no other purpose than to stigmatize inner-city youth as dangerously different in the best case and inferior in the worst. As if a school uniform, a golf shirt, or a pair of khakis bought at the Gap or J C Penney can fill the social and educational gaps promoted by racism, malnutrition, poverty, community violence, and structural violence. Additionally, in this context, Thernstrom's description of the school environment is terribly disingenuous. The image of disorder does not seek support from the dominant classes to improve inner-city schools; it simply reinforces the image of inner-city youth as practitioners of incivility. For the most part, however, claims like this pass unquestioned under color blindness because she did not state "Black youth practice incivility," just students in inner-city schools do. Caricatured claims like these become operative and carry much racial power because inner-city youth are presumed to be youth of color. Simply, her claims do not have to be explicitly racial (racist?) to play on racist worldviews and to effect racialized consequences, such as influencing dominant voters' choices to perpetuate disinvestment in inner city public schools attended by students of color.

This is the precise point. Thernstrom's argument, cast under the color-blind guise of improving public education and creating racial equality in educational achievement while stigmatizing urban youth, is about eliminating urban public schools. Thernstrom argues, however fallaciously, that the privatization of inner-city schools is the best mechanism to improve educational achievement (see Bracey, 2005). According to Thernstrom, urban public school administrators are "obstructed" by burdensome state regulations in taking responsibility of their schools, hiring and firing teachers, and expelling unwanted students. Meddlesome unions, which are prohibited in charter schools, protect underperforming teachers and stagnate the wages of competent teachers, forcing them to leave needy schools, according to Thernstrom. For Thernstrom, zero tolerance is a weapon of exclusion exercised on youth in urban public schools until they can be saved and privatized by charter or for-profit schools. She doesn't claim that urban charter schools or suburban, White public schools need zero tolerance or need to be privatized. Inner-city youth in public schools are quite literally disabled consumers. Until their schools are privatized, and when students and parents become clients and consumers, the most effective policy to improve equality in educational achievement is, ironically, to exclude students of color. The only challenge left, then, is to convince powerful voters to cast ballots for the privatization of urban public schools because their tax dollars are supporting uncivilized students of color who can only be saved by the market.[23] Needless to say, this version of color blindness is not the color blindness of which the great Martin Luther King Jr. was dreaming. Clearly, this position is not only significantly flawed but also fundamentally antidemocratic, because despite its carefully chosen language, it is about the unequal provision of social and political resources to a group marked historically by racial oppression.

Arguments like this, made by influential political actors, suggest much about the conditions of struggles over scarce social, political, and economic and the role color blindness and zero tolerance play in them. As the state is further weakened, or weakens itself, by neoliberal policies, more funds are diverted to militarization and criminalization, and middle-class livelihoods and social groups are rendered insecure by mobile and global capital. Economic and social inequality widens, throwing the social strains of poverty and structural neglect into sharp relief, and fierce individualization of social risks and atomization of social relationships lodge deeper into the body politic. The way to maintain power and status is not only to insist on the irrelevance of the racialized processes that made racial power possible, but also to ignore the persisting processes and relationships that reproduce and secure racialized group power. This is the logic of color blindness and the symbolic racial exclusions and historical expulsions it promotes; the practice of zero tolerance simply aids and abets the disposal.

Conclusion

Although color blindness and zero tolerance operate on different registers, the discourses supporting them and the practices enacting them emerge from similar historical contexts. They occupy similar racial ground and produce a similar racial effect—exclusion. That context is the consumer society and its concomitant private investment-police state, which scarcifies public goods and individualizes social risks by pitting individuals in heated battles over limited social, political, and economic resources that are redirected upwards (Duggan, 2003) towards the processes of militarization and criminalization. The racial ground is, as it always was, the terrain between dominant Whites and less dominant African Americans, but at a time when post-civil rights discourses claim that race is irrelevant and racism is all but a historical artifact; spheres of social interaction are not only highly commercialized and atomized but also markedly resegregated and other less dark minorities try to make claims on the privileges of whiteness (Bonilla-Silva, 2003a); when Whites of most classes feel the downward economic and social insecurity brought on by neoliberal state and social policies, recasting them as anxieties of being under siege.[24] The racial effects are different but constitutive forms of racialized social and political exclusion because deindustrialization, the privatization and commercialization of public goods, and social, economic domination coupled with cultural stigmatization, is no longer a viable mechanism for racial subordination. Actually, the latter form of racism calls attention to the racist structure that has not been eliminated by color blindness. In consumer society, social and political exclusion of African Americans, the disposal of disabled consumers and redundant workers, becomes the principle mode of racial domination. Its consequences are more easily portrayed as the result of personal flaws: irresponsible individuals, lack of initiative, moral depravity, and criminality.

Race, and its principle mechanism of production, racism, are not reducible to the economic. Race and racism are categories, structures, and processes, bound up in the state, market, and civil society—the official structure of governance and the sphere in which governance is effected and experienced through the modality of culture and the various media and practices involved in the production of meaning. Race and racism simply get refigured, at least until and unless racial inequalities of any kind are rectified, as the state is reconfigured and modes of cultural practice are transformed by and transform the social and material conditions in which they take place. Shifts in the conditions in which dominant social actors make meaning produce changes in the justifications they provide for racial inequality. Without a substantive, democratic, and public social sphere, Whites are held or make themselves virtually unaccountable to the privileges they reproduce and the discourse they use to explain them.

In this way, color blindness is still an ideology, a set of discourses and meanings enacted in the service of racial power. In large measure, it inheres, promotes, and borrows from a particular logic that would be incomprehensible under different social, political, and economic conditions. Color blindness is about the disposal of history, the elision of the present, and the individualization of the terms, practices, and consequences of structural and individual racism. To a great degree, trashing history, masking the present, and the atomization and privatization of racialized social relations and racism take hold. A society that is generally counterpoised to history and its impacts on the present, and collective social identities and commitments, is the consumer society. Because the consumer society relies on the production of consumers and their social and historical amnesia, it requires anxieties or desires that impell consumers to keep consuming. These anxieties create flawed consumers who drag on the competent consumer's power because they divert hard earned tax dollars to urban public schools, community-based organizations, healthcare, and social support, not to Walmart, the country club, or fruitful portfolios and private retirement accounts. In the era of happily delusional proclamations of racial equality, these anxieties must simultaneously be produced and disposed of. Consequently, color blindness can be seen as the racial logic and project of the consumer society. It allows for the maintenance of racial hierarchies and the exclusion of the history(ies) that produced them.

Zero tolerance, alternately, as it was from its inception, is a set of laws and an ideology that targets and stigmatizes individual social behaviors believed to be manifest in areas of gross social, political, and economic inequality. Although it now seems normal that we have zero tolerance for sleeping in public, hanging around street corners after a certain hour, trading in or self-medicating with noncommercial drugs, or disagreeing with a teacher or any other authority figure, it would seem absurd if we had zero tolerance for disinvestment in cities, the elimination of social welfare that expels individuals and groups from formal housing and places them in the streets, local control initiatives that help suburban areas hoard public monies and provide good schools and community centers, while these very institutions are attacked and closed in cities, rampant use of anti-depressants and other authorized psychotropic drugs in the middle- and upper middle-classes, and for a system that burdens urban public schools with overcrowded and underfunded classrooms and punitive testing schemes that mechanistically and routinely resort to exclusion as a way to deal with nonviolent classroom behaviors. Like color blindness, zero tolerance would have a difficult time taking hold in a society in which collective, public decisions and actions were used to deal with social pathologies. But in the privatized and individualized consumer society, zero tolerance is the strategy of choice. Like color blindness, zero tolerance provides consumer society and the private investment and police state with a mechanism to dispose of unnecessary, unwanted consumers in a very literal way.

Zero tolerance and color blindness are difficult phenomena to counter. This is true because they both have their own trajectories and are fundamentally interrelated at this point in history. But because they are difficult is not an adequate reason to avoid dealing with them. To the contrary, the stakes are too high. Both democracy and another generation of people of color are threatened with disposal by zero tolerance and color blindness. Democracy demands inclusion and collective involvement in mediating its shortcomings. For full inclusion, people of color need not only to have access to primary spheres of social interaction and reproduction, but also to have their history, which is part of White American history, be accounted for, and to gain the requisite public hearing they deserve.

CHAPTER 5

Against Zero Tolerance

The Struggle for the Democratic Legacy of Public Schooling and the Promise of Democracy

[H]ope is constituted in the need to imagine an alternative human world and to imagine it in a way that enables one to act in the present as if this alternative had already begun to emerge.

—Roger I. Simon, 1992, p. 4

*Z*ero tolerance both symbolizes and institutionalizes the lack of a public vision regarding the democratic legacy of schooling and the promise of democratic public life. This lack of vision is manifest in the use of zero tolerance as a primary weapon in the low-intensity warfare of social exclusion inflicted on students and youth of color; the criminalization of student behaviors in general; and the modeling of public schools on the prison and the military, when they are not modeled on the test center or shopping mall. As a powerful ideology supported by exclusionary practices, zero tolerance is a destructive phenomenon indicative of a contemporary war on youth and the future, in particular, a democratic future. Consequently, zero tolerance demands not simply public school reform but, more centrally, an urgent struggle over connecting schooling to democracy and working cooperatively, as mutually responsible members of a shared social fate, for the larger conditions that make democracy possible.

149

In this way, zero tolerance points to the necessity of two interrelated, public struggles: One is over the democratic legacy and promise of public schooling (Noguera, 2003), the other over democratic public life. Both sets of efforts also must be rooted in the promise and hope of a democratic future, and guided by interests in constructing and making good on an inclusive democratic social contract. Hope is fundamental to these broader efforts. It becomes operative in, and a guiding principle for, public struggles over the mission and functions of education and the definition of teacher, student, and citizen subjectivities that are consonant with invoking and reproducing democratic social relationships. As a guiding principle for developing democratic social relationships and the material conditions that foster them, a critical, educated hope is central to these efforts because it provides an ideological referent capable of contesting and transforming the cynicism implied in zero tolerance's ideology of no alternatives and the culture of fear that supports it, by suggesting that there are more humane and democratic strategies for dealing with the symptoms of deep-rooted social pathologies in public schools and their wider communities. Most critically, as educated hope squarely situates struggles over the future in efforts to reconstitute the democratic legacy of schooling and democratic public life, hope also contests the ideology of zero tolerance by recognizing that any opposition to zero tolerance must understand and accommodate the centrality of youth to a democratic future.

The Democratic Legacy of Public Schooling

The democratic legacy of public schooling is constituted by the belief that public schools are crucial facets in promoting the social, political, and cultural vitality of a democratizing society. This means that educators, schools, their communities and, by extension, the broader society, work to ensure that both the form and content of school-community relationships are conducive to such a project. The democratic legacy of public schooling is consequently the belief that public schools are spheres of common interaction, interest, and responsibility, where fostering the private interest, or self, is inseparable from the moral and ethical imperatives of enriching and extending the common good. In other words, the freer development of the individual is contingent upon the freer development of all. More generally, the democratic legacy of schooling is the guiding belief that public schools can and should play a role in not only maintaining social order and providing the affectivities and skills—or docility (Foucault, 1977)—appropriate to market demands, but also, and more centrally, in providing the conditions and experiences that encourage students, as future citizens, to gain the tools and learn the languages—and to develop the dispositions—critical to remaking social order when it is found to be antithetical to the promise of democracy.

This legacy can be approached by way of two obvious, but all too often unasked questions in contemporary public discourse regarding public schooling: If public schools are not in the business of encouraging both the affective investments and social competencies crucial to protecting and extending the democratic fabric of society, then what other institutions at the public's disposal can undertake such an enterprise? Or, if public schooling fails to assume the role of guarantor to democratic public life, can it be presumed that under the demands of an ever complex global society and without other institutions capable of assuming such a position, democratic public life stands a faint chance of being reproduced and, when necessary, reconstituted? These questions are important because the answers to them, regardless of their content, bear consequences for everyone. These questions are ethical, a primary and unavoidable part of both the practices of and discussions about schooling. They concern the status of schooling, the direction of social order and, thus, potential implications to be shouldered by future generations. These questions are also important for another reason central to the issue at hand.

These questions were given much thought, albeit in starkly different historical conditions, in the formative stages of public schooling in the United States and across much of the first half of the 20th century.

Often considered to be the founder of modern public schooling in the United States, Horace Mann took these questions seriously. He claims, in reference to public schools, that "A republican form of government, without intelligence in the people, must be, on a vast scale, what a mad-house, without a superintendent or keepers, would be on a small scale" (Mann, 1848). For Mann, education was clearly directly related to governance. Without schooling, society would be as it was for the enlightenment philosopher Thomas Hobbes in a different way, no more than a war of all against all. According to Mann's vision, schooling was more than merely a mechanism to produce social order in the sense of strict regulation or constraint. To paraphrase him, schooling is the equalizer in the social machinery of society. In other words, public schooling was not simply about any type of social order, because even tyrannical authoritarian regimes can produce order, but about the formation of the preconditions for an expanding and never finished democratic social order. These founding principles of modern, public schooling suggest that schooling assists in governance by producing an informed citizenry capable of engaging public life. It also equalizes access to and the means for participation in the polity (see also Cremin, 1957). These assumptions also underpinned much of the work of John Dewey and social reconstructionists in the first half of the 20th century. Dewey did not believe that democracy was infallible, but that it was the most appropriate, and the most effective, form of social and political organization for bringing together diverse groups of people and tapping and augmenting their social capacities—in Dewey's terms, their human nature (see Dewey, 1940, 1997, 1998). For Dewey, like Mann, this orchestration of humans and their drives was an act requiring practice, or experience, in appropriate forms of reflection, public action, dialogue and debate, and the public school was an ostensible site in which such experience could be promoted.

Critics in the 1950s, even relatively conservative ones such as historian Arthur Bestor (1985 [1953]), railed against what they believed to be the watering down of public schooling as a result of the use of basic life skills or life adjustment curricula for students perceived to be unworthy of academic learning. Bestor thought this was an affront to civil society and the role education plays in it. Instead, Bestor and others asserted that public schools need to provide the skills, knowledges, experiences, and expectations that would enable all students to be productive members in a complex civil society and changing economic order. As Bestor claims "a republican system of government requires citizens who are highly literate, accurately informed, and rigorously trained in the processes of rational and critical thought" (p. 12). Here, especially, one cannot overlook the central insight about public schooling that emerged from the various civil rights struggles over school desegregation. Unless all American students were provided equal and not separate forms of schooling, democracy would be thwarted.

These theoretical positions and public interests butted up against many social forces in the early stages of public school formation and throughout the 20th century, and they are threatened today in different, more intense ways. Early forms of urban education were based more on paternalism and domestication for ethnic groups perceived to be lacking in American values than on critical learning, political engagement, and democratic social transformation (see Tyack & Cuban, 1995). In other instances, education was to serve explicitly the demands of a burgeoning industrial order. Later in the 20th century, education was used as the bulwark against Cold War tensions, and the imperatives of schooling shifted to emphases on science and mathematics to aid in the development and production of military technology (see Dow, 1991). And, of course, despite the courageous efforts of the early Civil Rights Movement that culminated in the decision of *Brown v. Board of Education* (1954), and some contemporary efforts, the United States has failed to reckon with resegregated and unequal public schooling (Hochschild, 2003; Kozol, 2005; Rothstein, 2004; Street, 2005). But in each of these moments, none of these social forces completely overrode public discourses concerning the civic mission of schooling. In other words, this was one primary way that the modern, liberal democratic social contract became operative for youth. In return for their compliance, public schooling would provide—albeit in racially and class differentiated forms—the conditions and resources to develop the competencies and dispositions conducive to both the world of work and the work of citizenship. These two facets—being capable of reproducing the economic order and participating in the political life of society—were seen as crucial elements in not only protecting national security but also making practical the ideals of the democratic credo on which the United States was based.

On various levels and in relation to an assortment of social forces, zero tolerance unequivocally subverts this legacy that is so basic to both democratic principles and the existing fragments of the democratic fabric of U.S. society. Zero tolerance also points to and reinforces the gaping vacancy in democratic public life, which has permitted such a destructive idea to pervade meaningful social interaction from the smallest levels of interpersonal communication in classrooms to, arguably, the vast and despairing levels of foreign policy decisions in the War of Terror.[1]

Opposition to Zero Tolerance

A guiding principle behind my analyses of zero tolerance is an axiom provided by the late educational philosopher and educator Paulo Freire (2004). Freire insists throughout his work and practice that the benefit of committed and sustained critique, what he called the denouncing of "reality as it [exists]," is the "announcing of a better world" (pp. 104-105). A public vision of a better, more inclusive and humane way of living and organizing socially, politically, and economically can not be worked toward, unless concerned citizens also know, as fully as possible, what they are working against. Moreover, but less apparent, inherent in public denouncing, even if it fails to provide an explicit alternative, are the conditions of possibility for an alternative vision to be produced (see also Bourdieu, 2001 [1991], pp.127-136). For this reason, much can be gleaned implicitly from my analyses as to what might be done to unravel the power of zero tolerance and the conditions that produce it. Moreover, it is not in the greater public interests to prescribe, verbatim, what should be done. Zero tolerance is a complicated phenomenon. It must be engaged by individuals and groups within the specificity of their local contexts and in relation to a broader, democratic public vision and project. Nonetheless, schematic terms will show what existing opposition to zero tolerance looks like and what might be considered in addition to these valuable efforts.

The Efforts of Groups Opposing Zero Tolerance

Existing opposition to zero tolerance has taken various forms and their motivating interests are related but, often, equally as various. Opposition to zero tolerance is found in the efforts of public service and nonprofit organizations. There is the Advancement Project, a legal advocacy group in Washington, DC, which works on an array of legal issues surrounding schooling, access, and equality, and host of other public concerns, zero tolerance being one of them. The Harvard Civil Rights Project, often in coordination with the Advancement Project, studies issues of school policy and reform, resegregation, and zero tolerance. The Student Advocacy Center in Ann Arbor, Michigan, provides legal advice and educational support for students excluded from schools. Also in Michigan is the Institute for Public Policy and Social Research, which devotes many efforts to identifying the consequences of education policy and offer alternatives to them. In addition, the organization studies other social issues. End Zero Tolerance provides a multitude of resources for parents and students subjected to school exclusion, legal advice, and a forum in which citizens concerned about zero tolerance can participate in discussions. Building Blocks for Youth, Justice Policy Institute, Center for Juvenile and Criminal Justice, and the Applied Research Center are notable organizations concerned, sometimes indirectly, with various issues pertaining to the democratic legacy of schooling, and they have provided alternatives to or modifications for zero tolerance. Additionally, Rethinking Schools is an invaluable resource for both educators and citizens, as it not only has done valuable work on zero tolerance and related issues but also provides helpful resources for teachers and other concerned citizens.

The opposition that these groups provide typically deals with zero tolerance in policy terms. Groups like End Zero Tolerance are concerned with the complete eradication of the policy. Many of the other groups, as they recognize that the policy will exist, at least until the next Federal education plan is issued, are working with schools and state legislators to make sure adequate safeguards are in place to protect against overt abuses. For instance, the Student Advocacy Center in Michigan has led coalition efforts to force state legislators to amend the state zero tolerance policy. This coalition, All Kids in School Action!, urged the state to end permanent expulsion and cap it at 180 days for only firearm violations, the provision originally set forth by the Gun-Free Schools Act 1994 (Public Law 103-227, 1994). They have also pressured the state to require alternative and adequate education placements for excluded students, in addition to enforcing precise definitions and practices of due process for parents and students awaiting possible expulsion. The Applied Research Center has provided alternative disciplinary measures to zero tolerance, and they also have pressured both state and federal legislators to ensure that adequate measurement mechanisms are in place for schools to monitor which students are being excluded, from what schools, and for what reasons, and to reduce the uniform and disproportionate exclusion of students of color and the arbitrariness by which schools seem to exclude them.

The efforts of these groups contesting zero tolerance in policy terms are important and hopeful for a number of reasons. First and foremost, these groups demonstrate, often in public ways, that individuals and groups with greater degrees of institutional leverage, legitimacy, and resources than individual parents or caregivers are willing to contest zero tolerance as a policy that is counterproductive to educational goals. These groups have shown, in multiple useful studies, the relationships between punitive discipline practices, lower educational achievement, and school dropout rates. They are usually nongovernmental and nonprofit, and they are not subjected to the same institutional constraints as a government agency or commercial enterprise, allowing for different and potentially more democratic ways of educating parents and citizens about zero tolerance. Importantly, the groups contesting zero tolerance as a policy and offering advocacy to parents and caregivers and students often provide crucial mediating mechanisms between parents or caregivers and students and the impersonal gauntlet of the bureaucracies of larger schools. For instance, as David Rubin (2004) points out, public schools sometimes wittingly or unwittingly fail to provide necessary information to parents and students. Although, these groups provide information and often advocate on behalf of parents, caregivers, and students when the school system is unresponsive to their inquiries and demands.

Opposition to zero tolerance is also waged by national medical and legal organizations. The National Mental Health Association, American Association of Pediatrics, and American Bar Association have issued condemnations of the law and practice of zero tolerance. They tend to see the consequences of zero tolerance in very specific terms of the individual, and are concerned with the impacts of exclusion, the denial of educational opportunity, and stigmatization on the mental health of children. The efforts of these health organizations are important because zero tolerance not only produces social consequences in terms of reinforcing group disadvantage, but also inflicts very real psychological trauma on individual students subjected to punishment and exclusion. This type of opposition provides another level of criticism that can be brought to bear on the social and political consequences of zero tolerance. In other words, by demonstrating and calling attention to the impacts of zero tolerance on the mental health of children, these groups underscore a different set of moral and ethical considerations involved in the use of zero tolerance.

In the case of the American Bar Association, the primary concern with zero tolerance is the abrogation of student and civil rights. For the American Bar Association, eradication of the law and policy is preferable but, until it is eliminated, they suggest schools take adequate measures to ensure that students' constitutional rights are being protected. The opposition waged by the ABA and related legal organizations is important because it highlights the multiple legal consequences implicated in zero tolerance. The efforts of legal groups show that as zero tolerance was legislated to curtail one set of problems, namely, firearms and weapons in schools, the practice of it has created a slough of other problems, namely, the violation of Fourth and Fourteenth Amendment rights and the right to educational opportunity—cornerstones of the United States's allegedly representative, constitutional democracy.

Opposition to zero tolerance and related issues has also been produced by teachers and teacher educators, legal scholars, and social scientists (see Ayers, Dohrn, & Ayers, 2001; Burstyn, et al., 2001; Skiba & Noam, 2002). They have identified the ways that zero tolerance is both discriminatory and harmful to individual students. The alternatives they propose, outside of eliminating the law and policy, typically focus on the formation of more humane school disciplinary policies and the adequate preparation of teachers who work with students much different than them (see Akom, 2001; Noguera, 2001). Interests in the psychological and social well-being of students generally underpin their concerns, and these groups generally provide a more nuanced and informative definition of school violence that indicates the multidimensionality of school violence and shows that students are not the only, or even primary, perpetrators of violent conditions and relationships in public schools.

The efforts of these groups, and the studies they have provided, are also hopeful and important. As practicing teachers have produced some of these studies, their work underscores the fact that a group of concerned educators not only recognizes the dangers of zero tolerance but also is courageous enough to speak out and work against it. Simply, the efforts of these groups, even in some small way, convey the critically important message that not all educators are against students, and that students have advocates where they are needed. Moreover, their work, particularly that associated with Ayers, Dohrn, and Ayers, has given, often in very disturbing ways, human faces to the occasionally abstract understanding of the consequences of zero tolerance.

However, zero tolerance has rarely been addressed and opposed as a pedagogical concern (see Burstyn et al., 2001; Butchart & McEwan,

1998; Casella, 2003a; Noguera, 1995; Robbins, 2005). It has rarely been criticized and opposed for the ways in which it operates against the understanding of pedagogy as a "moral and political practice" that "provide[s] students with the knowledge, skills, and experiences that [can] enable them to understand, engage, and shape the symbolic and institutional conditions that influenc[e] their lives" (Giroux, 2001a, p. 107). These efforts demonstrate very clearly that issues of zero tolerance—as they pertain to the organization of students and teachers within public sites, the relationships between teacher authority and knowledge and student experience and voice, and how school members mediate broader social forces as they play out in the context of everyday classroom and school relationships—need to invoke and contest the deeply moral, ethical, and political implications of punitive school practices and exclusion. This work often shows that discipline strategies, whatever their normative bent, are concerned with the dissemination of authoritative messages that influence the emergence of certain sets of social relationships as opposed to others, the misallocation of life chances, and the construction of visions of future social relationships.

Additionally, the broader public, administrators and teachers miss, purposefully or incidentally, the various youth and community-based organizations that oppose zero tolerance and other laws that target and disproportionately punish youth of color. For instance, Inner City Struggle (www.schoolsnotjails.com), a Los Angeles-based organization, includes youth and adult community members from Boyle Heights in Los Angeles and East Los Angeles. This group not only provides a forum in which members of historically marginalized groups can gather and collectively work on social justice efforts, but also provide resources for dealing with and media exploring the devastating consequences of harsh laws like zero tolerance, three strikes, and Proposition 21. Schools and teachers could benefit from collaborative work with groups that are directing their efforts to self- and social-transformation (see Ginwright & Cammarota, 2002). By working with groups who have had direct experience with the consequences of zero tolerance and other weapons of oppression parading as legal devices, teachers and administrators could access the requisite knowledge and experience they need in order to better communicate with and meet the needs of populations who they consciously, or subconsciously, find disruptive or threatening to the school environment. Further, by reaching out to their communities, teachers and administrators could also contest a tacit but powerful consequence of zero tolerance: Instead of turning public schools away from their communities with the use of zero tolerance, teachers and administrators would be turning toward the very people for whom they have a moral and ethical responsibility.[2] Teachers and administrators could, in this instance, use their authority to make their schools operate as democratic public spheres in which various community members would be engaged as participants in social strategies directed toward the transformation of hierarchical and exclusionary school-community relationships. Further, as Jean Anyon (2005) and Shawn Ginwright, Julio Cammarota and Pedro Noguera (2005) poignantly demonstrate, these efforts directed at involving youth in socially just transformation vis-à-vis the process of education typically have the crucial benefit of both embracing and challenging students' cultural capital, a critical facet in the politics of exclusion attendant to the not-so-hidden curriculum. Rather than being rejected by the institution of school, students' cultural capital and modes of cultural production can be leveraged to strengthen communities and their access to vital resources (i.e., produce social capital); produce student attachment to the community and the educational process, whether in the school, the community, or in linking school and community energies and interests; and increase the involvement of parents, caregivers, and other community stakeholders in the radical possibilities of community and societal transformation. All this while helping students develop multiple literacies in public talk and engagement through pursuing research and writing reports relevant to addressing particular community needs; creating and performing presentations to politicians, business people, and other powerful groups; organizing and conducting public forums and performances; and producing and distributing multiple forms of literature throughout the community and to other local, regional, national, and international communities.

This list of groups and the characteristics of their efforts is not all inclusive. It is provided only to demonstrate that viable possibilities exist for opposing zero tolerance as a law, policy, and practice. There are many other groups working on similar and equally as valuable efforts. Existing opposition, however, could be augmented by articulating their various specific efforts around a common project of reconstituting the democratic legacy of schooling. (1) Coordinating efforts around a common project would better demonstrate how many specific consequences are related. They are not mutually exclusive problems and, taken together, they could signal something entirely different than the loss of opportunity, psychological trauma, abrogation of student rights, or disproportionate exclusion of students of color. Calling attention to and working to resolve these specific consequences of zero tolerance are important, but when these consequences are perceived collectively, a much larger problem manifests: an attack on youth and public schools—two central facets in the promotion of a democratic polity. (2) Coordinating their efforts around a common project of reclaiming the democratic legacy of schooling would provide the most effective counter to zero tolerance because it allows for widening the terms and conditions of publicness by which the problem can be approached and contested, that is, concerted efforts directed at contesting zero tolerance as an affront to schools as democratic public spheres, and democratic public life, which could provide the social relationships capable of contesting the ideological power of zero tolerance and the structures of fear that it reinforces. As is demonstrated in much of this research, zero tolerance is not necessarily new; the disproportionate exclusion of students of color and poor White students was well-ingrained in the structure of public schooling before zero tolerance. Zero tolerance simply intensifies and makes acceptable the push-out process in schools. Thus, articulating their interests around a common project of reconstituting the democratic legacy of education provides the conditions in which these and other groups of concerned citizens can better address the wide-ranging historical trappings and social moorings of zero tolerance.

It is worth reemphasizing the importance of the relationships between school organization and funding, teacher practice, and the use of zero tolerance. What is conveyed here not only suggests why existing opposition to zero tolerance needs to be connected and centered on a common project of making public schooling democratic, but also suggests what might be better emphasized in the preparation of teachers. Noguera (1995, 2001, 2003) and Casella (2001) have succinctly addressed the related issues of school organization, teacher practice, and zero tolerance. A brief look at these relationships will tacitly lead to the broader issues and social struggles that should be considered and taken up in order to reclaim the democratic legacy of public schooling and, by default, oppose zero tolerance in its ideological form.

School organization and funding structures, coupled with a punishing accountability scheme, play an underlying, sometimes unrecognized or ignored role in zero tolerance (see also Noguera, 2003; Johnson, Boyden, & Pittz et al., 2001; Zweifler & De Beers, 2002). (By school organization,

I mean the characteristics of the structure and practices of power (author-ity) in schools. In an individualized and competitive broader social order, it is unsurprising that corporate models of early forms of school admin-istration and teacher authority still exist. These forms of school admin-istration and teacher authority are highly individualized. The organization of curricula, time and space, teacher labor, and student relationships in cellular fashion are divorced from each other and the wider social, po-litical, and economic relationships in which they are moored (see also Noguera, 1995; Giroux, 1988). This historic shortcoming is only inten-sified and further embedded in both the structure of school relationships and the psyches of administrators, teachers, and students by an account-ability scheme that understands and constructs funding not along the lines of the common public good or school-community needs, but in the terms of punishments and rewards. It casts public schooling not as a given and precondition for democratic social order, but as a prize in a com-petition that takes place in and supports an iniquitous market order (see Pepper, 2006). From the school district to the classroom, school profes-sionals and students are pitted in a fierce, individualized competition over scarcified social resources by being held accountable—on grossly unequal resources—for achievement on a limited range of skills and knowledges. Preexisting to zero tolerance, this testing process was widely noted to have disadvantaged students already disadvantaged by racial oppression and class inequalities (see Orfield & Kornhaber, 2001). Moreover, this form of variable support and disinvestment in public schools has simply been superimposed on preexisting, disparate school funding formulae based on a combination of local property tax, state funds, and federal allocations. Consequently, students already placed at risk are seen as risks to teacher competency evaluations and school funding. Zero tolerance comes to the rescue by pushing these students, who are socially con-structed as the most needy (Noguera, 2003), out of school, because the resources needed to undo their neediness are scarcified and redistributed upwards to students who can perform well on tests, and to wealthier schools and districts.

However, zero tolerance does two destructive things, and these consequences are reinforced when zero tolerance operates at the same time as other punitive forces, such as unequal funding, school segrega-tion, and testing-punishment schemes. One, zero tolerance demeans teachers and dehumanizes students. It encourages teachers to ignore their own deficiencies in understanding the social and cultural capital of students (Akom, 2001; Noguera, 1995, 2001; Robbins, 2005), and to abdicate professional responsibility for correcting that deficiency and learning how to use student knowledge as a resource for democratic classroom and social relationships that are structurally, intellectually, emotionally, socially, and physically safer. As Donaldo Macedo and Lilia Bartolome (1999) point out in a different context, "Acknowledging and using existing student language and knowledge makes good pedagogical sense, and it constitutes a humanizing experience for students traditionally *de*humanized and disempowered in the schools" (p. 131).

The underlying issue, specifically in relation to school organization, funding structures and accountability regimes, is that zero tolerance prohibits teachers and professionals from developing "political clarity" (Macedo & Bartolome, 1999) about the nature and effects of their work. Zero tolerance permits already burdened and increasingly pressured teachers to lose sight of the broader political forces that strip them of their professional dignity, making it, even if operating at a subconscious level, seem appropriate or natural to strip students of their dignity. Further, zero tolerance taps preexisting administrator beliefs about their work. As zero tolerance is an individualized and highly instrumentalized practice, it reinforces the technocratic rationality by which administrators deal with social and political antagonisms in schools and communities (see Larson, 1997). Zero tolerance does this because it works ideologically by referencing a broader social structure of fear, surveillance, punishment, and exclusion that blinds teachers—or encourages them to blind themselves—to the classroom, school, and social conditions and relationships that pit them against "dangerous," but more typically unwanted, students. Simply, zero tolerance dangerously reduces the conditions of possibility by which teachers and other school professionals can work, and the diverse histories from which they emerge, in a shared process of meaning-making—the production of "existential significance" (see Freire, 1997; Staples, 2000) for which they are not only mutually responsible but also to which they can equally contribute.

Two, zero tolerance helps constitute teacher, administrator, and school authority as an incontestable given that is protected from self-, student, and social critique. The underside to this consequence is not only an authoritarian conception of authority, but also the promotion of teachers' inabilities to recognize their authority as a shared force in producing inclusive, democratic school relationships. For instance, zero tolerance suggests that teachers have the right to choose which students, under what conditions, and for what reasons are excluded, implying that teachers are completely cognizant of all the contextual factors informing student behavior and unquestionably competent in responding to them. Zero tolerance thus strips teachers of responsibility for punitive decisions, while reinforcing the misconception that teacher knowledge is omniscient and teacher authority should be dominative and abusive. Because the underlying conditions of classroom and school relationships go unchanged, and because they pass unquestioned or unquestionable, zero tolerance permits teacher authority to be conceived in authoritarian terms. It also reproduces the subconscious structures of fear that mobilize sedimented beliefs about what students pose the most dangers to classroom and school life. How else, as Pedro Noguera (2003) points out in a related context, can the uniform and disproportionate exclusion of African American, Latino, and poor white students in disparate school contexts, and as a result of equally disparate definitions of zero tolerance, be explained?

This (de)skilling and abdication of teacher practice and responsibility and demeaning of students, with the assistance of zero tolerance, obviously is not the result of a few irresponsible teachers. It suggests more than a subversion of the democratic legacy of schooling. In part, these processes of (de)skilling and demeaning are the result of zero tolerance as the glue that binds authoritarian forms of school organization, iniquitous funding structures, and punitive, often politically misinformed, teacher practices. And, it goes without saying, these forms of school organization and teacher practices, while being enacted in the classroom and schools, gain meaning and power in relation to a wider set of relationships. Schools and, more specifically, classrooms are primary sites for the practice of zero tolerance, but the whole way of life in the contemporary United States under the survival of the fittest rule of neoliberalism is the site of production for zero tolerance. For this reason, any opposition to zero tolerance, especially considering its ideological power, must also be concerned with the wider social forces that not only promote and temporarily benefit from the antidemocratic organization and support of public schooling, but also use zero tolerance as a smokescreen for the dangerous school, community, and social relationships they produce. Put differently, zero tolerance does not simply countermand the democratic legacy of public schooling, it negates the promise of democracy from which the democratic legacy of schooling emerged by justifying the conditions of individualization, fear, and punishment that have become central features of U.S. society under neoliberalism and social conservatism.

The relationship between zero tolerance and fear can not be understated. Fear is a powerful political tool, as Corey Robin (2004) convincingly demonstrates. For this reason, teachers and school professionals must be aware of how zero tolerance and fear are mutually constitutive, especially in a political climate in which individualization, atomization, suspicion, and brute force are animating categories of social (inter)action. As zero tolerance garners considerable power, teachers, administrators, and concerned citizens need to ask central questions about the negative social consequences of zero tolerance on students of color, and about who or what class benefits from the practice of zero tolerance, how zero tolerance undermines safe and democratic school relationships, how zero tolerance subverts teacher responsibility and authority, how fear, instead of political courage, guides teacher practices, sometimes against teachers' better interests, and how zero tolerance is related to a sweeping assault on youth in general, the democratic legacy of schooling, and democracy itself.

Conclusion and Beginning: The Promise of Democracy and Hope

To say zero tolerance functions ideologically in a whole way of life, is to say that zero tolerance is the catchword for a set of discourses, "captivating images," and meanings that are used by "groups and classes of people" in attempts to explain and understand the world(s) in which they live (see Hall, 1996). According to this understanding of ideology, zero tolerance is not merely symbolic—that should be obvious from the previous analyses of the phenomenon in this study. Since zero tolerance is supported by a set of discourses that are produced by the social relationships of classes of people in relation to other classes and groups of people, it tacitly refers to the hierarchies of power and the material conditions in which those discourses gain meaning. To whom does zero tolerance apply? For what behaviors is zero tolerance used? Under what conditions is zero tolerance practiced? To what effects is zero tolerance practiced? Who primarily wins, and who loses, as a result of zero tolerance? How do practitioners of zero tolerance explain the need for it? How do they mediate the gaping distance between the need for zero tolerance and the practice of it? How do predominant public discourses support or reject the ideology of zero tolerance? What classes and factions promote discourses about zero tolerance? In relation to what other discourses and social forces is the imagined need for zero tolerance mobilized?

Zero tolerance was a bipartisan strategy, constructed at the contradictory but powerful interstices of neoliberalism and social conservatism. It deals with the social symptoms of a new economic order, erasing the social contract, and perpetuating racism in a color-blind consumer society. It was, then, obviously brought to public schools, as they were one of the last substantive public spaces that had not been infected by the material and symbolic terrorism of neoliberalism. As a partisan strategy, zero tolerance has helped to justify other processes conducive to partisan interests: criminalization and militarization. The combined consequences of a new economic order, the waning social state, and the processes of criminalization and militarization are a significantly altered, if barely existent, democratic public sphere and, due to the lack of democratic public intercourse, a rampant culture and industry of fear. Consequently, what was originally a partisan strategy has become more or less a commonsense ideology under conditions in which individuals have little time or space to discuss not only their needs but also how the relationships producing those needs could be otherwise. Here, I am thinking of core existential needs that demand social and political structures and conditions to support them, but are undermined, in part, by zero tolerance: safety, security, and certainty (see Bauman, 1999).

Think of the various and highly disparate manifestations of zero tolerance that, in their own ways, produce unsafety, insecurity, and uncertainty. Zero tolerance was the guiding metaphor behind the now publicly apparent, dubious rationale for the War of Terror's devastation in Iraq, and the global disdain and hostility that is responding to it, even if the corporate media fail to report on this consequence of the War of Terror. The strategy of choice for dealing with a perceived threat to national security is not sustained investigation and public debate, but punishment, atrocity, and spectacle on a vast scale. Zero tolerance is the backdrop to attacks on dissent, parading as patriotic missions to protect U.S. interests. In this case, it acts under the name of U.S. democracy to shut down what plays a fundamental part in democratic public life. Zero tolerance underpins attacks on the social state writ large. Constituencies of politicians, democrats and republicans alike, are to be intolerant of sponges and lazy people, but be compassionate for the needy. As if in the ever shifting terrain of the construction of public enemies most citizens can distinguish between who might be lazy or needy. The United States is chided about a burdensome, inefficient government, at the same time the other side of that government extracts over $700 billion annually for the Department of Defense alone and creates multitrillion dollar debt through repeated tax cuts for the wealthiest 1% of income earners. On any register that it has been deployed, zero tolerance has not, in any qualitative capacity, made people safer, more secure, or their futures more certain. It has, in a very deep sense, reinforced the structures of fear and violence they inhabit in a privatized and individualized social order. The list above could proceed almost endlessly, but it points to a clear but by no means easy alternative: a renewed interest in reconstructing democratic public life.

The clear alternative to zero tolerance is a renewed interest in democratic public life; struggles over the larger conditions would make it possible for at least three reasons. One, zero tolerance is simply antithetical to democratic public life and the form of government that is required to protect it. Zero tolerance is, first and foremost, exclusionary. Democracy, as a political form, and democratization, as a social agenda, is inclusionary. This is because tolerance is a precondition for the basic socialities fundamental to a shared social existence. This is not to suggest that tolerance be an end to democracy, rather, it is to suggest that, without tolerance and an ontological sense of responsibility for the other, people are unable to engage each other in ways that would allow them to produce mutual respect for each other and a common commitment to widening the social conditions in which others could do the same. The excessive, often unjust exclusions that are encouraged by zero tolerance simply countermand the conditions and modes of sociality that are capable of making such a commitment possible. What remains in the absence of tolerance and inclusive social practices is one form of violence responding to the symptoms of another form of violence through social exclusion.

Two, democratic public life and efforts to produce it provide the forms of social interaction and the production of existential significance that, in turn, ensure greater safety, security, and certainty. With more publicness, transparency of behaviors, and shared responsibility for the conditions in which citizens live, safety is an ostensible by-product. This is, for instance, something that has been documented in studies of small schools. By having enriched interactions with others for whom one (or a group) feels responsible, a greater sense of security is produced, as potential threats to individual or collective safety are reduced. The publicness enabled by spheres of common interaction, trust, respect, support, debate, dialogue, dissensus, and consensus—the democratic public sphere—provide the conditions in which individuals and groups can develop mutual, if also contested and contestable, interests and investments in the future, in other words, develop greater certainty about the "mode" by which the future will function (see Grossberg, 2001, p. 133). This implies that citizens would be able to create new, revised, or reclaimed narratives and ideologies that not only reflected the relationships in which they participate but also provide the common terms by which they could become more responsible for one another. This is a critical facet of reconstituting democratic public life, while promoting safety, security, and certainty, as Nick Couldry (2004) and Paulo Freire (1997) point out in different but related ways. Couldry notes that, in large part, citizens are the incomplete stories they tell themselves, and without the stories one is left incomplete. Without knowing the stories others tell, one may be insecure, unsafe, and uncertain about one's place and role in the order of things. Freire claims repeatedly that common social interaction and committed inquiry into its conditions of possibility, and the conditions of possibility for other forms of human existence, is the foundational element in the human "ontological vocation" (Freire, 1997, p. 54) —that becoming more human(e) is a social process which, a fortiori, can only be done in the company of others.

Three, a consequence to one and two, a renewed interest in democratic public life cannot take shape unless individuals and groups make demands on the social state to devolve the provisions that both enable greater material, social, and political safety, security, and certainty, and protect the conditions in which citizens can take greater control over the terms of governance. Such a struggle might entail shifting social values away from mass violence, or the tacit support of it, by diverting social and economic resources from the military-prison-entertainment-industrial complex to the democratic-public, welfare-shared social responsibility complex. As William DiFazio (2003) notes, a provision could also be made to reduce the work week to 30 hours, without less pay, so individuals and groups, particularly those strapped by time and lack of resources, can participate in civic life. A default provision here would have to be reinvestment in, which presupposes recommitting to, the democratic legacy of public schooling. This would be necessary so students could learn the skills and develop the social identities crucial to participating in democratic public life. As Zygmunt Bauman (1999) argues, democratic social order is not possible unless it supports institutions in their efforts to educate future citizens about civic life.

Although reconstituting democratic public life is an immense order beset by any number of challenges, it is a pivotal part in the process of reclaiming the democratic legacy of public schooling and contesting zero tolerance. More importantly, the dangers of not participating are too despairing: constant fear, paranoia, and cynicism; building more prisons and fewer schools; making more criminals and less citizens and generating more fear, punishment, and exclusion; the tacit support of wanton violence on local, national, and global scales, and critically, the concomitant rejection of both the past and future that results from the absence of a space-time through which the past and future can be claimed, contested, reconstructed, and articulated in the interests of a more just democratic existence.

In these closing thoughts, I will skim the surface of why hope, a critical, educated hope, must be the guiding force and binding element between the related projects of reconstituting the democratic legacy of public schooling and protecting the promise of a democratic future. Hope, as Roger I. Simon (1992) points out, is not mere wishing or delusions of grandeur. Hope is the composite of private dreams translated into public visions and commitments, one that expands human possibility. As Simon states, hope is the driving principle of a "political project" that enables people "to assess and pursue knowledge forms in relation to their power to contest axes of material and symbolic violence" (p. 17). Hope inherently has a critical edge. It enables people to identify—and implicitly denounce—the social relationships and conditions that do violence, in any form, by claiming publicly that a different type of human existence is possible and desired.

By taking account of possibility, and its conditions of possibility, hope is reasoned. This is what David Halpin (2001) calls "ultimate hope:"

[I]t refracts back on the present, holding up to it the prospect of a better way of life—for oneself, for others and for society generally—while recognising (sic) there are likely to be obstacles on the way that need to be *challenged* and *overcome*. (italics added. p. 397)

In this way, hope places demands on citizen capacities to read material and symbolic violence and critically interrogate the ethical actions to undo it. Hope should be given pedagogical grounding and developed as "educated hope" (Giroux, 2004). Educated hope is the underlying principle of a pedagogical process that

makes concrete the possibility for transforming politics into an ethical space and public act that confronts the flow of everyday experience and the weight of social suffering with the force of individual and collective resistance and the unending project of democratic social transformation. (p. 137)

Critical, educated hope is fundamental to reconstituting democratic public life because if it is understood and practiced as sketched immediately above, it recognizes that the promise of democracy is never completely fulfilled. The promise of democracy is the other side of hope, the forward push of the future, or the possibility of a democratic future, which allows hope to take root in the present. Hope keeps issues of justice, fairness, respect, social responsibility, and social transformation on the public agenda. Without hope, there is no need for such questions. Hope is constituted in social relationships and, for that reason, requires a democratic public space for those relationships to emerge, ensuring the space will exist for future generations (see Arendt, 1958). Without educated hope, the ability to construct and cast visions of different, more desirable futures—a peculiarly human capacity, we cease to be human (Bauman, 2004b).

Hope must also be part of the struggles to reclaim the democratic legacy of public education. Being critical and educated, hope has the sober recognition of the present, what has made it such, and what needs to occur for it to be otherwise. It also places ethical demands on how we approach the future. What would hope be if it did not refer implicitly to youth? Consequently, the foundational opposition to forces such as zero tolerance is hope. Public education still has a central role in keeping the promise of democracy open. Where, if not in public schools, can youth struggle over the definition of subjectivities and social identities skilled and courageous enough to work for the wider conditions that make democratic public life possible and articulate a just, more inclusive future? This hope has been enunciated. The challenge now is to have the respect, openness, trust, and civic courage to act, as mutually responsible members of a shared social fate, as if the future mattered, and has already begun to emerge, by talking and acting as if youth matters.

Appendix

Studies About or Related to Zero Tolerance

Studies About or Related to Zero Tolerance

Types	Authors	Themes
Legal	Beger (2002); Bell (2001); Blankenau & Leeper (2003); Blumenson & Nilson (2002); Browne (2003); Dunbar & Villarruel (2002); Eskenazi, Eddins, & Beam (2003); Ginsburg & Demeranville (2001); Hunter, Russo, & Brown (2002); Losen & Edley (2001); Rubin (2003); Schwarz & Rieser (2001); Sughrue (2003); Zweifler & DeBeers (2002)	• Deviation, distortion, extension of zero tolerance in legislative process • Increase in school-based arrests • Circumvention of special education laws codified in IDEA 1975 • Violation of Fourth Amendment rights, particularly around issues of reasonable/unreasonable searches • Violation of Fourteenth Amendment rights, particularly around issues of due process and Miranda • Zero tolerance law and practices exist amidst complex of demographics and resource distribution
Educational opportunity	Advancement Project/Harvard Civil Rights Project (2000); Blumenson & Nilson (2002); Gordon, Piana, & Keleher (2000); Michigan Public Policy Initiative (2003); Morrison et al. (2002); Polakow-Suransky (2000); Richart, Brooks, & Soler (2003); Skiba & Peterson (1999); Skiba (2000 & 2001); Stone-Palmquist (2004); Zweifler & DeBeers (2002)	• Suspension and expulsion through zero tolerance is a process rather than merely an event • Middle-years students (of color) primary victims of suspension and expulsion; correlation between school exclusion and later school drop-out or push-out (10th grade) • Overrepresentation of students with disabilities or identifiable risk factors in exclusions since legislation of zero tolerance • Schools linked directly to criminal and juvenile justice system through zero tolerance policies; damaging effects of youth being detained in detention centers for nonviolent, previously noncriminal behaviors; excluded students and families have difficulty finding alternative education placements, or alternative education placements are wanting and undersupervised

Studies About or Related to Zero Tolerance (*continued*)

Types	Authors	Themes
Social-cultural contexts in public schools	Akom (2001); Ayers, Dohrn, & Ayers (2001); Casella (2001); Dohrn (2001); Donahue et al. (1998); Ladson-Billings (2001); Noguera (1995, 2001, 2003)	• Media representations of and political discourses about youth are racialized and not only inform and shape (zero tolerance) policy, but also teachers' responses to students • Zero tolerance is imposed on preexisting organizational structure of schools and further polarizes and atomizes student-teacher relationships, leaving conditions for reproduction of fear unaltered • Violence is produced on different levels in schools, and exists on continuum of violence in rest of society
Critical	Giroux (2003)	• Neoliberal economic and cultural policies empty democratic public life by commercializing and militarizing public institutions and space, and eliminating critical and democratic forms of citizenship • Zero tolerance is a law and practice that helps rationalize other forces impacting schools (e.g., testing, standardization, choice) and operating in society (e.g., politics of fear, individualism, competition, etc.)

As mentioned in chapter 1, articles on zero tolerance have appeared in venues ranging from alternative weeklies to esteemed legal journals. This list of studies is not exhaustive, but it is provided as a reference for the broad themes addressed by studies of zero tolerance. I chose these works because in some cases 1) experts on zero tolerance wrote them, 2) they are relatively comprehensive perspectives on zero tolerance, or 3) due to a study's unique approach to a particular consequence of zero tolerance, it provides pertinent observations about the law and practice of zero tolerance in general.

Notes

Introduction

1. This rate of disproportionality for African American school exclusion translates into a national rate of exclusion of 33%, while African American students are only 17% of the national school population. Office of Civil Rights, U.S. Department of Education, Fall 1998 "Elementary and Secondary School Civil Rights Compliance Report: National and State Projections (2000). Washington, DC: Government Printing Office.

2. The preeminent sociologist C. Wright Mills (2000 [1959]) suggested that responsible intellectuals "will try to do [their] work in awareness of its assumptions and implications, not the least of which are its moral and political meaning for the society in which [they] work . . ." (p. 77). In this spirit and in brief terms, I wish to introduce here the assumptions and potential implications of this work. C. Wright Mills, *The Sociological Imagination* (Fortieth Anniversary Edition), (New York: Oxford University Press, 2000 [1959]).

3. The issue of the changing public perception of and involvement with public schools is what will later background my analyses of zero tolerance, not that public schools strongly served the interests of an inclusive democracy and processes of democratization in the past.

Chapter 1

1. My choice to place a particular study in one category or another is purposeful, mindful of the particular features of zero tolerance being addressed. For instance, Browne's *Derailed: The Schoolhouse to Jailhouse Track* is a sweeping study that could be addressed in the legal, educational opportunity, or social-cultural contexts in/of schools sections, but it provides central insights to both the specific and general legal implications of zero tolerance. Thus, I address it in the legal implications section. J. Browne, *Derailed: The Schoolhouse*

to Jailhouse Track (Washington, DC: Advancement Project, 2003). Alternately, Dohrn's (2001) "Look out kid, It's something you did" is similarly a wide-ranging analysis of zero tolerance that is primarily concerned with the proliferation of laws that criminalize youth/youthful behaviors. However, Dohrn's study is helpful in understanding the contemporary political climate and shifting political discourses on youth. Thus, I review Dohrn's study in the social-cultural contexts in the schools chapter. See B. Dohrn, "Look out, kid, It's something you did": Zero Tolerance for Children, in Ayers, Dohrn, and Ayers (Eds.), *Zero Tolerance: Resisting the Drive for Punishment in Our Schools* (New York: Basic Books) 2006, pp. 89–113. For easy reference to the many studies of or related to zero tolerance, see the Appendix.

2. Although the denial of educational opportunity is indeed a legal concern, I approach the relationship between zero tolerance and educational opportunity as a separate category. I make this distinction in the studies because the articles that deal with the legal implications of zero tolerance generally focus only on explicit law-related concerns. The studies I place under the educational opportunity section take a more holistic approach to the impacts on educational opportunity by drawing out the long-term social consequences of the denial of educational opportunity.

3. The Gun-Free Schools Act of 1994 states: "No assistance may be provided to any local educational agency under this Act unless such agency has in effect a policy requiring the expulsion from school for a period of not less than one year of any student who is determined to have brought a weapon to a school under the jurisdiction of the agency." See Public Law 103-227.

4. Michigan is not alone in expanding teachers' power to remove students without administrative oversight. In 2000, New York City Mayor Guliani passed the SAVE Act, which permitted teachers and school security officers to remove students from schools for up to four days without administrative oversight.

5. Sansbury reports that in the Fall 2003, DeKalb County Schools in Georgia alone spent $8.9 million on "digital security upgrades." What's more, in the aftermath of 9/11, President Bush set aside $350 million for schools to purchase security devices. See J. Sansbury, "Schools Go Eye Tech, County Spending nearly $9 Million on Upgrades," *Atlanta Journal-Constitution,* September 25, 2003, p. JA1. All of this is purchased, ironically, when schools are failing to provide updated computer technologies, qualified teachers, adequate infrastructure, and quality curricular resources. These observations will be elaborated in chapter 3.

6. Recall that students are excluded from schools in the majority of cases for disruption and disorderly conduct.

7. Cases regarding zero tolerance violation of Eighth Amendment rights (e.g., protections against cruel and unusual punishment) have been heard. But,

again, because state and federal courts defer, in most instances, to local school autonomy, appeals on this violation have been rejected. See J. A. Sughrue, "Zero Tolerance for Children: Two Wrongs Don't Make a Right," *Educational Administration Quarterly* 39(2) (2003), 238–258. See also D. Rubin *Michigan's failure to provide due process rights for children*. Unpublished manuscript. Ann Arbor: University of Michigan Law School and the Student Advocacy Center, 2004.

8. These protections are as follows: notice of time frame for hearing and parental contact, accommodation of student's and parents' schedule for meeting dates, sufficient notice, explanation of evidence and the opportunity to be heard, students and parents/guardians are informed of school's conduct code, and the provision of a rudimentary adversarial meeting.

9. Browne's examples are telling. Browne notes that "a six year-old was arrested in Palm Beach County Florida for trespassing on school property . . . [as] [t]he student was walking through the school yard, after school hours, on his way home" (p. 11). She cites the case where elementary students in Mississippi were arrested and taken to the local jail "for talking during assembly" (p. 11). Browne documents how a student with emotional and behavioral disorders was arrested 18 times between fourth and fifth grade. One of his arrests and subsequent school exclusions was for "projecting a deadly missile onto an occupied structure," after he threw "a rock at a portable classroom building" (p. 27). Richart et al., (2003) found school exclusions and school-based arrests to occur on similar grounds with high frequency in Kentucky during the 2000–2001 school year. See D. Richart et al., "Unintended Consequences: The Impact of "Zero Tolerance" and Other Exclusionary Policies on Kentucky Students" (*Building Blocks for Youth*, http://www.buildingblocksforyouth.org/kentucky/kentucky.html, 2003).

10. While Eskenazi et al., quantify this relationship between resources and behaviors, it is a long-standing caveat of even behavioral strands of educational psychology: If students are engaged in meaningful learning environments, they are less prone to participate in inappropriate behaviors in those environments. See Eskenazi et al., *Equity or Exclusion: The Dynamics of Resources, Demographics, and Behavior in the New York City Public Schools* (Fordham University: National Center for Schools and Communities, 2003).

11. This useful analogy comes from Stuart Henry (2000). See S. Henry, "What is School Violence? An Integrated Definition," in W. G. Hinkle and S. Henry (Eds.) *School Violence* (pp. 16–29). The Annals of the American Academy of Political and Social Science Vol. 567 (Thousand Oaks, CA: Sage, 2000).

12. I would like to enter an important caveat here. Obviously, not all teachers conduct their classrooms in this fashion. However, all teachers conduct their classrooms in an intensely individualized and competitive educational climate that, as will be addressed later in this chapter, is simply prohibitive for teachers to use and incorporate these more social considerations.

13. Many of the "Narratives" in Ayers, Dohrn, and Ayers (2001) provide compelling stories of this process. See Ayers, Dohrn, and Ayers, *Zero Tolerance: Resisting the Drive for Punishment in Our Schools* (New York: Basic Books, 2001). Stone-Palmquist's (2004) miniethnography also provides insights to the difficulties students and parents face when trying to find alternative educational placements. They are provided conditions in which they learn to devalue the educational process, simply cannot provide for alternative education placements, or the students are deterred by the possibility that an alternative placement will not allow them to complete their schooling in a timely manner—a consideration that obviously impacts class minorities (of any color) more than those students of wealthier backgrounds who can procure adequate alternative education placements and for whom time is not so preciously coveted and scarce. See P. Stone-Palmquist, "Education after Expulsion," Unpublished manuscript (Ann Arbor, MI: Student Advocacy Center, 2004). See also, S. Polakow-Suransky, "America's Least Wanted: Zero Tolerance Policies and the Fate of Expelled Students," in V. Polakow (Ed.), *The Public Assault on America's Children: Poverty, Violence, and Juvenile Justice* (New York: Teachers College Press, 2000), pp. 101–129.

14. Similar patterns in rates of exclusion and disproportionality along racial lines were found in Florida, Maryland, Texas, California, and Kentucky. See Browne op. cit, and Richart et al., op. cit.

15. In recent years, zero tolerance for phones and paging devices has lessened. In fact, Maryland and other states have since changed their zero tolerance laws regarding cell phones and pagers. Although these changes are promising in that they demonstrate some states' willingness to alter their zero tolerance policies, this particular issue does not come without a racial or, possibly, racist subtext. Pagers and cell phones were initially seen as tools of the alleged drug economies and gang activities of black urban youth, thus the previously stringent policies against them. However, as a *New York Times* writer states, "Rather than banning the phones outright, as many once did, [school administrations] are capitulating to *parent demands and market realities*, and allowing students to carry phones in school—though not to use them in class" (italics added. Richtel, 2004, p. A1). Apparently, once the consequences of a punitive policy hit wealthier and whiter schools and a market rationale can counter the policy, then things like cell phones are no longer racialized symbols of thugs, drugs and danger, but "tools used by parents to keep in touch with, and keep track of, their children" (Richtel, p. A1). As if some angst-ridden White, suburban teens are incapable of using cell phones to contact friends outside of school to carryout a school shooting or make contacts for after-school drug deals, or as if Black parents could not have previously used the cellphones and pagers to keep track of their kids. See M. Richtel, "School Cellphone Bans Topple (You Can't Suspend Everyone)," *New York Times*, January 4, 2004, A1, A16.

16. These seemingly absurd, if not brutal, practices of zero tolerance occur frequently. See http://www.ztnightmares.com/html/zero_tolerance_nightmare_.htm.

17. Internal citations from these works will refer to Ayers, Dohrn, and Ayers (Eds.) op. cit. Although other studies (Giroux, 1999; Males 1996) are deeply instructive in this area, the works from Ayers, Dohrn, and Ayers are used because they focus on the relationship between zero tolerance and the redefinition of youth. See, H. A. Giroux, *Stealing Innocence: Youth, Corporate Power, and the Politics of Culture* (New York: St. Martin's, 1999). M. Males, *The Scapegoat Generation: America's War on Adolescents* (Monroe, ME: Common Courage Press, 1996).

18. Internal page citations will reference Noguera (1995), "Preventing and Producing Violence: A Critical Analysis of Responses to School Violence," *Harvard Educational Review*, 65(2), pp. 189–212. Casella (2001), *At Zero Tolerance: Punishment, Prevention, and School Violence* (New York: Lang).

19. Casella (2003a) has since extended this earlier study of zero tolerance, studying it specifically within strands of rationale choice theory predominating wider criminal justice policy. Rationale choice theory suggests that, all things being equal, individuals will make a conscious choice to participate or not in criminal activity when given explicit deterrents against it. Of course, as Casella points out, such an understanding of social action elides how conditions informing crimes are unequal and the underlying factors of certain criminal acts in specific contexts don't fit the universal rationale of the law. See Casella (2003a), Zero Tolerance Policy in Schools: Rationale, Consequences, and Alternatives, *Teachers College Record, 105*(5), pp. 872–892.

20. For a sophisticated analysis of the relationship between fear and learning, see Paulo Freire, *Pedagogy of the Oppressed* (New York: Seabury Press, 1970).

21. In this section, I will not specifically address the colorline. The impacts of zero tolerance on youth of color were clearly enumerated earlier; it goes without saying that with the features of neoliberalism and zero tolerance to be addressed in this section, youth of color and youth marginalized by class inequalities bear a substantially greater brunt of the consequences from the problem of zero tolerance.

22. Internal citations will refer to Giroux (2001a), "Youth, Domestic Militarization, and the Politics of Zero Tolerance" in *Public Spaces/Private Lives*, Lanham, MD: Rowman & Littlefield, pp. 29–54.

23. Consider Clinton's PRWORA 1996 welfare reform. Of the many things this reform does, it forces predominantly single women with children, without government-sponsored childcare, into low wage jobs and, when receiving their time-sensitive social support, they are monitored closely for criminal behavior such as alcohol abuse and drug use, conditions for revoking their funds. For a concise analysis of PRWORA 1996, see Polakow, op. cit. See also,

G. Delgado (Ed.), *From Poverty to Punishment: How Welfare Reform Punishes the Poor* (Oakland, CA: Applied Research Center, 2002).

Chapter 2

1. Although I understand that the liberal social contract came under attack most fiercely with the Reagan presidency beginning in 1981, a large portion of the attack having been waged on public schools, I tentatively include 1991 as the reference point where public education started to be turned away from its responsibilities to the social contract, as this was the year in which the first steps to zero tolerance in schools were taken in the passage of the Gun-Free School Zones Act.

2. In *Between Fear and Hope: Globalization and Race in the United States* (Lanham, MD: Rowman & Littlefield, 2003), A. Barlow demonstrates how as the government reduces, if not entirely cuts, social provisions, the state is used to support practices of private investment and accumulation, as opposed to those which support public investment and social gain.

3. For a sharp analysis of how public schools, when engaged primarily in the service of economic interests, are used for private gain and operate as commodities, see L. Bartlett et al., (2002), "The Marketization of Education: Public Schools for Private Ends," *Anthropology and Education Quarterly*, *33*(1), 5–29. See also, A. Molnar, *Giving Kids the Business: The Commercialization of America's Schools* (Boulder, CO: Westview Press, 1996).

4. Although I recognize that the social contract has a long history, extending to enlightenment philosophers such as Hobbes, Locke, and Rousseau, I am purposefully invoking a different tradition. For instance, Hobbes's notion of the social contract has much more in common with George W. Bush's ownership society than it does with the socially protective and augmenting tendencies of the social contract associated with the welfare state. Hobbes's conception of the social contract was an agreement between the state and wealthy propertied, White males that suggested the government was to protect only propertied interests (and, in some cases, promote the conditions that made the accumulation of more property possible, directing power and resources continually upward).

5. I will take up the process of criminalization later in this chapter and more specifically in chapters 3 and 4. Militarization, and especially its current impacts on schools, will be addressed fully in the next chapter.

6. The operative word here is place. Although some students actively choose these tracks which can serve useful functions when adequately supported and maintained within a broader economic context that engage students who go through them, the question is under what conditions, with what

consequences, and to whose benefit are certain students placed in these tracks. For an elaboration of these points, see R. Casella, *At Zero Tolerance: Punishment, Prevention, and School Violence* (New York: Peter Lang, 2001).

7. It goes without saying that public schools are not the only sites of deregulation. Social welfare has been reduced and, in some cases, the management of it has been turned over to corporations. The prison system has, during the last 20 years, become dominated by corporate entities such as Wackenhut, CCCA, and others, who have made a multibillion dollar per year industry out of the criminalization of non-violent offenders. See G. Delgado (Ed.), *From Poverty to Punishment: How Welfare Reform Punishes the Poor* (Oakland, CA: Applied Research Center, 2002) and V. Polakow (Ed.), *The Public Assault on America's Children: Poverty, Violence, and Juvenile Justice* (New York: Teachers College Press, 2000), especially 1–18, for analyses of the social welfare system.

8. What follows in this section will be explored in greater detail in chapter 4.

9. In *No Equal Justice: Race and Class in the American Criminal Justice System* (New York: The New Press, 1999), Cole provides an incisive analysis of quality of life policing. In particular, he notes that many civil liberties of African Americans and other minorities were violated regularly by what some critics call Giuliani's reign of terror. Individuals were stopped and frisked routinely, often for simply trying to avoid confrontation with police.

10. These practices associated with the hidden curriculum in public schools seem to have forecasted the undue, if not unconstitutional, shift of powers to the executive (Bush) branch of government with its spearheading and authorizing of domestic wiretapping and infiltration and monitoring of peace groups.

11. Cole again demonstrates clearly how this dimension of the law works. On one level, poor people and people of color are excluded from the authoring process of laws. Thus, laws a priori target behaviors in which the general constituency of the law's authors does not participate. On another level, there is a legacy of police brutality and intimidation of people of color; these people will obviously feel less inclined to resist or contest that same authority. If adults have this experience, why would a young person of color with the precarious citizenship of youth have any less difficulty contesting police or other authority figures in situations potentially involving the law?

12. See the various studies in Appendix.

13. I will return to this later: learning is a process contingent upon resources, how they are used, and the conditions in which they are engaged. A basic question to ask, it seems to me, is what will or should students learn when academic and social resources are sacrificed for security technologies and pedagogies of panic?

Chapter 3

1. Casella (2003b and 2003c) has explored the practices of the security industry. I agree with the main arguments of his studies—that the predominance of the security industry in schools must be viewed as questionable at best and potentially dangerous at worst, and that the security industry alters broader societal relationships by engaging consumers in their own surveillance and redefining public space. Casella also suggests that much of the security industry was bolstered by the nascent military-industrial complex of the early Cold War period, but after that period he presents the security industry as a relatively autonomous force, unmoored from the deeper process of militarization. However, I want to augment this understanding by demonstrating that the security industry is still bound up with the military and gains much of its commercial footing and social legitimation by way of the process of militarization and the ideology of zero tolerance. Although the security industry does have its own "determinations," as it were, its acceptability, use, and prevalence in schools, I believe, is inseparable from the militarization of schools and society. This formulation of the security industry's role in schools changes how we might understand both the security industry's impacts on schools' spatial and temporal codes and how it relates to zero tolerance. See R. Casella, "Security, Schooling and the Consumer's Choice to Segregate," *The Urban Review, 105*(5) (2003b), 129–148. Casella, "The False Allure of Security Technologies," *Social Justice, 30*(3) (2003c), 82–93.

2. Urban students of color, often harassed by police and who witness police brutality in their neighborhoods, would hardly believe increased police presence in their schools represents a sign of safety and trust.

3. To be sure, biometric devices are not simple or politically sound technologies. Biometric technologies include devices that are capable of performing "positive identification through the scanning of unique body characteristics such as fingerprints, eyes, facial features or voice patterns," Goldberg, "Creating Safer and More Efficient Schools with Biometric Technologies," *T. H. E. Journal, 31*(2) (2003), p. 18.

4. I will return to this issue in the next subsection. For now, it's important to note that this strategy is linked to what Haggerty and Ericson call the "militarization of policing in the information age," and, like zero tolerance, it has its own "unintended consequences." See Haggerty & Ericson, "The Militarization of Policing in the Information Age," *Journal of Political and Military Sociology, 27* (1999), 233–255. By March 2007, the security force in New York Public Schools topped 4,600.

5. The *New York Times* recently reported the efforts of a middle- and working class, suburban Houston district to use "card swipe" technology on its buses to track students coming and going from school. This security measure

alone cost the district $180,000, which does not include the cost of mainte-
nance and supervision of it. See Richtel, "In Texas, 28,000 Students Test an
Electronic Eye," *New York Times*, (November 17, 2004), pp. A1, A18.

6. M. Davis explains how in the early 1990s the use of information
technology and databases to track gang activity in Los Angeles not only altered
the practice of surveillance but had the inherent consequence of profiling
youth of color who were not actually involved in gang activity. See M. Davis,
"Uprising and Repression in LA: An Interview with Mike Davis by the
CovertAction Information Bulletin," in R. Goodling-Williams *Reading Rodney
King: Reading Urban Uprising* (New York: Routledge, 1993), 142–154.

7. C. Katz shows how the security industry is not only intruding on
schools but also the home. She argues that as a result of the state's disinvestment in social reproduction, increasing work schedules, and less family time,
"[t]he child protection industry is part of the $1.1 billion home surveillance
industry brought about by the migration of spy technologies and logics across
the domestic frontier" (p. 48). The underside of this relationship is that not
only are youth subjected to ever more intense forms of surveillance, but also
that state disinvestment in matters of social reproduction can be translated into
matters of fear and punishment, not to mention the process of privatization.
See C. Katz, "The State Goes Home: Local Hypervigilence and the Global
Retreat from Social Reproduction," *Social Justice*, 28:(3) (2001), 47–56.

8. One assumes that the percentage of schools with police presence
would increase greatly if the U.S. Department of Education study asked if
schools had routine or regular police presence such as that provided by schools'
DARE police liaisons' weekly visits.

9. Since these data were collected from schools in the school year
following the Columbine tragedy, one would assume that the relatively high
visibility and use of security measures in 1999–2000 were a response to it.
However, in the 1996–1997 school year, the other year from which this type
of data was collected, similar disparities existed in the use of security measures,
the only category showing a significant decrease was whether schools had
open or closed lunches. See Kaufman et al. (1998). 1998, Table A3.

10. I must note that Eitle and Eitle's study complicates typical studies
of strain, where conditions of high poverty, stigmatization, and racial injustice
are correlated with higher rates of violence. Nonetheless, their study is useful,
suggesting that not only might important factors be missing from structural
analyses of race and violence, but also how studies of strain might inadvertently
pathologize areas of concentrated poverty and racial oppression. See M. Tonry,
Malign Neglect: Race, Crime, and Punishment in America, (New York: Oxford
University Press, 1996).

11. In an insightful essay, P. Molloy calls this process the creation of limit
zones in which youth are stripped bare of any political protections. While I

agree with most of her argument, to say that zero tolerance and the security industry potentially strips all youth of political protections is to ignore how youth of color are robbed systematically and disproportionately of their political and social capacities. See P. Molloy, "Moral spaces and moral panics: High schools, war zones, and other dangerous places," *Culture Machine*, 4 (2002). http://culturemachine.tees.ac.uk/Cmach/Backissues/j004/Articles/molloy.htm.

12. JROTC cadets who complete the program and enlist upon high school graduation receive $250 per month more than an enlistee from the general school population, thus showing, in part, that the JROTC is used to boost recruitment.

13. As of 2005, 67% of Troops-to-Teachers taught in areas defined as cities, and 63% were White (see Feistritzer, 2005, p. 17, 16).

14. Of course, it must not be ignored that these programs can provide some students the structure they need to remain in school. The issue is that some students are given a choice of being kicked out of school through zero tolerance or entering the JROTC, and their choices to enter the JROTC are conditioned by the paucity of resources in their communities and schools, which are made more scarce by policies such as the JROTC and Troops-to-Teachers program that eat up public money that could be used on educational resources.

15. Pedro Noguera (2003) provides many useful insights in this regard. He suggests that, by routinizing the exclusions of so-called problem students, or students who will be identified as problem students, teachers and schools promote a bad apple syndrome—the idea that if a problem student is removed, the problem will be solved. However, by identifying the student, rather than the underlying school conditions and social relationships, as the problem, the problem remains, and thus more bad apples will grow on the tree, to continue the metaphor. See Pedro Noguera, "Schools, Prisons, and the Social Implications of Punishment: Rethinking Disciplinary Practices," *Theory into Practice, 42*(4) (2003), 341–350.

16. I am purposefully appropriating Lutz's definition of militarization. By doing so, I not only want to rework her definition in terms of what it might mean for democratization, but also to underscore implicitly the sharp contrasts between U.S. commitments to militarization and its contemporary disinvestments in democratization.

Chapter 4

1. Noguera (2003) argues convincingly that the uniform punishment of the neediest students, who are typically students of color and poor White students, is primarily the result of the breaking of the social contract in schools,

a process that has encouraged (urban) public schools to routinize punitive disciplinary practices. He recognizes the social forces impacting urban communities and schools (e.g., segregation, unequal funding, state disinvestment in urban areas), but he largely abdicates the proponents of these forces of culpability in shaping the politics of punishment in (urban) public schools. In other words, he argues that the disproportionate punishment and exclusion of the neediest students is a problem mostly inhered in school organization and relationships, operating relatively free of broader social, political, and economic determinants, like the active efforts of well meaning color-blindnists and neoliberal gurus like Abigail Thernstrom, and John McWhorter and the think tank(s) with which they are affiliated and which play a formidable role in shaping policy formulation and public discourse. One of Thernstrom's arguments will be visited later in this chapter and will show that, unlike Noguera argues, there are visible proponents of discourses that variably support and encourage the routinization of punitive practices in schools. See P. A. Noguera, "Schools, Prisons, and the Social Implications of Punishment: Rethinking Disciplinary Practices," *Theory into Practice, 42*(4), 341–350.

2. Watts and Erevelles (2004) provide a different analysis of the racial politics involved in school exclusion. They argue that the construction of violent students in urban public schools, their subsequent exclusion, and the continued processes of segregation and disinvestment operating on urban communities are components of an updated version of internal colonization. Although Watts and Erevelles present a formidable analysis of oppressive school conditions and school relationships and how they racialize students through normative processes of inclusion and exclusion, internal colonization seems to be an inappropriate theoretical position from which to analyze the social, political, and economic forces operating on urban communities and schools, as there appears to be little societal or state interest under the rule of neoliberalism in dominating these populations for the purposes of economic exploitation. See I. E. Watts and N. Erevelles, "These Deadly Times: Reconceptualizing School Violence by Using Critical Race Theory and Disability Studies," *American Educational Research Journal, 41*(2), 271–299.

3. Much of this claim was touched upon in chapter 2 in terms of neoliberalism's attack on the social contract. Nonetheless, I will pursue this claim in detail in this chapter, because the assault on the social state, which was and is largely responsible for maintaining commitments to the social contract, is interrelated with the use of zero tolerance and the hegemony that colorblind ideology current exercises on racial justice. The illustrative term "private investment state" comes from A. Barlow. See A. Barlow, *Between Fear and Hope: Globalization and Race in the United States*, (Lanham, MD: Rowman & Littlefield, 2003).

4. As is the case with most any generalization, exceptions to this exist. Some upwardly mobile African Americans, who have been enlisted by the

social conservative neoliberal regime, promote the ideology of colorblindness. Think here of Ward Connerly who spearheaded the Proposition 209 initiative in California to end affirmative action in college admissions, Supreme Court Justice Clarence Thomas who has worked against affirmative action, and Black intellectuals such as John McWhorter and Shelby Steele who are noted for their arguments that cast racial inequality in the privatized and color-blind terms of initiative, self-responsibility, and guilt.

5. Needless to say, even this tepid support for diversity was undone in Michigan in November of 2006 when Michigan voters backed Proposal 2: The Michigan Civil Rights Initiative, which, in Orwellian fashion, disposed of affirmative action in public or publicly-supported institutions and agencies.

6. While individuals (particularly those of color) are instructed to cobble together their own strategies to be upwardly socially and economically mobile, little is mentioned, of course, in the discourse of colorblindness and other individualizing discourses that are in vogue and power, how those at the top have safety nets in place so they remain relatively fixed at the top, seen, for instance, in repeated tax cuts for the wealthiest 0.5%, tax shelters and the loosening of cost-intensive environmental regulations for corporations.

7. While Goldberg focuses, in this instance, on quite literal forms of devaluation (e.g., diminished property values in Black neighborhoods), I believe that my emphasis on the symbolic and discursive devaluation of blackness vis-à-vis colorblindness is appropriate to his general argument on racelessness and colorblindness. See D. T. Goldberg, *The Racial State* (Malden, MA: Blackwell, 2002).

8. This rationale or vision for (urban public) school order is a direct heir to James Q. Wilson's broken window philosophy that has guided get-tough strategies since the 1970s, and which was not bashful in its racial overtones, implications, and desired applications. Consider one of his claims: "[U]ntended behavior . . . leads to the breakdown of community controls. A stable neighborhood of families who care for their homes, mind each other's children, and confidently frown on unwanted intruders can change in a few years, or even a few months, to an inhospitable and frightening *jungle*. A piece of property is abandoned, *weeds* grow up, a window is *smashed*. Adults stop scolding *rowdy* children; the children, emboldened, become more *rowdy*" (italics added. 1985 [1975], pp. 78–79). Later, I will show how these same codes are operative in an argument against public schools and in support of zero tolerance. See J. Q. Wilson, *Thinking about Crime* (New York: Vintage Books, 1985 [1975]).

9. I disagree with Watts's and Erevelles's (2004) conclusions about these practices being used for internal colonization, but their analysis of the school and social processes that construct the violent student is notably instructive. See Watts and Erevelles, 2004, op. cit.

10. The term "private investment" state comes from Andrew Barlow's instructive study of the changing characteristics of racism in a globalizing era. See Barlow, *Between Fear and Hope* op cit.

11. In recent years, especially with the Bush II administrations, these overt and covert forms of coercion have become only academic distinctions. I demonstrated in chapter 3 two ways in which these forms of coercion operate in tandem through the militarization and correctionalization of urban public school space. Giroux (2004) and Piven (2004) have demonstrated how the use of the military abroad is coupled with state-supported market fundamentalism and antidemocratic operations at home, eroding civil liberties and devouring resources for social infrastructure, with the sum effect being the concentration of economic and political power in the hands of the corporate elite. Wolin (2003) also demonstrates how the modern state of the United States is totalitarian, just not in the classical political sense. Instead of the state controlling the market and civil society, Wolin argues, with due cause, that the market controls the state and continues to colonize civil society. One only has to think of any number of instances where this can be seen: the state's support for corporate plunder of natural resources in Bush's Clean Skies and Healthy Forests initiatives; the state's negligence in monitoring massive pharmaceuticals; tax cuts for the super rich, and disintegrating schools, lack of healthcare, and work privilege taxes for the poor and not-so-rich; and continued consolidation of a rightward, corporatized mediasphere. Thus, whether individuals voluntarily acquiesce to the market order or are coerced into it is a dubious distinction, when an authentic choice between the two forms of coercion is nonexistent. See H. A. Giroux, *The Terror of Neoliberalism: Authoritarianism and the Eclipse of Democracy* (Boulder, CO: Paradigm Publishers, 2004); F. F. Piven, *The War at Home: The Domestic Costs of Bush's Militarism* (New York: The New Press, 2004); and S. Wolin, "Inverted Totalitarianism: How the Bush Regime is Effecting the Transformation to a Fascist-like State," *The Nation* (May 19, 2003), 13–15.

12. For an historical analysis of Bush's recommendation to go shopping, see Robert H. Zieger, "Uncle Sam Wants You . . . To Go Shopping: A Consumer Society Responds to National Crisis, 1957–2001, *Canadian Review of American Studies*, 34:(1) (2004), 83–103.

13. In recent years, there have been high-profile examples, such as the Enron, Tyco, and Martha Stewart heists, that counter this claim.

14. Of course, the new convention districts of urban trade centers counter this claim, at least superficially. The primary users and beneficiaries of these areas, however, are not local residents, but jet-setting conference goers and financiers. See C. Parenti, *Lockdown America: Police and Prison in the Age of Crisis* (New York: Verso, 1999).

15. When imprisoned Latinos are considered, people of color account for 63% of the prison population, while Blacks and Latinos constitute roughly a combined 25% of the aggregate population.

16. Think, for example, of the still-popular *Cops* and the ubiquitous crime shows that almost always feature urban people of color as the perpetrators of disorder and crime; on the other side, recall the LAPD's abuse of Rodney King in 1992, the NYPD's horrific abuse of Abner Louima in 1997 and their killing of the unarmed Amadou Diallo with 41 shots in 1999, and the Cincinnati police officer's shooting of unarmed, nineteen year-old Timothy Thomas in 2001.

17. It is important to note how these broader racial dynamics seem to be quite analogous to those that have emerged in urban public schools, especially under zero tolerance.

18. One only has to think here of the Rodney King incident in 1992, or the recent rash of Black house burnings perpetrated by White suspects in Washington suburbs, if African Americans are seen to be freely (and potentially upwardly) moving out of their place.

19. Cole (1999) documents many abuses of this policy, one of which is the life sentence of a man who stole a slice of pizza. See D. Cole, *No Equal Justice: Race and Class in the American Criminal Justice System* (New York: The New Press, 1999).

20. Zero tolerance, the education policy, was also passed in 1994. Its history was detailed in the introduction and chapter 1 and it does not bear repeating here.

21. The racial underpinnings and racialized consequences of this bill hardly need enumeration. If a middle-class White youth was denied grants or federal loans for a drug charge, one can presume that s/he could find comparatively better means to replace the lost grant money than a poor Black youth, in addition to being positioned in better-equipped social networks that could absorb the consequences of not attending college, or at least not attending it until he procured the necessary funds. This law simply does not apply to upper-middle-class and elite students, not because they don't participate in drug use but because they don't qualify for grants anyhow. This consideration, however, is moot: Blacks are profiled more stringently for drugs than Whites, despite proportionate rates of use and possession (Cole, 1999), thus they have a greater chance of being arrested and subsequently denied aid for education. See Cole, op. cit.

22. I am assuming a critical definition of culpability here: Whether the primary stakeholders in GFSA 1994 consciously supported, legislated, and enacted zero tolerance in schools for the purpose of producing these unintended consequences is ancillary to the fact that zero tolerance and the battery

of other get-tough initiatives were already noted and criticized for their dev-astating effects on urban people of color in the wider society.

23. One could imagine that, under current conditions, the next argu-ments made by concerned, conservative pundits like Thernstrom will be about the inadequacy of publicly run prisons and the need to privatize them, so corporations can compete with each other over the production and housing of criminals. For some indications of this possibility, see S. Abramsky (2004), "Incarceration, Inc.," in *The Nation*, (July 19–26), pp. 22–25.

24. Think here of the boom industry of gated communities that has emerged in recent housing trends and of the popularity of security devices that has taken sway of the dominant public mind.

Chapter 5

1. Think here of the strategy of pre-emptive strike. The rationale for zero tolerance is to punish students severely for breaking a school rule and sometimes for even threatening to do so, in the hopes that other students will be scared from doing the same. Zero tolerance is not concerned with context, history, questioning, debate, dialogue, public oversight and administration and so on; if it were, it would cease to be zero tolerance. The rationale of preemp-tive strike is very similar, just on a different scale, striking others before they strike or striking others if they are perceived to be a threat, and it has the same disdain for context, history, questioning, debate, dialogue, and public oversight. The distance and difference between zero tolerance and preemptive strike is more a matter of geography than meaning and effects.

2. This type of work in which teachers and administrators could in-volve themselves seems not only invaluable but crucially necessary. For ex-ample, the Philadelphia school system has in recent years experienced not so much an increase in student violence, but increasing instances where parents and caregivers are attacking school professionals. This issue has only recently been brought to the broader public's attention and the reasons for such behav-ior has not been studied critically. It would be safe to assume that this type of behavior is informed and influenced by a number of complex factors, one of which is that a set of school-community relationships are in place, which encourage certain parents and caregivers to perceive school professionals as actual enemies instead of advocates. See Associated Press, "Philadelphia Schools Faced with Challenge of Adult Combativeness," *Centre Daily Times* (March 21, 2005), p. A5.

References

Abramsky, S. (2001, August 21). Hard-time kids: Handing down adult prison sentences to juvenile criminals isn't solving their problems—or ours. *The American Prospect.* pp. 16–21.

Abramsky, S. (2004, July 19/26). Incarceration, Inc. *The Nation.* pp. 22–25.

Adams, A. T. (2000, January). The status of school discipline and violence. In W. G. Hinkle & S. Henry (Eds.), *School violence* (pp. 140–156). *The Annals of the American Academy of Political and Social Science:* Vol. 567. Thousand Oaks, CA: Sage.

Akom, A. (2001). Racial profiling at school. In W. Ayers, B. Dohrn, & R. Ayers (Eds.), *Zero tolerance: Resisting the drive for punishment in our schools* (pp. 51–63). New York: The New Press.

American Academy of Pediatrics. (2003, November). Policy statement: Organizational principles to guide and define the child health care system and/or improve the health of all children—Out-of-school suspension and expulsion. *Pediatrics, 112,* pp. 1206–1209.

American Bar Association. (2001, February). Zero tolerance policy: Report. Retrieved October 15, 2007, from http://www.abanet.org/crimjust/juvjus/zerotolreport.html

Ansell, A. E. (1997). *New right, new racism: Race and racism in the United States and Britain.* New York: New York University Press.

Anyon, J. (1980). Social class and the hidden curriculum of work. *Journal of Education, 162,* 67–92.

Anyon, J. (2005). *Radical possibilities: Public policy, urban education, and a new social movement.* New York: Routledge.

Arendt, H. (1958). *The human condition.* Chicago: University of Chicago Press.

Aronowitz, S. (2003). *How class works: Power and social movement.* New Haven, CT: Yale University Press.

Associated Press. (2005, March 21). Philadelphia schools faced with challenge of adult combativeness. *Centre Daily Times* (State College, PA), p. A5.

Ayers, W. (1997/1998, Winter). Politicians promote lock 'em up mentality. *Rethinking Schools, 12*(2). Retrieved October 15, 2007, from http://www.rethinkingschools.org/archive/12_02/kids.shtm.

Ayers, W., Dohrn, B., & Ayers, R. (Eds.). (2001). *Zero tolerance: Resisting the drive for punishment in our schools.* New York: The New Press.

Aziz, N. (2002). Colorblind: Whitewashing America. *The Public Eye, 16*(2), pp. 1–13.

Barlow, A. (2003). *Between fear and hope: Globalization and race in the United States.* Lanham, MD: Rowman & Littlefield.

Bartlett, L., Frederick, M., Gulbrandsen, T., & Murillo, E. (2002). The marketization of education: Public schools for private ends. *Anthropology and Education Quarterly, 33,* 5–29.

Bauman, Z. (1999). *In search of politics.* Stanford, CA: Stanford University Press.

Bauman, Z. (2001). *Work, consumerism, and the new poor.* Philadelphia: Open University Press. (Original work published 1998)

Bauman, Z. (2002). *Society under siege.* London, UK: Polity.

Bauman, Z. (2004a). *Wasted lives: Modernity and its outcasts.* Cambridge, UK: Polity.

Bauman, Z. (2004b, November/December). To hope is human. *Tikkun 19*(6), 64–67.

Bay Area School Reform Collaborative. (2003). The color of discipline: Understanding racial disparity in school discipline. Retrieved October 10, 2004, from http://www.basrc.org/Pubs&Docs/EquityBriefJan01.pdf (Original work published January 2001)

Beger, R. R. (2002). Expansion of police power in public schools and the vanishing rights of students. *Social Justice, 29,* 119–130.

Bell, J. (2001). Education, delinquency, and incarceration. In W. Ayers, B. Dohrn, & R. Ayers (Eds.), *Zero tolerance: Resisting the drive for punishment in our schools* (pp. 136–142). New York: The New Press.

Berlowitz, M. J., & Long, N. A. (2003). The proliferation of JROTC: Educational reform or militarization. In K. J. Saltman & D. A. Gabbard (Eds.), *Education as enforcement: The militarization and corporatization of schools.* New York: Routledge/Falmer.

Berube, M. (2000). Jail/Yale. *Teachers for a democratic culture.* Retrieved July 2, 2003 from http://www.tdc2000.org/pin/packets/ed1_editorial.html

Bestor, A. E. (1985). *Educational wastelands: The retreat from learning in our public schools* (2nd ed.) Urbana: University of Illinois Press. (Original work published in 1953)

Blankenau, J., & Leeper, M. (2003, November). Public school search policies and the "politics of sin." *Policy Studies Journal, 31,* 565–584.

Blumenson, E., & Nilsen, E. S. (2002). How to construct an underclass, or how the war on drugs became a war on education. Retrieved August 12, 2007, from http://endzerotolerance.com/Underclass.pdf

Boggs, C., & Pollard, T. (2007). *The Hollywood war machine: U.S. militarism and popular culture*. Boulder, CO: Paradigm.

Bonilla-Silva, E. (2001). *White supremacy in the post-civil rights era*. Boulder, CO: Lynne Rienner.

Bonilla-Silva, E. (2003a). "New racism," color-blind racism, and the future of whiteness in America. In A. Doane & E. Bonilla-Silva (Eds.), *White out: The continuing significance of racism* (pp. 271–284). New York: Routledge.

Bonilla-Silva, E. (2003b). *Racism without racists: Color-blind racism and the persistence of racial inequality in the United States*. Lanham, MD: Rowman & Littlefield.

Bourdieu, P. (1998). *Acts of resistance: Against the tyranny of the market*. New York: The New Press.

Bourdieu, P. (2001). *Language and symbolic power*. Cambridge, MA: Harvard University Press. (Original work published in 1991)

Bourdieu, P. (2003). *Firing back: Against the tyranny of the market II*. New York: The New Press.

Bourdieu, P. & Passeron, J. C. (1977). *Reproduction in education, society, and culture*. Beverly Hills, CA: Sage.

Bracey, G. (2005, January 4). Data point to failure. *USA Today*. p. A14.

Brooks, K., Schiraldi, V., & Ziedenberg, J. (2000). School house hype: Two years later. *The Justice Policy Institute*. Retrieved September 17, 2007, from http://www.justicepolicy.org/article.php?id=46

Brown, E. R. (2003). Freedom for some, discipline for "others": The structure of inequity in education. In K. J. Saltman & D. A. Gabbard (Eds.) *Education as enforcement: The militarization and corporatization of schools* (pp. 127–151). New York: Routledge/Falmer.

Brown, F., Russo, C. J., and Hunter, R. C. (2002, Summer). The law and juvenile justice for people of color in elementary and secondary schools. *Journal of Negro Education, 71*, 128–142.

Brown, M. K., Carnoy, M., Currie, E., Duster, T., Oppenheimer, D. B., Shultz, M. M., and Wellman, D. (2003). *Whitewashing race: The myth of a colorblind society*. Berkeley: University of California Press.

Browne, J. A. (2003). *Derailed: The schoolhouse to jailhouse track*. Washington, DC: Advancement Project.

Browne, J. A. (2005). *Education on lockdown: The schoolhouse to jailhouse track*. Washington, DC: Advancement Project.

Brumble, M. (2003, December 5). Bossier school board upholds Advil expulsion: Girl had over-the-counter pills in purse in school. *The Schreveport Times*. Retrieved March 4, 2004, from http://www.shreveporttimes.com/html/AE0F03BF-76FC-4300-8564-695F1898F37C.shtml

Bureau of Labor Statistics. (2004a, March 21). Occupational outlook handbook, 2004–05 ed., correctional officers. *U.S. Department of Labor*. Retrieved July 6, 2007, from http://www.bls.gov/oco/ocos156.htm

Bureau of Labor Statistics. (2004b, May 18). Occupational outlook handbook, 2004–05 ed., teachers—preschool, kindergarten, elementary, middle, and secondary. *U.S. Department of Labor*. Retrieved January 9, 2005, from http://www.bls.gov/oco/ocos069.htm

Burstyn, J. N., Bender, G., Casella, R., Gordon, H. W., Guerra, D. P., Luschen, K. V., et al. (2001). *Preventing violence in schools: A challenge to American democracy*. Mahwah, NJ: Erlbaum.

Butchart, R. E. and McEwan, B. (Eds.). (1998). *Classroom discipline in American schools: Problems and possibilities for democratic education*. Albany: State University of New York Press.

Butler, J. (1993). Endangered/endangering: Schematic racism and white paranoia. In R. Goodling-Williams (Ed.), *Reading Rodney King/Reading urban uprising* (pp. 15–22). New York: Routledge.

Casella, R. (2001). *At zero tolerance: Punishment, prevention, and school violence*. New York: Peter Lang.

Casella, R. (2003a, June). Zero tolerance policy in schools: Rationale, consequences, and alternatives. *Teachers College Record, 105,* 872–892.

Casella, R. (2003b, June). Security, schooling and the consumer's choice to segregate. *The Urban Review, 35,* 129–148.

Casella, R. (2003c). The false allure of security technologies. *Social Justice, 30,* 82–93.

Castoriadis, C. (1991). *Philosophy, politics, autonomy: Essays in political philosophy*. New York: Oxford University Press.

Castoriadis, C. (1997). Democracy as procedure and democracy as regime. *Constellations, 4,* 1–18.

Center for Juvenile and Criminal Justice. (2002). School house hype: Two years later. Retrieved December 2, 2003, from http://www.cjcj.org/pubs/schoolhouse/shh2.html#reality

Chicago Public Schools. (2004). At a glance. Retrieved November 23, 2004, from http://www.cps.k12.il.us/AtAGlance.html

Cole, D. (1999). *No equal justice: Race and class in the American criminal justice system*. New York: The New Press.

Cole, D. (2003). *Enemy aliens: Double standards and constitutional freedoms in the war on terrorism*. New York: The New Press.

Comaroff, J., & Comaroff, J. L. (2000). Millennial capitalism: First thoughts on a second coming. *Public Culture, 12,* 291–343.

Corbett, J. W. and Coumbe, A. T. (2001, January/February). 40 JROTC: Recent trends and developments. Combined Arms Center Military Review. Retrieved November 16, 2007, from http://www.leavenworth.army.mil/milrev/English/JanFeb01/corbett.htm

Couldry, N. (2004). In the place of a common culture, what? *Review of Education, Pedagogy, and Cultural Studies, 26,* 1–19.

Cremin, L. (1957). *Republic and the school: Horace Mann on the education of free men.* New York: Teachers College Press.

Cross, B. (2001). A time for action. In T. Johnson, J. E. Boyden, & W. Pittz (Eds.), *Racial profiling and punishment in u.s. public schools: How zero tolerance and high stakes testing subvert academic excellence and racial equity* (pp. 5–8). Oakland, CA: Applied Research Center.

DANTES. (2007a). Troops to teachers. *Defense Activity for Non-traditional Educational Support.* Retrieved November 11, 2007, from http://www.dantes.doded.mil/Dantes_web/troopstoteachersoverview.asp.

DANTES. (2007b). Troops to teachers. *Defense Activity for Non-traditional Educational Support.* Retrieved November 11, 2007, from http://www.dantes.doded.mil/Dantes_web/library/docs/ttt/statusreport.pdf

Darling-Hammond, L. (2000). New standards and old inequalities: School reform and the education of African American students. *Journal of Negro Education, 69,* 263–287.

Darling-Hammond, L.(2001). Apartheid in American education: How opportunity is rationed to children of color in the United States. In T. Johnson, J. E. Boyden, & W. J. Pittz (Eds.), *Racial profiling and punishment in U.S. public schools: How zero tolerance and high stakes testing subvert academic excellence and racial equity* (pp. 39–44). Oakland, CA: Applied Research Center.

Davis, A. (1998, Fall). Masked racism: Reflections on the prison industrial complex. *Colorlines, 1*(2). Retrieved November 15, 2007, from http://www.arc.org/C_Lines/CLArchive/story1_2_01.html

Davis, M. (1993). Uprising and repression in LA: An interview with Mike Davis by the *CovertAction* information bulletin. In R. Goodling-Williams (Ed.,) *Reading Rodney King/reading urban uprising* (pp. 142–154). New York: Routledge.

Delgado, G. (Ed.). (2002). *From poverty to punishment: How welfare reform punishes the poor.* Oakland, CA: Applied Research Center.

Dell'Angela, T., & Cholo, A. B. (2004, August 17). Critics say budget cuts don't add up. *Chicago Tribune,* p. 1.

Delpit, L. (1995). *Other people's children: Cultural conflict in the classroom.* New York: The New Press.

Denzin, N. (2002). *Reading race: Hollywood and the cinema of racial violence.* Thousand Oaks, CA: Sage.

Deparle, J. (2004). *American dream: Three women, ten kids, and a nation's drive to end welfare.* New York: Viking Books.

Detroit News (Associated Press). (2004, February 22). Educator admits he planted drugs, cop says: Assistant principal said he hoped student would be expelled for marijuana. Retrieved March 2, 2004, from http://www.detnews.com/2004/schools/0402/22/c06-70811.htm

DeVoe, J. F., Peter, K., Kaufman, P., Ruddy, S. A., Miller, A. K., Planty, et al. (2003). Education statistics quarterly: Elementary and secondary education. Indicators of school crime and safety. Retrieved January 5, 2004, from http://nces.ed.gov/programs/quarterly/vol_5/5_4/3_6.asp

Dewey, J. (1940). Creative democracy—The task before us. In S. Ratner (Ed.), *The philosopher of the common man: Essays in honor of John Dewey to celebrate his eightieth birthday* (pp. 220–228). New York: G. P. Putnam's Sons.

Dewey, J. (1994). *The moral writings of John Dewey.* (J.Gouinlock, Ed.). New York: Prometheus Books.

Dewey, J. (1997). *Democracy and education.* New York: Free Press.

Dewey, J. (1998) [1938] *Education and society* (60th anniversary ed.) West Lafayette, IN: Kappa Delta Pi.

Diamond, L. (2004, September 28). JROTC in Gwinnett: Here come the cadets—high school programs offer a quick route into the military or simply a way to build confidence and leadership skills. *The Atlanta Journal-Constitution,* p. JJ1.

Difazio, W. (2003). Time, poverty, and global democracy. In S. Aronowitz & H. Gautney (Eds.), *Implicating empire: Globalization and resistance in the 21st century world order* (pp. 159–178). New York: Basic Books.

DiIulio, J. (1995, December 15). Moral poverty. *Chicago Tribune,* Sect.1, p. 31.

DiIulio, J. (1997, June 11). Rule of law: Jails alone won't stop juvenile superpredators. *Wall Street Journal,* p. A23.

Doane, A. (2003). Rethinking whiteness studies. In A. Doane & E. Bonilla-Silva (Eds.), *White out: The continuing significance of racism* (pp. 3–18). New York: Routledge.

Dohrn, B. (2001). "Look out kid/it's something you did": Zero tolerance for children. In W. Ayers, B. Dohrn, & R. Ayers (Eds.), *Zero tolerance: Resisting the drive for punishment in our schools* (pp. 89–113). New York: The New Press.

Donahue, E., Schiraldi, V., & Ziedenberg, J. (1998). School house hype: The school shootings, and the real risks kids face in America. Washington, DC: Justice Policy Institute. Retrieved October 16, 2003, from http://www.justicepolicy.org/article.php?id=42

Dorgan, B. (1994, June 8). Guns in schools. Cong. Rec. S6587. Retrieved January 25, 2004, from http://thomas.loc.gov/cgi-bin/query/D?r103:2:./temp/~r103pbDyRF::

Dow, P. (1991). *Schoolhouse politics: Lessons from the Sputnik era.* Cambridge, MA: Harvard University Press.

Duggan, L. (2003). *The twilight of equality: Neoliberalism, cultural politics, and the attack on democracy.* Boston: Beacon.

Dunbar, C., & Villarruel, F. A. (2002). Urban school leaders and the implementation of zero tolerance policies: An examination of its consequences. *Peabody Journal of Education, 77,* 82–104.

Eitle, D., & Eitle, T. M. (2003, December). Segregation and school violence. *Social Forces, 82,* pp. 589–615.

Epstein, H. (2003, October 12). Enough to make you sick? *New York Times Magazine,* pp. 75–81, 98, 102, 104–105, 108.

Epstein, R. J. (2003, November 6). School suspends teen for rap lyric. *Milwaukee Journal Sentinel.* Retrieved July 26, 2004, from http://www.jsonline. com/news/wauk/nov03/183108.asp

Eskenazi, M., Eddins, G., & Beam, J. M. (2003). Equity or exclusion: The dynamics of resources, demographics, and behavior in the New York City public schools. Fordham University: National Center for Schools and Communities.

Expect More. (2006). Detailed Information on the Junior Reserve Officers' Training Corps Assessment. Retrieved May 8, 2007, from http://www. whitehouse.gov/omb/expectmore/detail/10003233.2006.html

Facts about . . . School Safety. (2002). *No Child Left Behind.* Retrieved August 11, 2007, from http://www.ed.gov/nclb/freedom/safety/keepingkids. html

Feinstein, D. (1994). The gun-free schools act of 1994: "It's time to stop making excuses about violence in schools." Retrieved June 12, 2003, from http:// www.senate.gov/~feinstein/booklets/gunfree.pdf

Feistritzer, C. E. (2005). *Profile of Troops-to-Teachers.* Washington, DC: National Center for Education Information.

Finkelstein, B. (2000). A crucible of contradictions: Historical roots of violence against children in the united states. In V. Polakow (Ed.), *The public assault on America's children: Poverty, violence, and juvenile justice* (pp. 21–41). New York: Teachers College Press.

Foucault, M. (1977). *Discipline and punish.* A. Sheridan (trans.). New York: Pantheon Books.

Foucault, M. (2003). *Society must be defended.* D. Macey (trans.). New York: Picador.

Freire, P. (1970). *Pedagogy of the oppressed.* New York: Seabury Press.

Freire, P. (1997). Pedagogy of freedom: *Ethics, democracy, and civic courage.* Lanham, MD: Rowman & Littlefield.

Freire, P. (2004). *Pedagogy of indignation.* Boulder, CO: Paradigm.

Friedman, M. (2002). *Capitalism and freedom.* Chicago: University of Chicago Press. (Original work published 1962)

Fuentes, A. (2003, December 15). Discipline and punish. *The Nation,* 17–20.

Fulbright, L. (2004, January 9). Sledder hurt in accident may be arrested. *Seattle Times.* Retrieved January 10, 2004, from http://archives.seattletimes. nwsource.com/cgi-bin/texis.cgi/web/vortex/display?slug= snowcrime 09e&date=20040109&query=Fulbright

Gagnon, J. C., and Leone, P. E. (2002). Alternative strategies for school violence prevention. In R. J. Skiba & G. G. Noam (Eds.), *Zero tolerance: Can suspensions and expulsions keep schools safe?* (pp. 101–125). San Francisco, CA: Jossey-Bass.

General Accounting Office. (2003, September). Military recruiting: DOD needs to establish measures and objectives to better evaluate advertising's effectiveness. http://www.gao.gov/new.items/d031005.pdf

Gingrich, N. (2005). *Winning the future: A 21st century contract with America.* New York: Regnery.

Ginsberg, C., & Demeranville, H. (2001). In W. Ayers, B. Dohrn, & R. Ayers (Eds.), *Zero tolerance: Resisting the drive for punishment in our schools* (pp. 155–164). New York: The New Press.

Ginwright, S., & Cammarota, J. (2002). New terrain in youth development: The promise of a social justice approach. *Social Justice, 29*(4), 82–95.

Ginwright, S., Cammarota, J., & Noguera, P. (2005). Youth, social justice, and communities: Toward a theory of urban youth policy. *Social Justice, 32*(3), 24–40.

Giroux, H. A. (1988). *Schooling and the struggle for public life: Critical pedagogy in the modern age.* Minneapolis: University of Minnesota Press.

Giroux, H. A. (1999). *Stealing innocence: Youth, corporate power, and the politics of culture.* New York: St. Martin's Press.

Giroux, H. A. (2001a). *Public spaces/private lives: Democracy beyond the politics of cynicism.* Lanham, MD: Rowman & Littlefield.

Giroux, H. A. (2001b). *Theory and resistance in education: Towards a pedagogy for the opposition.* Westport, CT: Bergin & Garvey.

Giroux, H. A. (2003a). Betraying the intellectual tradition: Public intellectuals and the crisis of youth. *Language and Intercultural Communication, 3,* 172–186.

Giroux, H. A. (2003b). *The abandoned generation: Democracy beyond the culture of fear.* New York: Palgrave/Macmillan.

Giroux, H. A. (2003c, July–October). Spectacles of race and pedagogies of denial: Anti-black racist pedagogy under the reign of neoliberalism. *Communication Education, 52,* 91–211.

Giroux, H. A. (2004). *The terror of neoliberalism: Authoritarianism and the eclipse of democracy.* Boulder, CO: Paradigm.

Giroux, H. A., & Giroux, S. S. (2004). *Take back higher education: Race, youth, and the crisis of democracy in the post-civil rights era.* New York: Palgrave/Macmillan.

Giroux, H. A., Penna, A. N., & Pinar, W. F. (1981). *Curriculum and instruction: Alternatives in education.* Berkeley, CA: McCutchan.

Giroux, H. A., & Purpel, D. (1983). *The hidden curriculum and moral education: Deception or discovery?* Berkeley, CA: McCutchan.

Goldberg, D. T. (1993). *Racist culture: Philosophy and the politics of meaning.* Malden, MA: Blackwell.

Goldberg, D. T. (1997). *Racial subjects: Writing on race in America.* New York: Routledge.

Goldberg, D. T. (2002). *The racial state.* Malden, MA: Blackwell.

Goldberg, L. (2003, September). Creating safer and more efficient schools with biometric technologies. *T.H.E. Journal*, 31(2), pp. 16, 18–19.

Goodman, D. (2002, January/February). Recruiting the class of 2005. *Mother Jones, 27*(1), pp. 56–61, 80–81.

Gootman, E. (2004, February 4). Metal detectors and pep rallies: Spirit helps tame a Bronx school. *The New York Times*, A1, C14.

Gordon, J. (2003, November 16). In schools, bad behavior is shown the door. *The New York Times*, p. 14 CN.1.

Gordon, R., Della Piana, L., & Keleher, T. (2000, March). *Facing the consequences: An examination of racial discrimination in U.S. public schools*. Oakland, CA: Applied Research Center.

Gordon, R., Della Pianna, L., & Kelcher, T. (2001). Zero tolerance: A basic racial report card. In W. Ayers, B. Dohrn, & R. Ayers (Eds.), *Zero tolerance: Resisting the drive for punishment in our schools* (pp. 165–175). New York: The New Press.

Gray, H. (1997). *Watching race: Television and the struggle for the sign of blackness.* Minneapolis: University of Minnesota Press.

Gress, J. R., & Purpel, D. (1988). *Curriculum: An introduction to the field*. Berkeley, CA: McCutchan.

Grossberg, L. (2001). Why does neoliberalism hate kids? The war on youth and the culture of politics. *Review of Education/Pedagogy/Cultural Studies, 23*, 111–136.

Grossberg, L. (2005). *Caught in the crossfire: Kids, politics, and America's Future*, Boulder: Paradigm.

Guinier, L., & Torres, G. (2003). *The miner's canary: Enlisting race, resisting power, transforming democracy*. Cambridge, MA: Harvard University Press.

Haggerty, K. D., & Ericson, R. V. (1999, Winter). The militarization of policing in the information age. *Journal of Political and Military Sociology 27*, 233–255.

Hall, S. (1996). The problem of ideology: Marxism without guarantees. In D. Morley & K-H. Chen (Eds.), *Stuart Hall: Critical dialogues in cultural studies* (pp. 25–45). New York: Routledge.

Hall, S. (1997). The centrality of culture: Notes on the cultural revolutions of our time. In K. Thompson (Ed.), *Media and cultural regulation* (pp. 208–236). Thousand Oaks, CA: Sage.

Halpin, D. (2001, December). The nature of hope and its significance for education. *British Journal of Educational Studies, 49*, 392–410.

Hardisty, J., & Williams, L. A. (2002). The right's campaign against welfare. In G. Delgado (Ed.), *From poverty to punishment: How welfare reform punishes the poor* (pp. 53–72). Oakland, CA: Applied Research Center.

Harvard Civil Rights Project. (2000). *Opportunities suspended.* Washington, DC: Advancement Project.

Henry. S. (2000). What is school violence? An integrated definition. In W. G. Hinkle & S. Henry (Eds.), *School violence* (pp. 16–29). *The Annals of the American Academy of Political and Social Science:* Vol. 567. Thousand Oaks, CA: Sage.

Herrnstein, R. J., & Murray, C. (1994). *The Bell Curve: Intelligence and class structure in American life.* New York: Free Press.

Herszenhorn, D. M. (2003, December 24). Mayor says he'll increase security at dangerous schools. *The New York Times,* p. B3.

Herszenhorn, D. M. (2004, January 29). Problems of school discipline system emerge at hearing. *The New York Times,* p. B6.

Hochschild, J. L. (2003). Social class and public schools. *Journal of Social Issues, 59,* pp. 821–840.

Human Rights Watch. (2000, May). United States: Punishment and prejudice—racial disparities in the war on drugs. Retrieved January 8, 2005, from http://www.hrw.org/reports/2000/usa/index.htm#TopOfPage

Human Rights Watch (2002). Human Rights Watch presentation to the United States sentencing commission. Retrieved September 12, 2004, from http://www.hrw.org/press/2002/03/ussc0314.htm

Hurst, J. (2004, February 4). Dogs sniff drugs at NHS. *Narragansett Times.* Retrieved February 12, 2004, from http://www.zwire.com/site/news.cfm?newsid=10908934&BRD=1714&PAG=461&dept_id=...

Institute for Public Policy and Social Research. (2002). Policy brief: Little tolerance for "zero tolerance." Retrieved June 18, 2003, from http://www.ippsr.msu.edu/policybrief.htm

Johnson, F. (2002, May 16). U.S. education spending. Adapted from "Revenues and expenditures for public elementary and secondary education: School year 1999–2000." U.S. Department of Education. National Center for Educational Statistics. *Almanac of Policy Issues.* Retrieved January 9, 2005, from http://www.policyalmanac.org/education/archive/doe_education_spending.shtml

Johnson, H. B. and Shapiro, T. M. (2003). Good neighborhoods, good schools: Race and the "good choices" of white families. In A. Doane & E. Bonilla-Silva (Eds.), *White out: The continuing significance of racism* (pp. 173–198). New York: Routledge.

Johnson, T., Boyden, J. E., and Pittz, W. (Eds.). (2001). *Racial profiling and punishment in U.S. public schools: How zero tolerance and high stakes testing subvert academic excellence and racial equity.* Oakland, CA: Applied Research Center.

Justice Policy Institute. (2002a). Cellblocks or classrooms. Retrieved September 21, 2004, from http://www.riseup.net/jpi/article.php?id=2

Justice Policy Institute. (2002b). Choosing cellblocks or classrooms. Retrieved September 21, 2004, from http://www.riseup.net/jpi/article.php?id=51

Justice Policy Institute. (2004, November 10). Prison numbers increase to 1.5 million despite decade-long drop in crime. Retrieved November 12, 2004, from http://www.justicepolicy.org/article.php?id=462

Karp, S. (2004, Winter). Leaving public education behind. *Radical Teacher, 68,* 32–34.

Katz, C. (2001, Fall). The state goes home: Local hyper-vigilance and the global retreat from social reproduction. *Social Justice, 28*(3), 47–56.

Kaufman, P., Chen, X., Choy, S. P., Chandler, K. A., Chapman, C. D., Rand, M. R., & Ringel, C. (1998). *Indicators of school crime and safety, 1998.* U.S. Departments of Education and Justice. NCES 98-251/NCJ-172215. Washington, DC.

Kennedy, M. (2004, January). Providing safe schools. American *School and University* 76(5). Retrieved January 15, 2004, from http://asumag.com/mag/university_providing_safe_schools/index.html

Kozol, J. (1991). *Savage inequalities.* New York: Crown.

Kozol, J. (2005). *The shame of the nation: The restoration of apartheid schooling in America.* New York: Crown.

Kraska, P. (1999, Winter). Militarizing criminal justice: Exploring the possibilities. Journal *of Political and Military Sociology, 27,* 205–215.

Kuipers, D. (2001, July 18). Less than zero: The new age of intolerance. *LA Weekly.* Retrieved July 24, 2004, from http://www.alternet.org/print.html?StoryID=11202

Ladson-Billings, G. (2001). America still eats her young. In W. Ayers, B. Dohrn, & R. Ayers (Eds.), *Zero tolerance: Resisting the drive for punishment in our schools* (pp. 77–88). New York: The New Press.

Larson, C. (1997, August). Is the land of oz an alien nation? A sociopolitical study of school community conflict. *Educational Administration Quarterly, 33,* 312–351.

Lavarello, C. (2003, February 10). NASRO calls upon congress for education homeland security act. Retrieved February 22, 2004, from http://www.nasro.org/PressRelHomelandSec021003.pdf

Lawson, B. (2001). *The language of space.* Boston: Architectural Press.

Levenson, M. (2004, September 7). Camp Chelsea high: Hard-pressed school taps military man as principal. *Boston Globe,* p. B1.

Lipman, P. (2002). Making the global city, making inequality: The political economy and cultural politics of Chicago school policy. *American Education Research Journal, 39,* 379–419.

Lipman, P. (2004, March). Education accountability and repression of democracy post-9/11. *Journal for Critical Education Policy Studies, 2*(1). Retrieved July 26, 2007, from http://www.jceps.com/?pageID=article&articleID=23

Lipsitz, G. (1998). *The possessive investment in whiteness: How white people profit from identity politics.* Philadelphia: Temple University Press.

Losen, D. J. and Edley, C. (2001). The role of law in policing abusive disciplinary practices: Why school discipline is a civil rights issue. In W. Ayers, B. Dohrn, & R. Ayers (Eds.), *Zero tolerance: Resisting the drive for punishment in our schools* (pp. 230–255). New York: The New Press.

Low, S. M. (2001, March). The edge and the center: Gated communities and the discourses of urban fear. *American Anthropologist, 103,* pp. 45–58.

Lutz, C. (2002). Making war at home in the United States: Militarization and the current crisis. *American Anthropologist, 104,* 723–735.

Lutz, C., & Bartlett, L. (1995). JROTC: Making soldiers in public schools. *Education Digest, 61*(3), 9–14.

Mabrey, V. (2004, February 4). Ambush at goose creek. *60 Minutes.* Transcript. Retrieved May 6, 2007, from http://www.cbsnews.com/stories/2004/02/02/60II/main597488.shtml?CMP=ILC-SearchStories

Macedo, D., & Bartolome, L. I. (1999). *Dancing with bigotry: Beyond the politics of tolerance.* New York: St. Martin's Press.

Madaus, G., & Clarke, M. (2001). The adverse impact of high-stakes testing on minority students: Evidence from one hundred years of test data. In G. Orfield & M. L. Kornhaber (Eds.), *Raising standards or raising barriers: Inequality and high-stakes testing in public education* (pp. 85–106). New York: Century Foundation Press.

Magdoff, F., & Magdoff, H. (2004, April). Disposable workers. *Monthly Review,* 18–35.

Males, M. (1996). *The scapegoat generation: America's war on adolescents.* Monroe, ME: Common Courage Press.

Mann, H. (1848). Report No. 12 of the Massachusetts School Board. Retrieved May 2, 2006, from http://usinfo.state.gov/usa/infousa/facts/democrac/16.htm

Marable, M. (2001). Racism, prisons, and the future of black America. *Zmag.* Retrieved June 9, 2003, from http://www.zmag.org/racismandblam.htm

Marable, M. (2004a, August 13). Globalization and racialization. *Zmag.* Retrieved August 15, 2004, from http://www.zmag.org/content/showarticle.cfm?ItemID=6034

Marable, M. (2004b, April 25). The new racial domain. *Zmag.* Retrieved June 3, 2004, from http://www.zmag.org/Sustainers/Content/2004-04/25marable.cfm

Martinot, S. (2003). *The rule of racialization: Class, identity and governance.* Philadelphia: Temple University Press.

Massey, D. (1994). *Space, place, and gender.* Minneapolis: University of Minnesota Press.

Mauer, M. (2003, June 20). Comparative international rates of incarceration: An examination of causes and trends—Presented to the U.S. Commission on Civil Rights. Washington, DC: *The Sentencing Project.* Retrieved

January 7, 2005, from http://www.sentencingproject.org/pdfs/pub9036.pdf

Mayo, P. (2003). A rationale for a transformative approach to education. *Journal of Transformative Education, 1*(10), 1–28.

McChesney, R. W. (1998). Introduction. In N. Chomsky (1999), *Profits over people: Neoliberalism and global order* (7–16). New York: Seven Stories Press.

McChesney, R. W., & Nichols, J. (2002). *Our media, not theirs: The democratic struggle against corporate media.* New York: Seven Stories Press.

Michigan Compiled Laws 380.1309. (2006). http://www.michigan.gov/documents/suspensions_118759_7.pdf

McRoberts, F. (2004, February 15). High school drug raid rattles town: Race is subtext as ex-Chicagoan joins lawsuit accusing S.C. officials of violating students' rights. *Chicago Tribune.* p. 10.

McWhorter, J. (2003, April–May). Don't do me any favors. *The American Enterprise, 14*(3), 22–27.

Medina, J. (2002, November 6). Metal detectors making students late, if not safe. *The New York Times*, p. A25.

Memmi, A. (2000). *Racism.* S. Martinot (trans.). Minneapolis: University of Minnesota Press.

Michigan Public Policy Initiative. (2003, January). Spotlight: Zero tolerance policies and their impact on Michigan students. Lansing: Michigan Nonprofit Association.

Miller, D. F. (2001). Quality time. In M. P. Soulsby & J. T. Fraser (Eds). *Time: Perspectives at the millennium (the study of time x).* Westport, CT: Begin & Garvey.

Mills, C. W. (2000). *The sociological imagination* [Fortieth Anniversary Edition]. New York: Oxford. Originally published in 1959.

Moller, J. (2003, December 12). No apology for Lafayette gay mom: School board decides discipline valid. *Times-Picayune.* p. O1.

Molloy, P. (2002). Moral spaces and moral panics: High schools, war zones, and other dangerous places. *Culture Machine, 4.* Retrieved September 27, 2007, from http://culturemachine.tees.ac.uk/Cmach/Backissues/j004/Articles/molloy.htm

Molnar, A. (1996). Giving kids the business: *The commercialization of America's schools.* Boulder, CO: Westview Press.

Molnar, A. (2005). *School commercialism: From democratic ideal to market commodity.* New York: Routledge.

Morrison, G. M., Anthony, S., Storino, M. H., Cheng, J. F., Furlong, M. J., & Morrison, R. L. (2002). In R. J. Skiba & G. G. Noam (Eds.), *Zero tolerance: Can suspensions and expulsions keep schools safe* (pp. 45–71). San Francisco, CA: Jossey-Bass.

Muhammed, D., Davis, A., Lui, M., & Leondar-Wright, B. (2004, January 15). *The state of the dream 2004: Enduring disparities in black and white.* Boston: United for a Fair Economy.

Muhkarjee, E., & Karpatkin, M. (2007). *Criminalizing the classroom: The over-policing of New York City schools.* New York: American Civil Liberties Union.

Myers, K. (2003). White fright: Reproducing white supremacy through casual discourse. In A. Doane & E. Bonilla-Silva (Eds.), *White out: The continuing significance of racism* (pp. 129–144). New York: Routledge.

National Center for Education Statistics. (2004). Common core of data. Retrieved October 10, 2004, from http://www.nces.ed.gov/ccd/

National Mental Health Association. (2003, June 8). NMHA position statement: Opposing the blanket application of zero tolerance policies in schools. Retrieved July 26, 2004, from http://www.nmha.org/position/zerotolerence.cfm

Navarro, V. (2004, June). Inequalities are unhealthy. *Monthly Review.* Retrieved June 15, 2006, from http://www.monthlyreview.org/0604navarro.htm

Noguera, P. (1995, Summer). Preventing and producing violence: A critical analysis of responses to school violence. *Harvard Educational Review, 65,* 189–212.

Noguera, P. (2001). Finding safety where we least expect it: The role of social capital in preventing school violence. In W. Ayers, B. Dohrn, & R. Ayers (Eds.), *Zero tolerance: Resisting the drive for punishment in our schools* (pp. 188–201). New York: The New Press.

Noguera, P. (2003, Fall). Schools, prisons, and social implications of punishment: Rethinking disciplinary practices. *Theory into Practice, 42,* pp. 341–350.

Oakes, J. (1985). *Keeping track.* New Haven: Yale University Press.

Oakes, J. (1999). Limiting students' school success and life chances: The impact of tracking. In A. C. Ornstein & L. S. Behar-Horenstein (Eds.), *Contemporary issues in curriculum* (2nd ed., pp. 224–237). Needham Heights, MA: Allyn and Bacon.

Oakes, J., & Rogers, J. (2003, October 5). Who needs data on race? The schools, for one. *Los Angeles Times,* p. M.2.

Office of Civil Rights, U.S. Department of Education. (2000). Fall 1998 Elementary and Secondary School Civil Rights Compliance Report: National and State Projections. Washington, DC: Government Printing Office.

Office of Juvenile Justice and Delinquency Prevention. (2003, December). *OJJDP juvenile justice bulletin: Juvenile arrests 2001.* Washington, DC: U.S. Department of Justice Office of Justice Programs.

Olson, M. (2003, August). Kids in the hole. *The Progressive, 67*(8), pp. 26–29.

Olszewski, L. (2003, August 27). Chicago schools to boost security. *Chicago Tribune*, p. 1.

Orfield, G., Eaton, S., & the Harvard Civil Rights Project. (1997). *Dismantling desegregation: The quiet reversal of* Brown v. Board of Education. New York: The New Press.

Orfield, G., & Kornhaber, M. (Eds.). (2001). *Raising standards or raising barriers: Inequality and high stakes testing in public education*. New York: Century Foundation Press.

Parenti, C. (1999). *Lockdown America: Police and prisons in the age of crisis*. London: Verso.

Parker, L., & Stovall, D. O. (2004). Actions following words: Critical race theory connects to critical pedagogy. *Educational Philosophy and Theory, 36*(2), 167–182.

Pepper, M. (2006). No corporation left behind: How a century of illegitimate testing has been used to justify internal colonialism. *Monthly Review, 58*(6). Retrieved November 22, 2006, from http://www.monthly review.org/1106pepper.htm

Piven, F. F. (2004). *The war at home: The domestic costs of Bush's militarism*. New York: The New Press.

Polakow, V. (2000). Savage policies: Systemic violence and the lives of children. In V. Polakow (Ed.), *The public assault on America's children: Poverty, violence, and juvenile justice* (pp. 1–18). New York: Teachers College Press.

Polakow-Suransky, S. (2000). America's least wanted: Zero tolerance policies and the fate of expelled students. In V. Polakow (Ed.), *The public assault on America's children: Poverty, violence, and juvenile justice* (pp. 101–129). New York: Teachers College Press.

Provenzo, E. F. (2003). Virtuous war: Simulation and the militarization of play. In K. J. Saltman & D. A. Gabbard (Eds.), *Education as enforcement: The militarization and corporatization of schools* (pp. 279–286). New York: Routledge/Falmer.

Public Law 103-227. (1994). *Gun-free schools act*. SEC 1031, 20 USC 2701.

Reinolds, C. (2004, October 7). Education notebook. The Atlanta Journal-Constitution. p. JQ10.

Richart, D., Brooks, K., & Soler, M. (2003). Unintended consequences: The impact of "zero tolerance" and other exclusionary policies on Kentucky students. *Building Blocks* for Youth. Retrieved September 20, 2004, from http://www.buildingblocksforyouth.org/kentucky/kentucky.html

Richtel, M. (2004, September 29). School cellphone bans topple (You can't suspend everyone). *The New York Times*, p. A1, A16.

Richtel, M. (2004, November 17). In Texas 28,000 students test an electronic eye. *The New York Times*, p. A1, A18.

Rimer, S. (2004, January 4). Unruly students facing arrest, not detention. *The New York Times*, p. A1.

Rios, V. (2006). The hyper-criminalization of black and Latino male youth in the era of mass incarceration. *Souls, 8*(2), 40–54.

Robbins, C. G. (2004). Racism and the authority of neoliberalism: A review of three new books on the persistence of racial inequality in the color-blind era. *Journal for Critical Education Policy Studies, 2*(2). http://www.jceps.com/index.php?pageID=article&articleID=35

Robbins, C. G. (2005). Zero tolerance and the politics of racial injustice. *Journal of Negro Education, 74,* 2–17.

Roberts, D. (2003). *Shattered bonds: The color of child welfare.* New York: Basic Books.

Robin, C. (2004). *Fear: The history of a political idea.* New York: Oxford University Press.

Robinson, C. (1993). *Race, capitalism, and the antidemocracy.* In R. Goodling-Williams (Ed.), *Reading Rodney King: Reading urban uprising* (pp. 73–81). New York: Routledge.

Rothstein, R. (2004). *Class and schools: Using social, economic, and educational reform to close the black-white achievement gap.* Washington, DC: Economic Policy Institute.

Rubin, D. (2004). *Michigan's failure to provide due process rights for children.* Unpublished manuscript, University of Michigan Law School and the Student Advocacy Center.

Safe Schools and Possession of Weapons. (2002). BEC 24 P.S.§13-1317.2. Pennsylvania Department of Education. Retrieved June 5, 2003, from http://www.pde.state.pa.us/k12/cwp/view.asp?A=11&Q=58859

Saltman, K. J. (2007). *Capitalizing on disaster: Taking and breaking public schools.* Boulder, CO: Paradigm.

Sansbury, J. (2003, September 25). Schools go eye tech, county spending nearly $9 million on upgrades. *Atlanta Journal-Constitution*, p. JA1.

Satellite News. (2004, August 2). GPS technology aids school-bus safety. *Satellite News, 27*(30), p. 1.

Saulny, S. (2004, October 19). City applies police strategy to it most troubled schools. *The New York Times*, p. A25.

Scaife, A. (2004, February 3). Chancellor high school student suspended for five days for having two Tylenol tablets. Retrieved July 26, 2004, from http://www.fredericksburg.com/News/FLS/2004/022004/02032004/1251201

Schaeffer-Duffy, C. (2003, March 28). Feeding the military machine. National Catholic Reporter. Retrieved October 7, 2007, from http://www.natcath.com/NCR_Online/archives/032803/032803a.htm

Schiraldi, V., & Ziedenberg, J. (2001). How distorted coverage of juvenile crime affects public policy. In W. Ayers, B. Dohrn, & R. Ayers (Eds.), *Zero tolerance: Resisting the drive for punishment in our schools* (pp. 114–125). New York: The New Press.

Schouten, F. (2004, March 21). Military schools producing army of solid performance. *USA Today.* Retrieved May 5, 2004, http://www.usatoday.com/news/nation/2004-03-30-defense-schools_x.htm

Schwartz, R., & Rieser, L. (2001). Zero tolerance as mandatory sentencing. In W. Ayers, B. Dohrn, & R. Ayers (Eds.), *Zero tolerance: Resisting the drive for punishment in our schools* (pp. 126–135). New York: The New Press.

Sentencing Project. (2002). Facts about prisons and prisoners. Retrieved September 21, 2004, from http://www.sentencingproject.org/pdfs/1035.pdf

Sentencing Project. (2004a). Facts about prisons and prisoners. Retrieved November 12, 2004, from http://www.sentencingproject.org/pdfs/1035.pdf

Sentencing Project. (2004b). New prison figures demonstrate need for comprehensive reform. Retrieved November 12, 2004, from http://www.sentencingproject.org/pdfs/1044.pdf

Simon, R. I. (1992). *Teaching against the grain: Texts for a pedagogy of possibility.* Westport, CT: Begin & Garvey.

Skiba, R. J., & Peterson, R. (1999). The dark side of zero tolerance: Can punishment lead to safe schools? *Phi Delta Kappan, 80,* 372–382.

Skiba, R. J. (2000, August). Zero tolerance, zero evidence: An analysis of school disciplinary practice. Policy research report #SRS2. Bloomington: Indiana Education Policy Center.

Skiba, R. J. (2001). When is disproportionality discrimination? The overrepresentation of black students in school suspension. In W. Ayers, B. Dohrn, & R. Ayers (Eds.), *Zero tolerance: Resisting the drive for punishment in our schools* (pp. 176–187). New York: The New Press.

Skiba, R. J., & Knesting, K. (2002). Zero tolerance, zero evidence: An analysis of school disciplinary practice. In R. J. Skiba & G. G. Noam (Eds.), *Zero tolerance: Can suspensions and expulsions keep schools safe* (pp. 17–44). San Francisco, CA: Jossey-Bass.

Skiba, R. J., & Noam, G. G. (Eds.) (2002). *Zero tolerance: Can suspensions and expulsions keep schools safe.* San Francisco, CA: Jossey-Bass.

Smith, S. (2004, September 1). JROTC builds skills, sense of belonging. *The Courier-Journal.* Retrieved October 15, 2004, from http://www.courier-journal.com/nabes/2004/09/01/A1-rotc0901ee-3982.html

Snyder, H. N. (2003, December). Juvenile arrests 2001. The Office of Juvenile Justice and Delinquency Prevention, The Office of Justice Programs. Washington, DC: U.S. Department of Justice.

Staples, J. S. (2000, January). Violence in schools: Rage against a broken world. In W. G. Hinkle & S. Henry (Eds.), School violence (pp. 30–41). *The Annals of the American Academy of Political and Social Science*: Vol. 567. Thousand Oaks, CA: Sage.

Stone-Palmquist, P. (2004, April). *Education after expulsion.* Unpublished manuscript, University of Michigan School of Social Work.

Street, P. (2005). *Segregated schools: Educational apartheid in post-civil rights America.* New York: Routledge.

Sughrue, J. A. (2003, April). Zero tolerance for children: Two wrongs don't make a right. *Educational Administration Quarterly, 39,* 238–258.

Thernstrom, A. (2003, November13). Education's division problem: Schools are responsible for the main source of racial inequality today. *Los Angeles Times,* p. A23.

Thompson, G. L. (2004, February/March). Playing god with other people's children. *The High School Journal, 87*(3), 1–4.

Tonry, M. (1996). *Malign neglect: Race, crime, and punishment in America.* New York: Oxford University Press.

Tyack, D., & Cuban, L. (1995). *Tinkering toward utopia: A century of public school reform.* Cambridge, MA: Harvard University Press.

United Health Foundation. (2003). Violent crime. Retrieved September 15, 2004, from http://www.unitedhealthfoundation.org/shr2003/components/violentcrime.html

USA Today. (2004, April 13). Pentagon could teach public schools some lessons. p. A22.

U.S. Census Bureau. (2003). Poverty rates in the United States. Retrieved January 3, 2005, from http://www.census.gov/prod/2003pubs/p60-222.pdf. P.8

U.S. Department of Education, National Center for Education Statistics. (1999). Safe gun-free schools act final report: School year 1997–1998. Retrieved September 20, 2004, from http://www.ed.gov/offices/OESE/SDFS/GFSA/title.html

U.S. Department of Education, National Center for Education Statistics. (2002). *Schools and staffing survey, 1999–2000; Overview of the data for public, private, public charter, and Bureau of Indian Affairs elementary and secondary schools.* NCES 2002-313, by Kerry J. Gruber, Susan D. Wiley, Stephen P. Broughman, Gregory A. Strizek, & Murisa Burian-Fitzgerald. Washington, DC.

U.S. Department of Education, National Center for Education Statistics. (2006). *The condition of education 2006,* NCES 2006-071. Washington, DC : U.S. Government Printing Office.

U.S. Department of Justice. (1995). Bureau of justice statistics bulletin: Prisoners in 1994. Washington, DC : Office of Justice Programs.

U.S. Department of Justice. (1997). Bureau of justice statistics bulletin: Prisoners in 1996. Washington, DC: Office of Justice Programs.

U.S. Department of Justice. (2004). Bureau of justice statistics bulletin: Prisoners in 2003. Washington, DC: Office of Justice Programs.

van Dijk, T. A. (2002). Denying racism: Elite discourse and racism. In P. Essed & D. T. Goldberg (Eds.), *Race critical theories* (pp. 307–323), Malden, MA: Blackwell.

Wacquant, L. (2002, January/February). From slavery to mass incarceration: Rethinking the "race question" in the U.S. *New Left Review, 13.* pp. 41–60.

Watts, I. E., & Erevelles, N. (2004, Summer). These deadly times: Reconceptualizing school violence by using critical race theory and disability studies. *American Educational Research Journal, 41,* 271–299.

Webber, J. A. (2004). Global youth: The great divide. *Workplace: A Journal for Academic Labor, 6*(1). Retrieved October 17, 2006, from http://www.cust.educ.ubc.ca/workplace/issue6p1/webbera.html

Williams, P. (1998). *Seeing a color-blind future: The paradox of race.* New York: Noonday Press.

Williams, R. M. (1993). Accumulation as evisceration: Urban rebellion and the new growth dynamics. In R. Goodling-Williams (Ed.), *Reading Rodney King: Reading urban uprising* (pp. 82–96). New York: Routledge.

Wilson, J. Q. (1985). Thinking about crime (Rev. ed.). New York: Vintage Books. (Original work published in 1975)

Winant, H. (1997). *Behind blue eyes: Whiteness and contemporary U.S. racial politics.* New Left Review, 225, 73–88.

Winant, H. (2001). *The world is a ghetto: Race and democracy since world war II.* New York: Basic Books.

Winant, H. (2004). *The new racial politics: Globalism, difference, justice.* Minneapolis: University of Minnesota Press.

Wolin, S. (2003, May 19). Inverted totalitarianism: How the Bush regime is effecting the transformation to a fascist-like state. *The Nation,* 13–15.

Wright, C., Weekes, D., & McGlaughlin, A. (2000). *"Race," class and gender in exclusion from school.* New York: Falmer Press.

Yates, M. D. (2004, April). Workers looking for jobs, unions looking for members. *Monthly Review,* pp. 36–48.

Zieger, R. H. (2004). Uncle Sam wants you . . . to go shopping: A consumer society responds to national crisis, 1957–2001. *Canadian Review of American Studies,* 34(1), 83–103.

Zweifler, R., & DeBeers, J. (2002, Fall). The children left behind: How zero tolerance impacts our most vulnerable youth. *Michigan Journal of Race and Law,* 8, 191–220.

Index

Abramsky, Sasha, 32, 189n23
Adams, A. Troy, 7
Advancement Project, 7, 73, 154, 172
African American, 15, 64, 77, 110, 119,
  122–23, 138, 143, 146, 181n9,
  188n18; and imprisonment, 136–37,
  141–43; and unemployment, 126, 136;
  and poverty, 126, 139, 141; and
  structural racism, 136; disproportionate exclusion of, 27–28, 30, 31, 67,
  73–74, 76, 115, 117, 163, 175n1;
  males, 2; representation of, 33–35, 78,
  96, 116, 121, 185–86n4; net worth,
  127; students, 48, 59–60, 61, 99–100,
  115, 118, 125, 143; youth, 12, 67, 73–
  74. *See also* colorblind discourse and
  ideology, color blindness, educational
  opportunity, exclusion, inequality,
  militarization, racism
agency, 65, 83, 84, 88, 104, 105–106
  Tab. 3.1, 116, 128; of social control,
  57
Akom, A.A., 29, 70, 157, 162. 173
alienation, 9, 12, 17, 29, 34, 36–37, 42,
  44, 82
American Academy of Pediatrics
  (AAP), 7
American Bar Association (ABA), 7,
  156, 157
angst, 34
Ansell, Amy E., 122
Anyon, Jean, 59, 159

Applied Research Center, 155
Arendt, Hannah, 13, 44, 169
Aronowitz, Stanley, 97, 123
assault, 21, 73, 103; military, 101; on the
  social, 41; on the social state, 185n3;
  on White privilege, 124; on youth,
  5, 164
authority, 8, 13, 19, 25, 41, 55, 59, 72,
  74, 76, 84, 89, 97, 102, 104, 105–106
  Tab. 3.1, 107–109, 110, 111, 158–59,
  161, 162, 164, 181n11
autonomy, 19, 24, 59, 60, 72, 73, 122,
  176–77n7
Ayers, Rick, 7, 157, 173, 176n1, 178n13,
  179n17
Ayers, William, 7, 33, 157, 173, 176n1,
  178n13, 179n17
Aziz, Nikhil, 115, 122

Barlow, Andrew, 115, 121, 123, 180n2,
  185n3, 187n10
Bartlett, Leslie, 24, 89, 98, 99, 101,
  180n3
Bartolome, Lilia I., 162
Bauman, Zygmunt, 13, 61, 132–33, 134,
  138, 143, 165, 168, 169
Beam, John M., 10, 27, 29, 60, 118,
  172, 177n10
Beger, Randall R., 9, 23, 25, 68, 72, 75,
  172
Bell, James, 29, 32, 172
Berlowitz, Marvin J., 98

Berube, Michael, 142
Bestor, Arthur E., 152
biometric technology, 8, 23, 69, 75, 84, 90, 92–93, 105 Tab. 3.1, 182n3. *See also* surveillance
Blankenau, Joe, 24, 72, 172
Blumenson, Eric, 29, 32, 140, 141, 172
Boggs, Carl, 98, 103
Bonilla-Silva, Eduardo, 115, 121, 123, 125, 146,
Bourdieu, Pierre, 53, 54, 132, 154
Boyden, Jennifer Emiko, 7, 160
Bracey, Gerald, 145
Brooks, Kimberly, 9, 117, 118, 172
Brown, Enora R., 99
Brown, Frank, 138, 140, 172
Brown, Michael K., 15, 31, 115, 121, 122, 138
Browne, Judith A., 6, 7, 11, 26, 49–50, 73, 75–76, 118, 172, 175n1, 177n9, 178n14
Brown v. the Board of Education (1954), 51 Tab. 2.1, 56, 153
Bureau of Labor Statistics, 142
Burstyn, Joan N., 157
Bush, George H.W., 140
Bush, George W., 1, 2, 64, 65, 100–101, 132–33, 141, 176n5, 180n4, 181n10, 187n11, 187n12
Butchart, Randall E., 157

Cammarota, Julio, 158, 159
Carnoy, Martin, 15, 31, 115, 121, 122, 138
Casella, Ronnie, 7, 9, 35–38, 42, 76, 89–90, 93, 118, 157–58, 160, 173, 179n18–19, 180–81n6, 182n1
Castoriadias, Cornelius, 112
Chicago Public Schools, 30, 93–94, 99, 117
citizenship, 17, 18, 36, 39, 41, 50, 56, 61–62, 63, 64–65, 67, 70, 72, 79, 80, 82–86, 104, 116, 121, 123, 124, 130, 133, 153, 173, 181n11. *See also* democracy, democratization, educational opportunity, life chances, rights

Civil Rights Movement, 119, 122–24, 153
Clinton, Bill, 126, 135, 140, 141, 179n23
Cole, David, 2, 64, 73, 119, 138, 142, 181n9, 181n11, 188n19, 188n21
colorblind discourse and ideology, 15, 115–16, 119–27, 137, 185n3, 185–86n4, 186n6, 186n7; and zero tolerance, 127–31. *See also* color blindness
color blindness, 15, 17, 115–16, 120–27, 128–30, 131, 132, 139, 143, 144, 155, 146, 147–48; practice of, 119
Comaroff, Jean, 135
Comaroff, John L., 135
consumer society, 116, 132–35; and color blindness, 143–46; and zero tolerance, 143–46; underside of, 135–43
Couldry, Nick, 167
Cremin, Lawrence, 152
crime, 6, 10, 13, 31–32, 34, 73, 84, 91, 94, 102, 136, 142, 179n19; distortion of, 35, 103, 188n16; juvenile, 35; youth, 38, 118
criminalization, 54, 62, 71, 145, 165, 181n7; as mode of regulation, 136; of school space, 109; of social policy, 40; of social problems, 15, 42; of society, 93; of students and youth, 35, 42, 81, 88, 95, 149; process of, 13, 16, 146, 180n5; relation to militarization, 13, 16, 39–41, 54, 62, 88, 108–10, 146, 165. *See also* exclusion, *Juvenile Crime Control Act* (1997), neoliberalism, racism, racial domination, security industry, Violent Crime Control and Law Enforcement Act (1994)
criminal justice, 5, 64; policies, 120, 141, 179n19; strategies, 69, 137; system, 11, 12, 19, 28, 31–32, 45, 73, 116, 119. *See also* crime, criminalization
Cross, Beverly, 30, 61
Cuban, Larry, 56, 153